Pedagogy

D0908011

12⁹⁵

Pedagogy: The Question of Impersonation
is Volume 17 in the series

THEORIES OF CONTEMPORARY CULTURE
Center for Twentieth Century Studies
University of Wisconsin-Milwaukee

General Editor, Kathleen Woodward

Pedagogy
The Question of Impersonation

edited by Jane Gallop

Indiana University Press

Bloomington and Indianapolis

The paper used in this publication meets the minimum require-
ments of American National Standard for Information Sciences—
Permanence of Paper for Printed Library Materials, ANSI
Z39.48-1984.

Manufactured in the United States of America

Library of Congress Cataloging-in-Publication Data

Pedagogy : the question of impersonation / edited by Jane Gallop.
     p.   cm.—(Theories of contemporary culture ; v. 17)
    Includes bibliographical references and index.
    ISBN 0-253-32536-6 (alk. paper).—ISBN 0-253-20936-6
    (pbk. : alk. paper)
    1. Teaching—Congresses. 2. Teacher-student relationships—
Congresses. I. Gallop, Jane, date. II. Series.
  LB1025.3.P436 1995
371.1'02—dc20   94-28325

1 2 3 4 5 00 99 98 97 96 95

Contents

    Indira Karamcheti

13. In-Voicing: Beyond the Voice Debate   *147*
    George Otte

14. *In Loco Parentis*: Addressing (the) Class   *155*
    Susan Miller

    Contributors   *165*
    Index   *167*

Acknowledgments

Any book of this sort, with a conference behind it, depends upon the effort and support of many people. Although I cannot possibly thank everyone who helped make the conference a wonderful event and bring this volume to light, I want to take the time here for two major acknowledgments.

The Center for Twentieth Century Studies has been my intellectual home for fifteen years now. Soon after I left graduate school, it took up that place as the site of learning, fulfilling at the same time the dream of community. I organized the conference and edit this book as a token of my gratitude (I could never repay what the Center has given me). I cannot count or even remember all the conferences, lectures, discussions, and chats at the Center that have shaped and bettered my work.

I've been to a lot of conferences, and no one runs them more gracefully than the Center. In that regard, this one was perhaps the most impressive. As I edited this book, I depended once again upon the considerable abilities and resources of the Center staff. I want here to thank Nicole Cunningham, Cathy Egan, Amelie Hastie, Brent Keever, Paul Kosidowski, Barbara Obremski, and Carol Tennessen. But above all, I want to thank Kathy Woodward for the intellectual leadership and personal warmth that make the Center at once a place of continual challenge and great comfort.

Although I wouldn't have done this book without the Center, I couldn't have done it without Chris Amirault. Chris was my research assistant for two years, the year I organized the conference and the year I edited this book. He has helped me every step of the way, from researching and choosing speakers to editing the essays (and as I write this he is editing my introduction for me). Working sessions with Chris transformed planning the conference and editing the book from duty to pleasure. In this volume, Roger Simon identifies a specific fantasy structuring teaching as "the desire for an intellectual partner." When I read Simon, I recognized this fantasy as central to my professional life. In working with Chris these last two years, I recognize its fulfillment.

A Personal Postscript, an Impostured Preface

David Crane

I FEEL LIKE such a brownnoser; worse yet, I might actually be a brownnoser. How else would I, alone of all my fellow classmates, end up here, writing a preface for the text my teacher has edited? How did I get called upon—or get myself called upon—to act like some sort of student representative from our—my fellow students', my teacher's, and my—class? What gives me the right, the authority, to move from the class to the head of this book, to impose myself this way?

Brownnosing, after all, is about imposing yourself somewhere you shouldn't be, about assuming a role and a posture that is not quite proper. It is an act approaching imposture, and as a student writing a preface to a book about pedagogy, I feel like an impostor even as I think it more than appropriate for students' "voices" to be represented here. But the problem is that I am alone (my fellow graduate student, my friend, Chris Amirault is also in this book, true, but he was not a member of the class I will be addressing). And the student voices (mine especially) in this book (or any book about pedagogy) are never there unless they are authorized by, are passed through, the teacher. So while my (pre)face ought to be held high, since it appears to head this book, it may in fact be forced somewhere else, which explains why the tone of my "voice" does not seem properly grateful.

Nobody likes a brownnoser. This term of accusation, reserved especially for use by and about fellow classmates, is usually used outside the actual classroom, or outside the teacher's presence, to deride what seems to be an improper student/teacher relationship. However, it is also often used by students resistant to the teacher's authority to delegitimate what seems to be a too proper teacher/student relationship. (And a cynic might say that the term perfectly describes the unspoken yet authorized graduate student/teacher relationship.) As a student, I've always hated brownnosers. As a teacher (true, a teaching assistant, but in this role I've usually been the sole instructor and acted like a "real" teacher), I've also hated them, but only when they've been too "obvious"; that is, when their performance is too easily seen, when their interest in me as a teacher is not "personal," but an act, false, an imposture—which may mean that it seems too personal. Yet (true) imposture—unlike impersonation—can't be seen too easily. An impostor, after all, relies on acting and seeming genuine, and that label only really fits after the ingenuity of that act—that blurring of false and true—has been revealed.

Playing the dual role of both teacher and student has helped make me more aware of fuzzy distinctions (or confusions), of the blurriness found in the distinction, especially when "sharp," between terms (such as "student" and "teacher"). That is why I used two—well, actually four, if you count the adjectives—distinct terms in my title, and why this is both a postscript and a preface—and neither. It falls between and outside each and attempts to mark out the temporal space in which a personal question of pedagogy becomes an impersonated one and a specific conference became a specific book. But more important, it is about how, in my personal observation, a specific class was erased, only to become (or to become only) a new word. It is a preface to this book only as it is simultaneously a postscript to that class.

The class I refer to, "Pedagogy: The Question of the Personal," was a graduate seminar offered at the University of Wisconsin-Milwaukee during the spring semester of the 1992–93 school year. It was offered in conjunction with the conference of the same name that in turn was the basis for this volume; its teacher was the conference coordinator, Jane Gallop—and because I know her personally, I'll refer to her here as "Jane." The class and the conference, temporary things that they are, have ended. Jane no longer plays the role of teacher or coordinator, at least in those contexts. She will continue, however, to play the role of this text's editor. You can see that yourself just by looking at the cover. And there, you will also see that between the time of the conference and the publication of this book, the title changed from "Pedagogy: The Question of the Personal" to *Pedagogy: The Question of Impersonation*. Odd, isn't it, that when the question was personal it was set in quotes, as if the personal question were in fact an act—or at least in question. Odder still, that when the question becomes impersonation, it merits the emphatic authority of italics, as if it were acting like a fact.

The question of impersonation was first broached in the class in question. In that place and time, it became one of our ways to explore the interaction between the frameworks and dynamics of pedagogy. So even though the class has ended, it will remain inscribed in the new title, in the changed word. In a sense, then, it continues to organize the essays in this book; it appears to, in part, entitle, if not authorize, them in some way. A small, yet significant, way. The teacher's, now editor's, way; for once the class and the conference have been transformed into a book, the students—except for me—have been removed from the question, and that should raise questions about any representations of pedagogical dynamics, whether they be posed as personal or impersonated (or impersonal) questions. And even this complaint can appear only if approved.

This returns us to the question: Why am I here? Why me? Well, I was called upon because I played a role in the title change. In a letter that in part notified me of the new title, Jane wrote: "You might also be interested to know that when I write the Introduction and explain the history of the (new) title I fully intend to work you in as a named character in the (true) story. I might, at that point, need your help in remembering what happened in what sequence." As you can see, since she wrote that letter, there's been another change. My character's role has expanded. I am now explaining the history of the new title myself, and this change involves another (true) story. This other story raises further, and perhaps deeper, questions about the shift from the personal and impersonation, as well as the theoretical and temporal space between those terms—especially in terms of what is included (and excluded) between the covers of this book. But the first story first.

The question of impersonation began as a class joke. In preparation for the conference, the class read essays submitted by the conference participants. Some of these essays dealt with pedagogy; others didn't. The aim was for us to become familiar with the participants through their work—to get a "personal" relationship with them via their texts before we would see them in person. One of these texts was by someone whom many of us already knew personally: Lynne Joyrich, an assistant professor at UWM (and a contributor to this book). Her essay (which has since been published in the journal *d i f f e r e n c e s*) was titled "Elvisophilia: Knowledge, Pleasure, and the Cult of Elvis" and includes an account of an Elvis Impersonators Convention in Chicago. Her discussion of the convention included a disagreement with another cultural theorist specializing in television studies, Lynn Spigel, who had previously published an account of that same convention.

Being one who always looks for a cheap joke in an intellectual argument, I asked if Lynne Joyrich might be acting like a Lynn Spigel impersonator. I got some laughs, though my question was half-serious. When the one Lynne quoted the other Lynn about how Elvis impersonators are "excessively aware of their pretense even as they hope to recover something true about themselves and their world," I was reminded of the "slight insecurities about the intellectual and cultural status of this essay" that Lynne presented in her opening lines. (I'll admit that I'm performing my argument better here than I did in the classroom.) Furthermore, the way that she assumed, and yet differentiated herself from, Spigel's position seemed to somehow enact—or impersonate—the pretense that Joyrich feared might appear in her own intellectual position. Well, maybe you had to be there to really get it.

We continued to discuss impersonation in the hallway outside of the classroom during break. Jane pushed the joke further, pointing out that Spigel (if an "e" were added) is German for mirror, and that that coincidence was amplified by the difference of an "e" in Lynne and Lynn (a close-reading joke). And if that were not coincidence enough, Lynne Joyrich then appeared in the hallway (she had just finished teaching a class). With Jane's prodding, I asked her in person if she thought she was a Lynn Spigel impersonator. She said she hadn't thought of that, but added that she had sometimes been confused with Lynn Spigel by people who knew them only through their work.

The conference began the next day. Joseph Litvak's paper ("Discipline, Spectacle, and Melancholia in and around the Gay Studies Classroom") kept the idea of performative pedagogy in circulation, and as we ourselves circulated during the breaks, members of the class continued to make impersonation jokes. (Our preoccupation with impersonation had in fact been foreshadowed by Joseph Litvak's essay, "Pedagogy and Sexuality," which addresses performativity, theatricality, mimicry, and sexuality in the classroom. But we never discussed this essay or these issues directly in class.) On the second day, impersonation entered the more official space of the conference. During a question-and-answer session, Jane noted that Madeleine Grumet "impersonated" her students as she read from their essays, which were incorporated into her paper ("*Scholae Personae*: Masks for Meaning"). At least Jane later told me she had done this, and that she had used the word as part of a publicly articulated private joke with me. Unfortunately, I had left the room to make a personal phone call, so I missed both the comment and the joke. Because I had missed this chance, Jane tried again later in the conference. Though I remember her using the word, for some reason I can't recall exactly when she said it, or to whom, or in what context. Odd, that I can recount the incident when I was absent better than the one when I was personally present. Odder still, that a teacher would insist on making a private, a personal, joke with her student as part of a public discussion of pedagogy. For while everyone in the audience would be able to understand her comments, and her use of impersonation, only a few people—only the students in the class—would get it. And since I first brought the idea up, I would not only get it, but appreciate it in a unique way. I could see not only how the word imposed our classroom (and extra-classroom) discussions into the confines of the conference, transforming, in what seemed at the time a small way, the framework of that discussion; I also could take special pleasure in the fact that my joke had been itself transformed, extended from a moment in a classroom dynamic into a way of addressing the dynamics of pedagogy: specifically, a way of addressing how a teacher represents students in her or his text.

That's the special thing about jokes: they have a way of making (though also hiding) surprising connections, a way of transforming and revealing (and again hiding) through their own rules and logics the rules into which they are imposed—the rules they impose upon. Their connections can even surprise the teller. This does not mean that they are transgressive. They can just as easily, and usually simultaneously, enforce other rules, even the ones they appear to break. That is why they are both fun and dangerous, and they are especially dangerous (and fun) because their humor often disguises their danger (or erases it) and makes them appear safe. And the special thing about my joke is that it emerged out of the pedagogy in class, only to see the class left out of the framework for thinking about pedagogy that it had, according to this (true) story, initiated. That may be what's at the heart of substituting a personal question of pedagogy for an impersonated one. Or it may be what's at the heart of a joke.

So let us move on to the second (true) story, the story of how I got here (assuming this text actually makes it into the book). But to (truly) tell that story, I need to explain why I initially signed up for the course—and I would like to distinguish a course from a class. A class is a course embodied; it has a certain temporal, locational, dynamic, and personalized makeup. It has a specificity that cannot be duplicated no matter how many times the course is offered or taken, no matter how its story is told; it is a course caught in the act.

My reasons for taking the course were primarily personal. During the first class session, as we introduced ourselves to each other and explained why we were there, I said half-jokingly that I enjoyed talking to Jane (whom I had not yet taken a course from) at departmental parties and receptions; I thought I should see how I would like her as a teacher. Liking Jane, then, was my reason, though I could not say that I liked her as a "friend"—only as an acquaintance, and as an acquaintance in quasi-institutional settings. One reason why I liked her was that we shared a similar sense of humor—a passion for jokes, which is a good way to make acquaintances (or even friends) at parties and receptions. I did worry, however, that I might not like her as much in a more official institutional setting. But as you can guess, this bond over jokes grew throughout the course of the class, and at the risk of again browning my nose, I must say that I liked her as much—if not more—by the end of the semester.

Actually, I'm not (truly) telling a story here—I'm retelling one, a story I told in an essay that I read to the class on its final day. I've even lifted much of the language here from that essay. Not only did I receive my best grade on that essay (my best grade of my graduate school career, in fact), but Jane asked if I would let her consider it for possible publication in this book. Actually, she was considering using other essays from our class in this book, as an act of including somehow the class's acting out of the subject of pedagogy. Obviously, that didn't happen, which speaks volumes about the difficulty in imposing the complex dynamics of pedagogy into a new context. The class's omission, then, marks with its absence the impossibility of representing temporal and temporary specificity within the static typeface of a book. Perhaps this impossibility can be achieved only through a joke.

So while I never felt entitled to have my essay included in this collection, I was, rightly or wrongly, angered by its omission. I was angered mostly, however, about the omission, the erasure, of the class. Once I was calmer, I met with Jane over lunch to discuss these omissions. In that discussion, she explained her reasons for changing the planned structure of the book and suggested that instead of playing a character in her (true) story, I could play author (not truly her words) by writing a preface. I'm not sure if she did this solely to please me, although it did (as it would any publication-seeking graduate student). In fact, the chance to preface a volume that includes some of the most influential writers on pedagogy seemed like a deal too good to pass up.

But the prospect also disturbed me, because it smelled too much like a deal. It seemed to position me not just as a possible brownnoser, not just as one who would use my personal relationship to the teacher to make my own gain, but also as being bought-off: as if I had traded my jokes for a special privilege, and in turn sold out the rest of the class. Or perhaps I was playing, or being played, into Jane's own specific pedagogical drama, not unlike (but not [truly] like) the man playing the student representative in Jane's reading of Helene Keyssar's retelling of her rehearsing of Susan Miller's "Cross Country"—the reading that can be found in this book under the title "The Teacher's Breasts."

I can only impersonate a student representative—no, I can only be an impostor; I was chosen not by my fellow students, but by the teacher; but also through my own imposition. And even though I have made you aware of my act, that does not quite turn my imposture into impersonation. That would simply be using my joke as a prophylactic, and one giving false protection, at that. Making you aware of my act too easily frees me from the risks of my own involvement, and infection, in the pedagogical drama. It is as false as placing the word "true" in parentheses (or quotes), as if that truly excuses my story's, and my drama's, true falseness. I can only hope that I have somehow infected this volume, and not simply to inoculate it (or me), but to make it aware of its weaknesses, to make it learn from its weaknesses, its deficiencies. I hope that I have restored some danger to my joke. But if I truly believe that I have, then my joke has probably again turned on me.

Pedagogy

1 | Im-Personation
A Reading in the Guise of an Introduction
Jane Gallop

On APRIL 15–17, 1993, the Center for Twentieth Century Studies of the University of Wisconsin-Milwaukee hosted a conference entitled "Pedagogy: The Question of the Personal." The present volume represents the transformation of that event into a book. As such, a number of changes have occurred: some papers presented at the conference have not been included; a few of the essays here were not presented (although all authors were major participants in the conference); all of the papers have undergone various degrees of revision since the conference. Such changes are typical of collections which are not, strictly speaking, "conference proceedings" but rather belong to a related hybrid genre—publications which originate in but grow out of conferences. This introduction will not comment on such typical changes (although I recognize their inevitable local historical interest). The purpose of this introduction is rather to gloss a more singular, more dramatic alteration—the new title.

How and why did "the personal" become "impersonation"? What does this substitution say about the two terms? In attempting to answer these questions, I propose to link them, through the hybrid term "im-personation." This introduction will try to theorize im-personation through reading its articulation in the essays collected here. But I want to begin by telling the how and the why of this change of garb. (A version of the first part of this story has already been told by David Crane.)

The semester of the conference, I taught a graduate seminar likewise entitled "Pedagogy: The Question of the Personal." Other Center conferences have been accompanied by graduate courses and such a pedagogical enactment particularly suited this topic. During the weeks just preceding the conference, the seminar read essays by the speakers (not the ones they would present but others which the speakers chose as related). The night before the conference the class was discussing Lynne Joyrich's article on Elvis impersonators and—in what for this class was not unusual behavior—began to play with applying the idea of impersonation in any direction we could make it go (vying for the honors of who could push it furthest). As we gathered in the hall for our mid-class break, we milked impersonation for all the fun we could get (beyond even our usual jocularity), moved by our excitement that the next day the people we had been reading would show up and talk to us in person. During our corridor impersonation shtick, Joyrich (who teaches at UWM) showed up and we couldn't resist turning our class joke on the person who was, without knowing it, its author. Although Joyrich attempted to get us to tell her seriously what we thought of the essay, she was nonetheless clearly amused to find that our boisterousness was in fact some version of response to her essay. This encounter with an actual speaker on the very eve of the conference seemed a foretaste of the possible surplus pleasures of group attendance at this public event.

One of the prime pleasures here is the group feeling itself, marked in this narrative by an undifferentiated first-person-plural subject: we, the class. My version of the narrative avoids either individuated students or any differentiation between teacher and students. This construction of the undifferentiated class "we" is explicitly taken up in several of the essays that follow. Naomi Scheman, Chris Amirault, Susan Miller, and my own essay all confront the teacher's desire to merge herself in the student group. Getting personal, or rather in this case social, playing a member of the class like any other, the teacher impersonates a student.

Crane's version of this story, unlike mine, focuses on individuals telling jokes (in particular, him and me). While casting this as a story about individuals, Crane troubles over the way a class dynamic is betokened by a special relation between teacher and individual student. Crane's worry finds its echo at the end of the book in Miller's pointed critique of the evasion of the class as a class through narrative dyads where the teacher interacts with one student. Such dyads not only crop up throughout the volume but—as instanced in Crane's and my story—are both unavoidable in and in fact constitutive of the present attempt to think pedagogy at the place where the personal becomes impersonation.

In considering the individual student, the teacher cannot help but take him, at least in part, as a token for the whole class of students. At the same time, any perception the teacher has of the class as a whole is necessarily focused and embodied by individual students.[1] Crane wittingly navigates the contradictions of his token position in his preface; my attempt to tell the story founders against narrative conventions which force me to choose between a personal story about individuals or a group history. It feels unseemly to tell this as a story of my relation to David and inaccurate to tell it as an undifferentiated story about my relation to the class. However I tell it, it is, inextricably, both.

The morning of the second day of the conference, after Madeleine Grumet's paper, I stood to ask about her "impersonation" of her student, referring to the thespian flair with which she had read her student's papers. The question, although unremarkable to the public audience, was a private communication, a wink reassembling the class in the corridor where we had accosted Joyrich. "Impersonation" was a code word, an in-joke that could communicate effectively to select individuals dispersed among a larger public which remained unaware that any private communication had even occurred. The question was itself an impersonation: posing as a serious intervention, it was in fact meant as something else. Even though I was in public and had a formal obligation as conference coordinator to relate to the public as a whole, I performed the question as class clown, to make the students laugh (to give them pleasure, to make them like me), to tell them I was still thinking of them, still with them.

We talk a lot about students trying to please the teacher. Sometimes we discuss this matter-of-factly as a structural necessity; sometimes it seems scandalous and exploitative. But I want to draw your attention to this incident in which my professional behavior (in a context which included peers whom I very much wanted to impress) was motivated by my desire to please the students. I flag it not because I believe it an unusual occurrence but rather because it seldom appears in our writing. We all know (and loudly proclaim) that we must not care if our students like us if we are to do our duty as teachers. As embarrassing as the identity of "brownnose" might be for students, it can be—and frequently is—justified as what students must do to succeed professionally. A teacher trying to please students doesn't have that rational, pragmatic excuse. I pause at this frequently experienced, generally denied scene of playing to the students, because I suspect it is a prime site where the personal tangles with impersonation.

I asked the question to make the class laugh, but it also must be said that I asked the question to make David laugh. In the jocular sociality of the class, David was my best audience, my best partner in repartee. When later I learned that David had been out of the room and not heard my question, I was disappointed.

That afternoon, after Cheryl Johnson's paper, I asked a second "impersonation" question, referring to her impersonation of academic discourse in the definition of the Afro which closes her paper. Had David been in the room for the first, I might not have asked this second question. Yet this question was for me more serious, not just played for laughs. Johnson had begun by talking about masks and went on to warn us that she was a trickster. When her definition marked its comic exaggeration with the word "quadrangle" (used to define the shape of the comb used for Afros), I glimpsed in her paper a reflection about performance which rendered what might have been an impertinent question pertinent.

Johnson spoke in the last session of the second day. The next day, the last of the conference, I frequently found myself thinking in terms of impersonation. But it was no longer a joke. I asked Naomi Scheman about her evident pleasure in reading to us bell hooks's scathing remarks about white feminists.[2] While I may have used the word "impersonation" in my question, I was no longer trying to get my class to laugh. My intention now was to get speakers to talk about their dramatic taking on of other's voices, what George Otte in this volume calls "in-voicing." No longer merely an enjoyable bit of social silliness, "impersonation" had become for me a productive category of analysis.

After the conference, the class met for four more weeks. During those four class periods, the term "impersonation" was frequently heard. Although it still retained some of the pleasures of an in-joke, it was now also clearly a useful category organizing our discussions. When the final assignment for the semester asked each student to write about the course, Marsha Watson devoted a page to the word "impersonation." I quote from her account:

> One of the words that has been weaving through the second half of the class is "impersonation." It has been both serious and comic; a topic for breaks as well as for papers; sometimes only appearing in a title, or in an off-hand comment in the middle of a discussion. First used in our classroom vocabulary late in the [semester], the concept now seems to me to have been undergirding the course from the start: Rousseau impersonated a father, Bloom impersonated Socrates, Freire impersonated Christ, feminist teachers impersonated students. . . .

I am fascinated by Watson's idea that "impersonation" was "undergirding the course from the start." No one had uttered the word until we read Joyrich three-quarters of the way through the semester. I who made up the syllabus and led class discussions had never thought of it. To illustrate that it was there from the start, Watson goes back and recaps our discussions of the books we read during the first half of the course, using the term "impersonation." The term works, is surprisingly appropriate to the discussions we had where it was never mentioned. It is in fact more effective for unifying our various class discussions than terms we used at the time.

Watson goes on to propose that "the term 'impersonation' caught hold in this course because of a view of pedagogy that we encountered in all our texts; a view that accepts that the aim of pedagogy is really reproduction." Although she introduces "reproduction" as overarching explanation, it is also a reference to another of the texts for the course—Bourdieu and Passeron's *Reproduction in Education, Society and Culture*.[3] In Bourdieu and Passeron's account, education involves, not only the specific case of the student as reproduction of the teacher, but the more general case of the student as impersonation of an educated person, taking on and reproducing the style and tastes of a class.[4]

Watson brings in "reproduction" in order to explain why " 'impersonation' caught hold." While the class's concern with "reproduction" does not, to my mind, seem to sufficiently explain the peculiar effect of the term "impersonation," I agree that the term "caught hold" with a vengeance that demands explanation. Furthermore I share Watson's sense that "impersonation" not only "caught hold" but was "undergirding the course from the start." This last idea is rich in epistemological implications. Her word "undergirding" connotes something that is hidden, not on the surface (hence the word was not in evidence, not used or even thought of) but structurally necessary to support what is on the surface. That a concept never considered should prove to have been a necessary structural support is surprising enough. But in our case, I want to draw attention to the accidental, marginal, and even silly derivation of this hidden structural principle.

Given the topic of the course, almost all the texts we read were about teaching. But since Joyrich had never written on pedagogy, when I asked her to recommend a relevant earlier paper, she chose the closest thing she had: an investigation into modes of knowledge. Because it was not at all about pedagogy, the paper on Elvis which introduced "impersonation" into the class was, of all the texts we read that semester, arguably the most marginal to the course.

Not only was our initial discussion of impersonation off the course's topic; it was also not serious. Using Joyrich's paper we could have had a considered discussion of the meaning and implications of impersonation, but we did not. I suspect that impersonation "caught hold" in our class precisely because we made a joke of it.

Not every joke is so successful. Perhaps because impersonation, always already "undergirding the course," was more than a joke—"both serious and comic, a topic for breaks as well as for papers," as Watson says. Whereas "papers" are arguably the most serious business of a class, the site of requirement, anxiety, and evaluation, "breaks" are the most social, personable part. Standing around drinking pop, smoking, or snacking during break, the class members (both students and teacher) relate casually, socially, "as if we were just people," rather than professionally. Yet a topic which could be "for breaks as well as for papers" crosses the line that would separate the social from the intellectual, the personal from the pedagogical, rendering that boundary porous and less decisive.

This double structure—"both serious and comic"—can be found not only in the odd effect of the word "impersonation" in our course; it also plays a major role in the professional performance that goes by the name impersonation. There are two major forms of such performance: Elvis impersonators and female impersonators.[5] Elvis impersonators, Joyrich explains, have an odd epistemological status; they both are and aren't believed, taken seriously as Elvis. While female impersonation is familiar stock comedy, Marge Garber demonstrates in *Vested Interests* how it can be understood as undergirding culture itself. Appreciating these two most organized forms as emblematic, I would argue that impersonation must be taken at one and the same time both as a joke and as serious. The general structure of impersonation would thus be not unlike the double structure Watson ascribes to the impersonation effect in our class.

By the end of the semester, I was convinced that "impersonation" was, for the class, both a great joke and a productive category. But when the semester and the class ended, I thought I was leaving impersonation behind. It was still a class joke and, however interesting it had become, you had to be there to get it.

I was sorry for that class to end. I felt considerable regret at the loss of the context in which the issues of the conference had grown more and more lively, complex, and fun. Despite my regret, by the end of May I had turned in my grades and read my student evaluations—the course was definitively over—and I turned to work on this book. George Otte's paper had opened the conference, so I began my editorial reading there. Three-quarters of the way through his paper, I came upon the following:

> If ventriloquism is dangerous for writing teachers, it may be just the thing for our students. . . . students are good at role playing, at in-voicing identities not their own.

Ventriloquism, role playing, in-voicing identities: I wrote "IMPERSONATION" in the margin and wished the class were still meeting so we could enjoy this together. Although I had read the paper before, I was completely surprised to find this material so resonant with impersonation in Otte's paper.[6]

Otte's paper never defined "in-voicing" and used the term only a couple of times in positions of very low profile. But having been sensitized, not only did I recognize the term as cousin to impersonation but I noted that, despite its low profile, it is in fact what he recommends writing teachers teach. Given the enormous preference writing teachers display for "personal" writing, Otte can be seen as trying to move writing pedagogy from the personal to in-voicing.

Otte's sense of in-voicing would also seem to share in some of the epistemological ambiguities of impersonation. In the sentence which immediately follows the above-quoted passage, he writes: "Typically, a student who inhabits some fictive scenario, who 'pretends' to write from the position of a public figure or literary character, shows a rhetorical sophistication well beyond what might have been taught or expected." The scare quotes around "pretends"—never glossed by Otte—suggest that the student is not simply pretending, that the student is in some way "really" in the position he is impersonating.

I was excited that Otte's paper seemed to bear out the class's sense of the aptness of impersonation. During the next twenty-four hours, although it was now summer, I saw first Marsha Watson and then David Crane and insisted on showing them the in-voicing passage from Otte. But it was only one paper, a lucky coincidence; I still felt "impersonation" belonged only to the class, not to the conference as a whole.

Halfway through my editorial review of the conference, I read Indira Karamcheti's "Caliban in the Classroom." A page before the end of her paper, I actually encountered the word "impersonator": "minority teachers can be figured as Calibans, Ariels, impersonators of Prospero."[7] This use of "impersonator" refers back a couple of pages to where she writes:

> The last of the potential roles . . . is . . . Prospero himself. The minority teacher can cast himself or herself as the . . . brilliant, no-nonsense professional for whom the personal has nothing to do with anything: John Houseman in racial drag.

Her use of "impersonator" picks up this idea of "racial drag." The phrase "in drag" derives from female impersonation; Karamcheti here implies one can put on a race in the way one can put on a sex. In this description of the Prospero role, impersonation is specifically contrasted with "the personal." The drag role, the impersonator, is here the "professional for whom the personal has nothing to do with anything."

While Karamcheti's actual use of the word "impersonator" in her paper partakes of the traditional opposition between the personal as authentic and impersonation as false performance, the paragraph immediately following acknowledges the inadequacy of that opposition and moves beyond it to the position I would call im-personation.

> However, the personal, at least as it concerns the genres of race and ethnicity in this country, is irrepressible. . . . it is inevitably part of the equipment with which one teaches, willingly or not. The only ways of speaking it are through a playful, inventive, eclectic use of preexisting genres. . . . the performance of race, of ethnicity, can provide a more supple . . . authority. But this should be a Brechtian performance, which alienates the viewer from the spectacle, discomforts rather than fulfills audience expectations. If we Calibans, knowing our hour has yet to come around, do not slouch toward Bethlehem, yet we may shuffle off to Buffalo as guerrilla theater or neo-blackface minstrel show.

While the description of the Prospero role as impersonation relies upon a contrast between real and assumed race, this paragraph proceeds to a more postmodern understanding in which the minority teacher playing a minority teacher would herself be in "racial drag." This "neo-blackface" performance involves performers whose "real faces" are not presumptively white. Yet the "real black person" underneath does not make the "blackface" any less a performance.

When I read this paragraph early last summer, I wrote a note to myself: "good theorizing of impersonation." Then I realized the surprising similarity between Karamcheti's prescription for minority teachers and Otte's recommendation for writing students. Both propose that the way beyond the debilitating opposition between personal and professional is to speak "through a playful, inventive, eclectic use of preexisting genres." Otte's and Karamcheti's papers had seemed to belong to widely different sectors of the conference topic—one was taking on personal writing, the other considering the dynamics produced in response to the minority teacher. Yet they both, quite separately, hit upon impersonation as a way out of long-standing binds. Marveling at this unexpected connection, I determined to place the two essays together in the volume. And then, I decided to put "impersonation" in the title.

Impersonation, it seems, had been undergirding the conference too from the start. Although no one used the word, the talks were rife with a sense of performance and repeated insistence that things were not what they seemed. The speakers had all responded to the call to address "the personal," but no one quite accepted the term. Madeleine Grumet confessed: "It's odd that I don't like the term, the personal. In my field, curriculum theory, that's what I'm known for. . . . I have systematically avoided the personal as an emblem for my efforts." Perhaps because of her association with it, Grumet may have been the most direct in expressing her dislike of the topic. Yet, in fact, each speaker addressed the personal with a swerve.

Cheryl Johnson tells us that she would have preferred to avoid the topic altogether: "by engaging in my own version of academic signifying . . . I hoped to escape or subvert the expressed interest/focus of this conference—to examine the personal." Johnson threatens to hide behind a series of masks. "There was the 'She's really smart' mask and the 'She is quite witty' mask . . . the 'She is Theoretical' mask . . . [and] the 'Oh, I didn't know she was Afrocentric' mask." This threat presumes the traditional view which opposes the personal (as naked, real face) and the mask, but Johnson tells us that the masks were discarded with earlier drafts of the paper. Her actual conference paper inhabits a different relation to the personal.

First, she tells us: "I will . . . put the masks aside." Then she gets real personal (or at least I take it personally): "the coordinator of this conference . . . would, over coffee or Maker's Mark, say, 'Now, Cheryl—' and I would feel the mask shift. So, I will give her partly what she wants." These two versions (appearing in the same paragraph) don't quite jibe. A mask that has "shifted" may be partially revealing, but it is not a mask removed. Perhaps we should read her putting the masks "aside" as putting them askew. In any case, the notion of partial revelation corresponds to her giving the coordinator "*partly* what she wants." If the coordinator asks "the question of the personal," Johnson will answer but only partly. Johnson closes her introduction: "Please be forewarned, however, that even as I put my masks away, that something of the trickster still informs my consciousness here; I am merely slouching toward the personal."

Johnson's "slouching" uncannily recalls Karamcheti's attempt to theorize "neo-blackface" performance. Johnson wants, at one and the same time, to get personal and to play the trickster (her vernacular term "signifying" can include both). Like Karamcheti she is slouching toward a new configuration in which the personal and the mask are not mutually exclusive alternatives. Grumet, motivated by her own ambivalence about the personal, discovers that this new configuration was in fact undergirding the personal from the start.

> My ambivalence about [the personal] . . . sends me to the *OED*. . . . Person is traced to the Latin verb *personare*, to sound through, later . . . a mask, the thing through which one sounds as in a play: dramatis personae. That is the first meaning of person, one that the *OED* admits hasn't made it into English. . . . And so I call this paper *"Scholae Personae*: Masks for Meaning" . . . to argue that the personal is a performance, an appearance contrived for the public, and to argue that these masks enable us to perform the play of pedagogy.

While Johnson's early drafts had her choosing masks as an alternative to the personal, Grumet asserts that the personal *is* a mask. The personal as mask is what I here propose to call im-personation, the personal as performance, as what one takes on. Following Grumet, I would argue that when the personal appears it is always as a result of a process of im-personation, a process of performing the personal for a public. If female impersonation is appearing as a female and Elvis impersonation is appearing as Elvis, I want to suggest that impersonation unmodified, the most general form, is *appearing as a person*.

Although Grumet is the only one to state flat out "the personal is a performance," when asked "the question of the personal" quite a few of the writers in this volume, as if by chance, turn to the performing arts. Karamcheti casts her understanding of the position of the minority teacher in terms of the roles in the *Tempest* plays by Shakespeare and Césaire. Joyrich approaches teaching through its cinematic representation in *The Prime of Miss Jean Brodie*. My own essay considers feminist pedagogy by focusing on a class that is literally putting on a play. Joseph Litvak confesses that he went into teaching because it resembled show business. Arthur Frank muses over the suggestion that university lectures be delivered not by the professors who write them but by professional actors. And Naomi Scheman, echoing Grumet's reading of the etymological sense of *personare* as sounding through, recalls her role in a school play to imagine her professional self as speaking through a microphone.

While Karamcheti, Joyrich, and myself use theatrical vehicles as primary structures in our papers, Litvak, Frank, and Scheman each seem to bring up performance as merely an amusing image on the way to their principal ideas. The central section of Scheman's essay opens with the story of her class play as a way into questions of power and authority. Although the play seems soon forgotten as the section gets into its serious material, a bit later the microphone makes a rather striking return. Already a few sentences into a paragraph, Scheman changes the subject, marking the abruptness of her transition with a simple declarative sentence that begins with "and": "And then there's the pesky question of that microphone." This sudden, bald switch of topic suggests that the microphone is indeed a "pesky question," one that comes up unannounced and inopportunely, one that Scheman can't quite leave behind. She stays with the microphone metaphor until the end of the paragraph and then it disappears again. The microphone makes a final appearance a page before the end of the essay, well into the last section which otherwise makes no mention of that microphone at all.

Even more than Scheman's, Frank's reference to performance initially seems merely a comic aside. He takes off from Goffman's view of the inefficiency of listening to a lecture (compared to reading the written text) to tell us:

> Goffman would have been amused by the recent remarks of Alberta's former Education Minister who wanted lectures given by professors to be replaced by videos scripted by academics but delivered by professional actors.

At the conference the audience greeted this with a burst of laughter at the expense of the unnamed philistine government official. Frank then comments that we shouldn't "superficially dismiss" this proposal since it would be a real boon to the efficiency both of students and professors. Since he makes it clear that efficiency is not the point of lecturing, we understand this comment as an ironic milking of the joke.

On the surface, Frank does dismiss the proposal as he goes on to contemplate what a lecture offers beyond efficiency. Yet what at first seems merely a joke reappears at the very heart of Frank's articulation of the personal and the pedagogical as enacted in the lecture.

> The self of the lecturer is split. . . . The part of the lecturer who could be replaced by an actor or a video machine is the "textual self," a talking head presenting verbally a text that could be more conveniently read. Giving voice to this text is another self, the "animator". . . .

The quoted terms—"textual self" and "animator"—are Goffman's. Goffman "would have been amused" by the scripted video scenario because it resonates with his view of the lecture. The Education Minister is proposing a professional impersonation. Yet even in the conventional lecture read by the person who wrote it, the one who appears in person is, Frank theorizes, im-personating the one who wrote the text.

This idea of performing the text one has written recalls Scheman's role in her school play.

> When I was in fourth grade a paper I wrote on evolution was turned into a class play, and I got to narrate, as Father Time. . . . on the day of performance, I was outfitted with a microphone. . . . But had I decided to deviate from the script (I wrote it, after all, so why not?) and called for a schoolyard insurrection, I'd have had the plug pulled on me.

Scheman specifically imagines a quite radical deviation from the script (in keeping with the "tenured radical" identity her paper is exploring), but the parenthesis opens another question, perhaps less identifiably radical but more theoretically poignant. The placement of the parenthesis signifies that Scheman is questioning not why she couldn't call for a schoolyard insurrection (she knows the answer to that question) but why she could not "deviate from the script" (deviation unspecified) which she herself wrote.

This is, I would suggest, a version of the "pesky question of that microphone." It is an experience of what Frank calls a split self, a self in performance, split between performing self and self performed. As performer, little Naomi had to follow the script as much as if it were written by another. Although the words are "hers," she cannot speak them as her own but must aim for an accurate im-personation. Scheman recounts this schoolgirl experience because it conveys something about how she continues to feel in the institution as a professor.

Although Scheman accepts the microphone as part of her professional responsibility, she remains personally troubled by its splitting effects. Like Scheman, Litvak takes us back to primary school to figure his relation to the profession, but he is thrilled to imagine himself at the microphone.

> Starting in about first grade, I cathected my teachers—and hoped to be cathected myself one day—in much the same way that I cathected my favorite stars of stage, screen, and television. (. . . I'm . . . delighted to read on a course evaluation: "Mr. Litvak should be an actor." And . . . one of the evaluations that I remember most fondly is the one that commented, "My friend and I referred to this class as The Litvak Show.")

Litvak's student evaluation uncannily seconds the Education Minister's suggestion that the professor "should be an actor." Like Frank, Litvak will proceed from this amusing, odd suggestion to the general proposition that "*all* teaching . . . is . . . theatrical." But Litvak goes even further.

> [T]he more-than-perversity, the defiant gayness, of the show biz analogy might bring out the ways in which *all* teaching, even by heterosexual men, is not just theatrical, but what it somehow seems appropriate to call "queer."

It is this specific association that determined me to place Litvak's essay first in the collection. Although Litvak never uses the word "impersonation," his emphasis on the gayness of performance corresponds to a primary aspect of the term. The exemplary form in which our culture knows impersonation is undoubtedly female impersonation. And female impersonation in our present cultural imaginary inevitably connotes male homosexuality (and even vice versa). More than other terms designating performance, the word "impersonation" carries the connection that Litvak underscores between spectacle and gayness.

Litvak points to this connection in order to posit that "*all* teaching, even by heterosexual men, is . . . 'queer.' " This is the move I wanted to foreground by placing Litvak first and by putting impersonation in the title. Just as Frank takes the kooky suggestion and uses it to illuminate the conventional case, Litvak takes the supposedly marginal queer figure and wants to apply it as the general rule. It is this sort of gesture I have in mind by attempting to move from the specific and relatively restricted case of impersonation proper to the generalized structure I am calling im-personation.

And it is no coincidence that this is first of all, in the present volume, located as a "queer" move. One branch of queer theory has devoted itself not to the identification or even celebration of a restricted queer minority but to the defiant perversion of any norm, working toward a notion of the queer as the generalized case. Litvak's move queers pedagogy—"every teacher, even the most reactionary custodian of the eternal verities, is . . . a pervert." This same sort of queer generalization can be seen in contemporary attempts to theorize female impersonation.

In a 1991 article, Judith Butler writes: "drag enacts the very structure of impersonation by which *any gender* is assumed. . . . Drag constitutes the mundane way in which genders are appropriated, theatricalized, worn, and done; it implies that all gendering is a kind of impersonation" (21).[8] In a May 1993 interview, Marge Garber likewise states: "what [cross-dressing] really suggest[s] is that every woman is a female impersonator in a sense, and every man is a male impersonator."[9]

While Elvis impersonation was certainly the exemplary form of impersonation in the class I taught, for this book the exemplar might well be female impersonation, or rather "drag." We begin with Litvak's general queering, and, as noted earlier, Karamcheti—who is the only contributor actually to use the word "impersonation"—introduces the phrase "racial drag." This phrase taps into gender theory to think about the performance of race or ethnicity. Karamcheti's implied expansion of racial drag to include the performance of one's own race corresponds to the contemporary radicalization in feminist and queer theory that views all gender as performance. Karamcheti's borrowing allows us to see this postmodern notion of impersonation entailing other so-called identities besides gender.

If "drag" is a synonym for female impersonation, it specifically means, my dictionary tells me, "women's clothing worn by a man." The emphasis on clothing leads us back to the moment when Grumet, ambivalent about the personal, turns to the *OED*, and this emphasis affords me the opportunity to fill in the ellipsis in the block quotation I presented above.

> . . . a mask, the thing through which one sounds as in a play: dramatis personae.
> That is the first meaning of person, one that the *OED* admits hasn't made it

into English. It offers many more, among them this pair: "The living body of a human being; either a) the actual body as distinct from clothing, etc., or from the mind or soul, or b) the body with its clothing and adornment as presented to the sight of others."

A—flesh or B—fashion?

And so I call this paper *"Scholae Personae*: Masks for Meaning," deliberately choosing fashion over flesh. . . .

Among the many definitions of the person, Grumet chooses "the body with its clothing and adornment as presented to the sight of others." The idea of "presented to others" fits her performative sense of the personal, and directly rejecting the first of the pair—the body as distinct from clothing—Grumet chooses im-personation with "clothing and adornment."

The most explicitly theatrical moment of the conference was Grumet's. Early in the talk, she connects "the personal" to her bathrobe and describes this garment in some detail. Immediately before her turn to the *OED* (just quoted), she says: "It is a robe I write in, not about. It is strange to see it move into the yellow letters on my screen. It is my robe, it has my smell, and as I present it to you. . . . " With this last phrase, she stopped reading, turned to Kathleen Woodward who was moderating the session, and said: "The robe, please." Woodward pulled a green bathrobe out of a shopping bag and handed it to Grumet, who hung it on a hanger next to the podium. Grumet then went back to reading her talk: "as I present it to you . . . it becomes my costume."

Through this performance, her own clothing, her very private, at-home, comfy clothing, becomes her "costume." She here quite explicitly performs im-personation, her personal self "as presented to the sight of others," and in presentation the personal becomes a costume. As she stood there lecturing, we were able to see the split self Frank told us about. The one reading the lecture was stylishly dressed for public appearance; on the hanger was the empty garment of the "animator," the self who wrote the text being read.

Grumet joins Frank and Litvak at the beginning of this collection, as the three of them provide the most direct theorization of pedagogy as impersonation. Yet the volume also includes a radically different vision of teaching. Susan Miller best represents that other pole.

Miller's paper fittingly ended the conference. Whereas every speaker more or less swerved from the personal, Miller directly turned on it and denounced it as a sham. Johnson threatened to escape the personal but ultimately chose to engage it, although only partly. Grumet, wanting to avoid the personal, reconfigured it as a mask. But Miller gave the final answer to "the question of the personal": she rejected it for another term.

Miller demonstrates with documents from the discipline of teaching English how "personal" relations between teachers and students have historically been recommended as a mechanism of regulation. She wants us to stop "applying a situationally inapplicable" personal and to start recognizing a situation that involves "managers of the vernacular and a linguistically managed class." Accusing us of "hid[ing] this . . . from ourselves in talk about personal relations to students and personal teaching histories," Miller asserts that "the personal" is a "fiction" and suggests that it be written "in quotation marks." Miller thus could also be construed as saying that "the personal is an impersonation," but only if we give this sentence a different interpretation.[10]

I placed Miller's essay last because I would not want to leave the topic of impersonation without taking seriously the gloomier side of the subject. In the attempt to generalize the structure of im-personation, moving beyond a naive belief in bringing the authentic self into the institution, it is necessary to bear in mind the idea of impersonation as motivated deception and exploitative strategy. I want to think impersonation in a way that includes both Litvak's celebration of performance as potentially liberatory and Miller's suspicion of deception as historically documented. The two are not worlds apart, for these essays (among many others here) share a style that is at once extremely funny and yet nonetheless earnest about its positions. Not worlds apart, but, at least for now, undeniably at opposite ends of our collective enterprise.[11]

Miller is, of course, not the only author in the volume to explore this troubling side of the personal. In fact, Litvak shares her concern with surveillance. As his title shows, he is interested not only in spectacle but also in discipline.[12] Miller's suspicion of concealment finds an echo in Amirault's reading of Bourdieu and Passeron. "For Bourdieu and Passeron, the radical pedagogical practices at 'liberal universities' actually reinforce [institutional] authority more effectively . . . by 'more fully mask[ing] the ultimate foundations of [their] pedagogic authority.' " Where Johnson is attracted to masks and Grumet embraces the mask, here "masking" seems a nefarious thing.

Miller elaborates on how this masking operates.

> [C]urrent reemergences of equalizing teaching techniques . . . reinstate unproblematized portrayals of "student" and "teacher" as merely "taking" roles they might easily, "individually," forego. . . . such techniques . . . prevent the distinct . . . student body from recognizing itself as different from the pedagogical moral technology that was designed to contain it.

These "equalizing" techniques are in part the subject of both Amirault's and my own essay in this volume. Like Miller, we critique the assumption that students and teachers are "not really different." Amirault specifically addresses the move of putting "student" and "teacher" in quotation marks, which Miller here typographically alludes to.

Miller's use of the phrase "taking roles" makes us see that these masking techniques involve an understanding of pedagogy as performance not unlike that often championed in the present volume. I would want to argue for a difference between this sort of role-taking and the im-personation proposed in this introduction. Miller's critique presupposes a restricted and voluntaristic understanding of performance—a role is taken on and understood to be distinct from the real. It is this liberal understanding of pedagogical performance, that these are *just roles* we are playing, that blocks understanding of the situation.

This whole question of "taking roles" is one Judith Butler astutely addresses in her theorization of drag.

> I do not mean to suggest that drag is a "role" that can be taken on or taken off at will. There is no volitional subject behind the mime who decides, as it were, which gender it will be today. . . . gender is not a performance that a prior subject elects to do, but gender is *performative*. . . . (23–24)

I cite Butler's distinction between drag as performance and as performative because it clarifies the distinction I am making between impersonation in the restricted, traditional sense and a generalized im-personation.

It is this notion of the performative which undergirds the present volume. Roger Simon is the most explicit: "As Judith Butler points out, the material or linguistic assertion of identity is not a question of offering an adequate representation of a preconstituted group; it is rather the performative invocation of an identity." Although Butler is specifically talking about gender, Simon is able to use these formulations to conceptualize "postmodern Jewish identity, a practice through which a Jew makes evident the constructedness of her or his identity." In Simon's essay "constructedness" clearly does not imply false as opposed to true; it does not mean a role that can be taken on or off at will. Simon is "really" Jewish and, if we are to understand the performative which appears not only in Simon's essay but, I would say, throughout this book as a whole, we have to think constructed somehow other than in opposition to authentic.

This turns out not to be so easy. In fact, the notion of the performative espoused by Butler and other postmodern theorists has been consistently misunderstood as a volitional "we can be whatever we want." Gregory Jay's essay can be understood as specifically arguing against this sort of weak postmodernism. The volitional misunderstanding results in two trends, both of which Jay takes on: the depersonalizing strain of poststructuralism that denies the connection between discourses and the bodies that produce them; and a consumer multiculturalism which encourages anyone to take on any identity they wish. Like Butler and Simon, Jay is trying to formulate a postmodern conception of identity which while recognizing its constructedness is still embodied and must be, as he says, "taken personally."

Grumet chooses to define the personal as what is "presented to the sight of others." Jay describes "taking multiculturalism personally" as "to see my own subjectivity *from the other's point of view.*" He hopes by that means to "achieve a sense of *my own* strangeness, my own otherness, and of the history of how my assumed mode of being came into being historically." It is through the sense of oneself as presented to others that one can get access to what Simon calls "constructedness." This apperception of one's own constructedness is for Jay not license to play at being whatever one likes but the only possibility of taking difference seriously. Jay's essay brings into focus the ethical side of im-personation. If we are persons only inasmuch as we become persons "in the sight of others," then we have a constitutive responsibility to take our audience into account.

Jay's sense of the ethics of taking identity personally resonates with the way Butler herself directly tries to counteract the widespread misunderstanding of the postmodern notion of the performative:

> To say that I "play" at being one is not to say that I am not one "really"; rather, how and where I play at being one is the way in which that "being" gets established, instituted, circulated, and confirmed. This is not a performance from which I take radical distance, for this is deep-seated play, psychically entrenched play. . . . (18)

While the particular "one" that Butler here plays at being is a lesbian, her sense of "deep-seated, psychically entrenched play" has, for me, immediate pedagogical relevance. I have used strikingly congruent formulations about being a teacher in a recent essay. Recalling my feelings about a student I taught when I was still a graduate student, I wrote:

> In relation to Mike, I was not only playing *the* teacher but was specifically playing my teachers . . . who were all male. . . . Finding myself in an analogous relation to Mike but in the opposite role, I felt I had switched genders. My concurrent sense of our "real genders," however, caused me to experience the pedagogical positions as drag performance, role-playing.
> Although "being the teacher" felt like a masquerade, I am convinced that Mike learned a lot from me. . . . This knot of pretense and reality is, I believe, the very paradoxical heart of my pedagogy. I was, and from the beginning, at one and the same time, a fake teacher and an effective one. I am—after twenty years of teaching, literally hundreds of students, as a "Full Professor"—still getting off on "playing teacher" even or especially while I actually teach. (216–17)

This knot of pretense and reality is what in this book I want to signal with the word "im-personation." If I am here constructing a reading of the volume which specifically explores that knot, it is certainly not unrelated to this experience and this sense that pedagogically I am an impersonator.

Like the above quotation, Amirault's essay in the present volume deals with the experience of teaching while still a graduate student, and his essay likewise leads into the knot of pretense and reality. With the guidance of Bourdieu and Passeron, Amirault reaches a dismal understanding of teaching as deception that is very close to Miller's diagnosis. Yet the end of his essay stalwartly affirms both that his teaching was a sham and, at the same time, "real." Following Butler, we can perhaps begin to see a way to make this double realization less painfully contradictory.

This knot of pretense and reality leads me back to Otte's essay, the first which suggested to me that this book was about impersonation. When earlier I told about reading Otte, I remarked in passing that in his explanation of in-voicing, he puts "pretend" in scare quotes, and I want now to return to his "pretend." Despite the dissimilarity in the subjects they are addressing, Otte is in fact quite close to Butler in stipulating that we take his sort of "pretend" very seriously.

> The point of in-voicing other voices is not to make for risk-free, semi-engaged games of pretend; on the contrary, it's to make apparent the risks of a practice we all constantly enact, speaking the already spoken whether by teachers or . . . talk show celebrities. Whatever is said is . . . mostly borrowed. . . .

To make his bid for in-voicing as not just a game, Otte performs the generalizing move. Taking on someone else's voice is no longer just a restricted, specific practice but becomes "a practice we all constantly enact"; not only the odd imitation but "whatever is said is mostly borrowed." Like so many of the authors in this volume, Otte here proceeds from impersonation to im-personation. And as he does, he makes clear that in this generalized in-voicing we cannot make the conventional distinction between performance and reality.

Otte's parallel between teachers and "talk show celebrities" recalls Litvak's show biz analogy; I want to draw attention to the specific form of professional performance Otte names. Talk shows, that typically postmodern entertainment genre, promise the pleasure of seeing people act like people. I share Otte's sense of the connection between teaching and talk shows (people "just being people" might be called im-personation). The personal in pedagogy acts not unlike the personal on talk shows, a performance that nonetheless functions as real.

When I changed the book's title from "the personal" to "impersonation," it was not to leave the personal behind. As so many of the authors answered the question of the personal, we seemed inevitably to think of performing: this move to performance was not a change of subject but a way of figuring the personal. I read the collection through the device of im-personation to get at this sense of the performative personal.

Notes

1. When Miller ends her essay by exemplifying a view of teaching that considers the class as a class, she inevitably focuses on the statements of a few individual students. It is interesting to note that the dynamic she presents also involves joking.
2. Scheman's paper at the conference is not included here; she has written a new essay especially for this volume.
3. The other texts for the first half of the course are, in the order Watson refers to

them: Rousseau, *Emile; or, On Education*; Bloom, *The Closing of the American Mind*; Freire, *Pedagogy of the Oppressed*; and Culley and Portuges, *Gendered Subjects*.

4. In the present volume, Amirault's essay considers the impersonation complex portrayed in Bourdieu and Passeron's vision of education.

5. "It is almost as if the word 'impersonator,' in contemporary popular culture, can be modified *either* by 'female' or by 'Elvis' " (Garber 372).

6. "In-Voicing" was not in Otte's original title; his new title is meant to resonate with the book's (new) title.

7. Although in the present volume the word "impersonation" appears three times in the concluding paragraph of Karamcheti's essay, it did not appear in the conference paper but was added in response to the new title of the book.

8. To back up her generalization of drag, Butler cites Esther Newton.

9. Interview by James Cummings in the *Dayton Daily News* 16 May 1993. Quoted in Donaldson.

10. These two interpretations of "impersonation" correspond to Gregory Jay's discussion in this collection of the two meanings of "agency."

11. The dilemma represented by the opposition between these two positions is explored in detail (although in somewhat different terms) in Joyrich's essay in the present volume.

12. He states not only that "every teacher, even the most reactionary custodian of the eternal verities, is . . . a pervert" but also that "every teacher, even the most avant-garde queer theorist, is a disciplinarian."

Works Cited

Bloom, Allan. *The Closing of the American Mind*. New York: Simon, 1987.

Bourdieu, Pierre, and Jean-Claude Passeron. *Reproduction in Education, Society and Culture*. Trans. Richard Nice. London: Sage, 1990.

Butler, Judith. "Imitation and Gender Insubordination." *Inside/Out*. Ed. Diana Fuss. New York: Routledge, 1991. 13–31.

Culley, Margo, and Catherine Portuges, eds. *Gendered Subjects: The Dynamics of Feminist Teaching*. Boston: Routledge, 1985.

Donaldson, Laura. "On Critical Cross-Dressers, Narrative Transvestities and Textual Passing: Authenticity and Feminist Identities at the Fin-de-Siècle." Conference Paper. Figuring Feminism at the Fin de Siècle. Scripps College. Nov. 1993.

Freire, Paulo. *Pedagogy of the Oppressed*. Trans. Myra Ramos. New York: Continuum, 1970.

Gallop, Jane. "Knot a Love Story." *The Yale Journal of Criticism* 5.3 (1992): 209–18.

Garber, Marjorie. *Vested Interests: Cross-Dressing and Cultural Anxiety*. New York: Routledge, 1992.

Joyrich, Lynne. "Elvisophilia: Knowledge, Pleasure, and the Cult of Elvis." *d i f f e r e n c e s* 5.1 (1993): 73–91.

Newton, Esther. *Mother Camp: Female Impersonators in America*. Chicago: U of Chicago P, 1972.

Rousseau, Jean-Jacques. *Emile; or, On Education*. Trans. Allan Bloom. New York: Basic, 1979.

2 | Discipline, Spectacle, and Melancholia in and around the Gay Studies Classroom

Joseph Litvak

1.

FOR ME, THE most chilling passage in Paul de Man's "The Resistance to Theory" is the one near the beginning, where he writes:

> Overfacile opinion notwithstanding, teaching is not primarily an intersubjective relationship between people but a cognitive process in which self and other are only tangentially and contiguously involved. The only teaching worthy of the name is scholarly, not personal; analogies between teaching and various aspects of show business or guidance counseling are more often than not excuses for having abdicated the task. (4)

The passage chills me because, to tell you the truth, the reason I got into teaching is precisely that it seemed to combine the best of both show business and guidance counseling. Starting in about the first grade, I cathected my teachers—and hoped to be cathected myself one day—in much the same way that I cathected my favorite stars of stage, screen, and television. (Much as I suspect a backhanded compliment, I'm in fact delighted to read on a course evaluation: "Mr. Litvak should be an actor." And though I *know* it was meant as a put-down, one of the evaluations that I remember most fondly is the one that commented, "My friend and I referred to this class as The Litvak Show.")

Nothing could be easier, I suppose, than to recognize this avowal as not just perverse but "perverted," as shamelessly solicitous of the stereotype not so much of the teacher as frustrated actor (Robin Williams in *Dead Poets Society*) as of what, even more embarassingly, stands behind it: the stereotype of the pedagogue as pederast, or, to flesh things out a bit further, as flamboyantly lovesick, stagestruck Gay Man. Overfacile opinion notwithstanding, there may be more to do with that stereotype than merely to send it up or to send it packing. To the degree that it *is* embarrassing, it may . . . have something to teach us.

For example: the more-than-perversity, the defiant gayness, of the show biz analogy might bring out the ways in which *all* teaching, even by heterosexual men, is not just theatrical, but what it somehow seems appropriate to call "queer."[1] It would not require much effort, after all, to show how the passage from Paul de Man "deconstructs itself," demonstrating a consummate showmanship in its very repudiation of showmanship, evincing about as much authentic antitheatricality as, say, Judy Garland turning her back on her audience at the end of a song to wring the last drops of pathos out of yet another virtuoso performance of triumph through pain.[2] Since the category of the performative in fact makes a disruptive return later in de Man's essay, albeit in necessarily abstract or disembodied form, such a "queer" reading would constitute not a carnivalesque impertinence but the staging of a difference already within de Manian performance. That is to say, such a reading would stage Paul de Man's melancholic relation to the performing, desiring body; it might also stage its own melancholic relation to Paul de Man himself—a teacher (and dissertation advisor) whom I was by no means alone in cathecting pretty intensely, and whom I may not be alone either in having a hard time differentiating from a few other men that got away.

2.

Based on a talk written for an MLA session entitled "Mourning, Trashing, Shaming, and Pogroms in and around the Gay Studies Classroom," this paper spends as much time "around" as "in" that classroom, on the assumption that "in" isn't really comprehensible *without* "around." And it interprets "around" rather broadly, casting a wider net than may seem altogether fitting and proper. Looking around, then, by looking back (way back), I ask you to consider the following primal scene of instruction.

It was in the summer of 1967. My father had taken me and two of my younger brothers on a vacation to what we now know to be the exceptionally antihomophobic town of Aspen, Colorado; my mother had "decided" to stay at home with my youngest brother, who, then less than one year old, was too young to travel. One night, after dinner, the four of us were lying around on the two double (or was it queen-size?) beds in the motel, listening to my father regale us with his reading, or deconstructive performance, of an ad from the back of *Harper's* magazine. The ad was for some Charles Atlas-type bodybuilding method, and it sported an enticing picture of an all-but-naked muscle man, supposedly the method's inventor, whose conventional narrative of self-transformation from ninety-six-pound weakling into incredible hulk constituted the enticing text. After showing us the picture, and pointing out its intrinsically suspect spectacularization of masculinity—those weren't his exact words, but the translation is accurate enough—my father proceeded to debunk the text itself by reading it aloud in the lisping, effeminate voice that we all on some level knew meant "fag."

Given both the homoeroticism of the scene (boys on the bed with dad) and the homophobia that we had already absorbed from the culture as a whole, it is hardly surprising that my brothers and I greeted my father's performance, even

egged it on, with delighted giggles, mine probably being the loudest of all insofar as I understood even then that in some menacingly implicit sense the
laugh was on me, the least butch of my father's sons. Gay theory has taught us,
of course, that heterosexual masculinity is not an identity that one simply has,
but an identification that one must be terrorized into; but if all boys in this culture are routinely subjected to the manifold operations of homophobic shaming,
boys whose parents and teachers worry that they might be or become gay obviously make especially inviting targets. That, for all the manic insistence and
protean versatility of homophobic role-modeling (Robin Williams in *Aladdin*),
some of those boys nonetheless *do* remain or become gay suggests not that they
are constitutively shameless but, to the contrary, that they are highly responsive
to shame—not, to be sure, in the same ways that their straight brothers are, but
in ways that have a logic, a history, and widely diffused cultural consequences
of their own.[3]

Despite the epic sweep of that last phrase, for now I am more locally interested in describing and following through the strands of the pedagogical and
performative relations structuring and structured by that scene in the motel
room. Not that the scene can't claim a certain exemplary status. Like another
primal scene, that of Freud's Wolf Man, it could indeed be characterized, in
Freud's words, as "entirely commonplace and *banal.*"[4] After all, what event more
drearily typifies masculinist culture—or gets played out in more motel rooms,
locker rooms, and "family" rooms all over America—than a father instructing
his sons in the intricate decorum of homophobic knowingness? Teaching me
and my brothers how to tell the difference between a real man and a self-dis-
crediting parody of one, my father was only doing his job, like millions of other
fathers and father figures before and after him.

And yet, just as the events of the Wolf Man's primal scene never manage to
look quite as banal as Freud anxiously insists they are, so my own primal scene
had something a little too exciting about it. I'm referring to its central feature,
my father's performance, which, while intending a lesson in homophobic deconstruction, in how to unmask (what he took to be gay) hypermasculinity, consisted most spectacularly in a parody of that parody, so that, in acting like a
"fag," however apotropaically, my father seemed, however fleetingly, almost to
become one. Taking charge of our character-building by steering us away from
the temptations of bodybuilding, showing us how the muscle man illicitly made
a spectacle of masculinity, my father, whether he knew it or not, made a spectacle of—that is to say, homosexualized—himself. When, as often happens, the
scene of instruction is also a scene of humiliation, the shame-agent can turn
into, or become readable as, a shame-object, and, on some spectators, that reversal or doubling can have powerful, because equally unstable, effects.[5]

Though I can't quite affirm a direct causal link between the scene in the
motel room in 1967 and the scene in the lecture room, say, twenty-five years

later, the former, I want to argue, emblematizes a lot of the forces that propelled me into and that keep me going in and around the latter. To put it most schematically: while the effect of my father's performance on my brothers, who turned out straight, seems to have been to make them "identify with" him—that is, with his homophobic heterosexuality—the effect of that performance on me was to make me "identify with" him—that is, with his homophobic homosexuality. Confronted with the uncanny, quasi-pornographic spectacle of the gay-hating yet gay father, I mimetically internalized the apparent contradiction he thus represented, hoping to take on his knowledge—his sophisticated ability to decipher the culture's sexual codes—with his power—not only the power that came with this knowledge, but also the power of *performance*, a power indistinguishable from the thrilling danger of exposing oneself as at once "overdeveloped" and underdisciplined, as shamefully in excess of the properly nonspectacular straight male body. With such a role model, is it any wonder that I became a teacher?

3.

But what does all this have to do with teaching *gay, lesbian, or queer studies*? A lot, I think. I tell this story not only because it hints at the intimate connection between witnessing and experiencing shame in childhood, on the one hand, and becoming a teacher, on the other, but also because, for me, teaching gay studies in large part means trying to reconfigure what passes for the "normal" relation between teaching and shame. And reconfiguring that relation means thinking about an issue dramatized less by the motel scene "itself" than by my rehearsal of it: the pedagogical uses, "normal" and otherwise, of mourning and melancholia.

I would propose that melancholia—the fantasmatic perpetuation of an ambivalent love one refuses to acknowledge, much less to mourn—plays a major, if uncredited, role in the non-gay-identified scene of pedagogy-as-usual. Judith Butler's *Gender Trouble* has become famous for its theorizing about performance, but it also has a lot to say about what Butler calls "the melancholia of gender." Butler suggests that melancholia virtually constitutes, for instance, heterosexuality, especially male heterosexuality, in which, as she says,

> The loss of homosexuality is refused and the love sustained or encrypted in the parts of the body itself, literalized in the ostensible anatomical facticity of sex. Here we see the general strategy of literalization as a form of forgetfulness, which, in the case of a literalized sexual anatomy, "forgets" the imaginary and, with it, an imaginable homosexuality. In the case of the melancholic heterosexual male, he never loved another man, he *is* a man, and he can seek recourse to the empirical facts that will prove it. (71)

This sounds like a pretty good account of my brothers' response to my father's pedagogical performance: it may well have turned *them* on, too, but their heterosexualizing identification with him took shape as a disavowal or forgetting of their love for him and an encrypting of it in or on their bodies. But Butler's denaturalizing narrative of melancholic heterosexuality also helps me make sense of my students' responses to *my* performance, particularly in classes that aren't conducted under the explicit rubric of gay studies. For if, following the example of my father, my teaching has attempted to combine the discipline of demystification (that is, of shaming others) with apparently *un*disciplined but no less self-conscious lapses into theatricality (that is, into shaming myself), many students consume that teaching in such a way that all that seems left of it, all that registers on their spectatorial bodies, is its most obviously disciplinary effects, whose most characteristic physical sign is the cool, narrow-eyed gaze that keeps everything, and everyone, under surveillance.

In other words, just as what my brothers learned from my father's performance was the discipline of heterosexuality, so it is as a disciplinarian that I, too, seem to leave my most visible mark on students in non-gay-studies classes. Of course, I like to think that the discipline *I* administer—call it "literary criticism," for want of a better term—differs from my father's in having not only greater intellectual substance but also the opposite political valence. If I've imitated my father's pedagogical style, I've tried, even in "straight" classes, to reverse his lesson's homophobic, sexist content. But "tried" makes things seem more conscious and volitional, less obtusely transferential, than they really are. For in teaching "straight"—indeed, throughout a long (and still not completely abandoned) career of heterosexual masquerade—I've necessarily picked up a little melancholia of my own: after all, even to internalize the father already means to deny not just that one has lost him but that one ever loved him in the first place. So that when, under the aspect of disavowal, one stages an imaginary rematch with this phantom, in which, instead of "losing" by surrendering to homophobia, one "wins" by speaking out against it, one may merely reinforce the spectral, specular rule of melancholia over the classroom.

Gay studies seems to arrive on this scene not as a mere antidote—in the crude sense that "gay" means the opposite of "melancholy" or "sad"—but, like coming out, as an opportunity for transformative truth-telling, for naming and narrating the constitutive melancholia of modern subject-formation as such. Insofar as the educational system itself—from grade-school drilling in "good citizenship" to college-level instruction in more sophisticated forms of ideological policing—seems designed to produce and promote this melancholia, that system also *needs* the "perversions," if only to encrypt them in each and every good middle-class subject as so many stages (suggestive term) through which he or she must pass. If every teacher, even the most avant-garde queer theorist, is a disciplinarian, every teacher, even the most reactionary custodian of the eternal verities, is also a pervert. But if one's fate as a teacher—especially as a teacher of literature—is to be lovingly forgotten both as the person who, for instance, laid down the law of "political correctness" *and* as the person who, for instance, "went too far" in the interpretation of texts, teaching gay studies seems to offer a way of intervening in this cultural work of (one's) compulsory encrypting. It seems, that is, to offer a way of prying open the crypts that have already been sealed, of keeping others from forming too quickly, of bringing out, or educing, or even *educating* loves, pleasures, and desires that education otherwise serves to put away.

Education as bringing out: does that mean gay studies as sexual harassment? In the class I taught where gay studies figured most prominently, and where I was most out, the students, especially the self-identified queer or bisexual students, seemed precisely to regard as invasive any attempt *not* to grant them the heterosexual privilege of spectatorial distance, and to resent any invitation to explore their encrypted desires and identifications, not from a developmental perspective, as stages or "phases" to be transcended, but in a more generously theatrical light, as parts (of themselves) to be revived and reinterpreted—maybe even enjoyed and celebrated—on a pedagogical stage where we might all act up together instead of just acting out against one another.

To this newer theatrical model, the students in that class, an advanced seminar on literary theory, seemed to prefer the melancholic norm in which the teacher is the only one making a spectacle of himself. At a couple points in the semester, in fact, their vigilance and tenacity in maintaining the proscenium arch that invisibly but no less stringently organizes pedagogical space, their commitment to keeping me on one side of the arch and themselves on the other, nearly had the effect, as I'll explain, of raising my spectacle to new melodramatic heights, pushing me, I'm both proud and ashamed to say, to the verge of tears. If I ultimately succeeded in acting like a man (or like *de* Man) and blinking back what would otherwise have been signs of a fatally discrediting "sensitivity," I continue to linger regretfully over similar lost or bungled opportunities I had that semester to deviate from—and thus perhaps to revise—the code of "professional" conduct that governs my pedagogical practice.

It was one such bungle, in fact, that precipitated one of the classroom scenes of borderline melodrama. Around the middle of the semester, the school newspaper published an article on gays and lesbians on campus, in which I was surprised to read that there was only one out gay or lesbian professor at Bowdoin— a colleague of mine in the sociology department. Having made a point of coming out in several classes, and having given a public lecture on campus *about* coming out, I was dismayed by the ease and the apparent eagerness with which I was suddenly inned. When I called the student who wrote the article to ask him where he got this information, he told me that he had learned it from two of the members of the lesbian/gay/bisexual student organization—one of whom, it turned out, was also in the theory seminar. This news was of course even more upsetting, especially since the student in question—I'll call her Lisa—was a student with whom I felt an unusual bond, not only because she was out as queer, but also because, well, she seemed to like me too. She had even come to see me at the beginning of the semester to thank me for coming out, to tell me how important it was for lesbian, gay, and queer professors and students to do so, and to come out herself. So what was going on?

I couldn't wait to find out, although, as you can no doubt predict, and as even I wasn't too enraged by my wounded narcissism to sense at the time, wait is precisely what I should have done. I picked up the phone immediately and called Lisa at home, which already felt like a transgression, a breach of the rigorous etiquette that, especially at the kind of small liberal arts school that claims to promote close teacher-student interaction, serves to keep that interaction from becoming *too* close. When Lisa rather sheepishly confirmed the reporter's account, explaining that she hadn't been sure if it was permissible to identify me as gay, I quickly lost what little cool remained to me, and she just as quickly responded in kind. Hearing how angry she was, I recognized the extent of my blunder and tried, frantically, to control the damage. I apologized for calling her at home, and for putting her on the defensive, but I also asked her to understand how I had felt erased, and to imagine me for a moment—I hesitate to say it—not as a professor but as a person. Repeating the phrase, I'm even more aware of its triteness and deconstructibility than when I first uttered it; but I hoped that, by being trite, I would sound appropriately *con*trite, and that the very naïveté of my plea would make me seem all the more lovably and forgivably human, all the less like the hateful representative of a phallic authority that had overstepped its bounds.

As my lesbian colleague in the sociology department pointed out to me, however, maybe the reason Lisa put me back in the closet in the first place is that she wanted to regard me not as a person but as a professor—that is, as a representative of phallic authority. And as a lesbian colleague from another institution suggested, when a man comes out as gay, it can feel, to those receiving the news, like the death of a son, a brother, or a father. No more immune from melancholia than anyone else, in other words, Lisa, in covering me up, may have wanted to *re*cover through me, for example, a lost paternal object. Whatever her motive, she responded to my personalizing strategy by personalizing me with a vengeance. Though I managed to make a tentative peace with her by the end of the phone call, it soon became apparent, both in and out of class, not just that she was still mad at me, but that I had stirred up in her undercurrents of hostility that would not let themselves be discussed, much less mitigated. If she persisted in casting me in the pedagogical role I like least—that of father figure—she added insult to injury by turning me into the *abusive* father, so that, where I had hoped, throughout the semester, to get beyond the only two models of teacher/student relations that our culture seems to allow—namely, melancholic heterosexuality and sexual harassment—I found myself stuck with the worst of both of those models, forced to play out an Oedipal scenario in which I acquired all the oppressiveness of the paternal function but none of its cultural prestige.

In the last class of the semester, we were supposed to discuss two essays on pedagogy from *Inside/Out*, the anthology of lesbian and gay theory. I had hoped to recuperate some of the painful moments in and around the class by getting the students to consider the essays' suggestions for a more humane pedagogy, one that would be unabashedly gay-affirmative and sex-positive. But the result, I'm afraid, was just one more painful moment. A few minutes into the discussion, one of the bisexual students asked, with what I can only describe as a straight face, how students could most effectively "police" the erotics of the classroom. Taking her cue from her classmate's rhetorical question, which performed the very policing it pretended merely to ask about, Lisa launched into a diatribe about teachers who practice "mindfuck" on their students, and who abuse their power by "masturbating in front of" them. It was this outburst that nearly provoked a symmetrical, if more pathetic, effusion from me. Twice warned, however, to clean up my act—to police *myself*—I would hardly have dared to pour forth tears destined to seem only slightly less obscene than the upshot of any autoerotic self-indulgence.

But I continue to wish that, instead of retreating obediently behind the *cordon sanitaire*, I had had the energy and the nerve to explore those tropes of "mindfuck" and of teachers "masturbating in front of" students. For as tropes, they operate like catachreses, intriguingly blurring the lines between the literal and the figurative, between the violently sexual and the perversely textual, between the personal and the professorial/professional. For all the disciplinary aggression with which they were mobilized, that is, they might have made it possible for us to articulate an alternative to sexual harassment and melancholic heterosexuality. What, after all, is a teacher doing when he masturbates in front of his students? Presumably, he isn't actually masturbating; but he isn't just letting himself be encrypted as the egghead-pervert either. Performing an apparently auto-affective and self-contained act but performing it *in front of* others, he might be trying to set up a new kind of relation across the footlights—a relation not between an assaultive pedagogical subject and a bunch of inert, empty pedagogical objects, but between desiring and performing subjects who, from their different positions as teacher and as students, might decide that there are better things to do with the erotics of the classroom than to police them—or who might, since policing *is* the dominant mode of eroticism in our culture, at least find ways to do the police in different vices.

Notes

I would like to thank Eve Kosofsky Sedgwick for inviting me to participate in the session at the 1992 MLA Convention at which the first version of this essay was presented. As always, I am grateful to Lee Edelman for his incisive comments and suggestions.

1. For a plausible (if non-gay-inflected) argument that "the academy is in a certain sense a branch of show business," see Graff. A distinctively "queer" recognition and exploration of the possibilities of show business in the academy, of the academy *as* show business, might be related interestingly to the current confluence of lesbian and gay studies and cultural (that is to say, mass-cultural) studies.

2. I owe this example to Richard Meyer.

3. For discussions of this issue in relation to the paradigmatic figure of Henry James, see "Making a Scene: Henry James's Theater of Embarrassment," chapter 6 of my book *Caught in the Act*, 195–234; and Sedgwick.

4. Freud 223. For a compelling account of why Freud needs to characterize this scene as banal, see Edelman, also forthcoming in *Homographesis: Essays in Gay Literary and Cultural Theory* (New York: Routledge, 1993).

5. On the unstable grammar and dynamics of shame (condensed exemplarily in the phrase "Shame on you"), see Sedgwick 7–9, MS.

Works Cited

Butler, Judith. *Gender Trouble: Feminism and the Subversion of Identity*. New York: Routledge, 1990.

de Man, Paul. "The Resistance to Theory." *The Resistance to Theory*. Minneapolis: U of Minnesota P, 1986. 3–20.

Edelman, Lee. "Seeing Things: Representation, the Scene of Surveillance, and the Spectacle of Gay Male Sex." *Inside/Out: Lesbian Theories, Gay Theories*. Ed. Diana Fuss. New York: Routledge, 1991. 93–116.

Freud, Sigmund. "From the History of an Infantile Neurosis." *Three Case Histories*. Ed. Philip Rieff. New York: Collier, 1973.

Graff, Gerald. "Preaching to the Converted." *English Inside and Out: The Places of Literary Criticism*. Ed. Susan Gubar and Jonathan Kamholtz. New York: Routledge, 1993. 109–21.

Litvak, Joseph. *Caught in the Act: Theatricality in the Nineteenth-Century English Novel*. Berkeley: U of California P, 1992.

Sedgwick, Eve Kosofsky. "Toward Queer Performativity: Henry James's *The Art of the Novel*." *GLQ* 1 (forthcoming).

3 | Lecturing and Transference
The Undercover Work of Pedagogy
Arthur W. Frank

MY TOPIC IS lecturing, specifically the daily lecturing in university courses that has been the major part of my teaching during the last eighteen years. My need to reappraise what I'm doing in the classroom comes from performing a good deal of non-university lecturing, primarily to groups of seriously ill persons and to professional caregivers. People attend my non-university lectures for the respite that comes from a sense of shared experience, shared both with me and with the others in the audience. Through these "other" lectures I have gained some perspective on my lecturing in courses. I've had to ask myself why people at my illness lectures are so much more appreciative and why I find those occasions so moving. Why, I ask myself, couldn't it be like this in the classroom?

Some obvious reasons present themselves. My illness lectures are what Erving Goffman calls "celebrative occasions" (168). People disrupt their daily schedules to come to hear me because they have self-consciously defined themselves as having emotional or practical needs; they arrive already prepared to be affected in certain ways. University lectures *are* people's daily schedules, and thus they are literally mundane. One sense of their mundanity is that both the students and I are there at least in part to fulfill a contractual obligation. Another sense is that the lectures occur with a frequency that dulls intense emotional involvement. These matters are what Goffman would call framing. They represent serious differences between the two types of lectures, but their recognition does not resolve the differences between the two types. My sense remains that in my university lectures both I and my students are getting a good deal less than what happens in my illness lectures.

My topic then is to consider the university lecture in relation to this sense of lack in my course lectures. I have not achieved any new lecturing pedagogy that fills this lack. On the contrary, my conclusion is going to be that the only "solution" is to make lack more thematic. As a contribution to theory, the call to make lack thematic is perfunctory. As pedagogical practice, however, thematizing lack is not without consequences.

The Lecturer as Undercover Agent

In 1971 Roland Barthes published a paper entitled "Writers, Intellectuals, Teachers" considering the university lecture in terms of three developments. The first was political crisis, the second was insights from Lacanian psychoanalysis, and the third was the recognition of the opposition between writing and speech.

Erving Goffman, in his 1976 lecture on "The Lecture," differentiates between lectures presented as "aloud reading" and those he calls "fresh talk" (171), though much of what is presented as fresh talk can be quite well rehearsed, and aloud reading seldom goes without improvisational asides. Goffman says (in the lecture he was giving) that he is reading a text, but that the future publication of his text (the publication I was reading) will omit many features of the spoken performance (just as my spoken quasi-reading of this text omitted these parentheses, and so on).

Barthes and Goffman both regard the text of the lecture as being a literal pretext. The lecture is a multilayered performance, and what is supposed to be going on hardly justifies the occasion. Goffman makes more than Barthes of the essential scandal of the lecture, its patent inefficiency. Of course we could read the written text more quickly. Goffman would have been amused by the recent remarks of Alberta's former Education Minister who wanted lectures given by professors to be replaced by videos scripted by academics but delivered by professional actors. The proposal cannot be superficially dismissed. We can hardly ignore the efficiency of students consulting videos that they could play and rewind, and professors then being free to spend their time updating scripts rather than spending hours delivering these scripts in front of students.

This sort of efficiency leads both Goffman and Barthes to ask what more the lecture has to offer beyond the written text that they saw as its rival or the video text we can now imagine. "What is lost," Barthes wrote, "is the supplement" (193). Goffman specifies this supplement as having two components. The first is the *access* the speaker affords to the audience by her personal presence (186–87). Even if the lecture is thoroughly scripted, auditors retain the belief that they can glean more about the speaker through personal delivery than they could learn from reading a written text. The spoken delivery is taken to be "candid" in ways that make the speaker uniquely available to the audience. Goffman's second aspect of the supplement is what he calls *ritual*, the "preferential contact with an entity held to be of value" (187). Clearly, access and ritual support each other, since the value of the entity is also what makes access valuable.

To buttress Goffman's argument I offer my perpetual fascination when students come to see me about papers or course performance. I ask them what questions they have. I gradually realize they have no specific questions; they only want, quite literally, to *see* me in an exclusive interview, as if that contact could confer something. Depending on my schedule, I can find these meetings frustrating, yet Goffman reminds me that I ought to be honored: I am being treated as an object that is valuable to encounter.

Goffman and Barthes tell us, then, that the content of a lecture is neither more *nor less* than what Goffman calls "the price [audience members] have to pay for listening to the transmitter" (186). Goffman and Barthes both describe the lecturer as one who presents something else "under cover" of the text that is only a pretext (Barthes 194; Goffman 191). Goffman describes this undercover work using a psychoanalytic metaphor that could be Barthes's: "As the manifest content of a dream allows a latent meaning to be tolerated, so the transmission of a text allows for the ritual of performance" (191). The problem with the Education Minister's video proposal is that this ritual of performance would be lost, and with this loss much of the pedagogy of the lecture would be lost as well.

Let me underscore the point that, for Barthes and Goffman, the pedagogy of the lecture is intensely personal. Yet both recognize that the lecture works precisely by *concealing* this personal essence; stated another way, the personal element is effective only *if* it is concealed. The manifest content must be that of conveying information and truth. Thus Barthes describes the defining characteristic of the lecture as its capacity to admit *summary*, this summary presumably giving the content a universal existence beyond the lecturer's particularistic presentation.

Goffman complements Barthes when he describes the lecture as being delivered in a style that is "serious and slightly impersonal, the controlling intent being to generate calmly considered understanding . . . truth appearing as something to be cultivated and developed from a distance, coolly, as an end in itself" (165). The cool, distant truth of the summary is the manifest content that conceals and thus makes possible the supplementary ritual of performance.

Thus, in Barthes's and Goffman's descriptions, lectures emerge as curious occasions. The lecture presents a text that is ostensibly independent of the lecturer but actually covers a ritual centering on the value of the lecturer's physical presence. Both Barthes and Goffman invoke a psychoanalytic metaphor, or even analog, for the lecture situation. I read each as suggesting that the truth of the occasion—as opposed to the truths spoken in the lecturer's text—exists on the other side of a repression. What the lecture speaks cannot be spoken directly but can only be smuggled in "under cover," to use the one phrase they both employ (at least as Barthes is translated).

This curious concealment also pervades Barthes's and Goffman's reluctant acceptance that the lecture is an exercise in authority. Barthes writes of "the role that makes every speaker a kind of policeman" (192), and Goffman emphasizes the "claim [to] some kind of intellectual authority" (195) that animates the lecture. This police authority is both real and a facade; the policeman *is* a control agent but also a smuggler, an undercover agent. What, then, is being smuggled into this most mundane and authoritative of occasions?

Truth and Transference

Course lecturers have to repeat our performance several times a week, and that is exactly what we have going for us: *time*. Lecturer and students pass time together, sufficient time to give rise to those particular relations that Barthes calls transference.

The basic analogy between the lecture and the psychoanalytic encounter rests on the relation of speech and silence. Writing in the *persona* of lecturer, Barthes says, "I speak, endlessly, in front of someone who remains silent . . . never knowing how that discourse is being received" (194, emphases omitted). For Barthes, "the teacher is the person analyzed" (194), and the students are "the Other [who] is always there, *puncturing* his discourse" (195).

Central to this puncturing are students' notes, which professors do not normally see. Barthes writes that the professor would not want to see his students' notes, for "fear of contemplating himself in a reduced state" (195). When the reception of our discourse does come back to us, it can be frightening, and professors act out of this fear in ways I'm not sure we are fully aware of.

I find Barthes's suggestion of transference relations in lecturing fascinating but underdeveloped. As I've experienced this relation, lecturing is a more complex inversion of psychoanalysis. True, the lecturer, like the analysand, speaks endlessly to a silent Other, and transferences certainly arise in the lecturer. The students, however, are forming transference relations of their own: the teacher is not the only person being analyzed.

Barthes says that the lecturer speaks endlessly; Goffman observes that lecturing as a form of talk is defined by one person holding the floor without limitation. However, precisely because of this endless talk, the lecturer is constructed by students as *one who never says what they want him to say*.

By virtue of organizational position and, we would hope, personal presence, and simply by holding the floor for so long, the lecturer becomes a version of Lacan's subject-presumed-to-know. The lecturer's true affinity with the subject-presumed-to-know is that she, like the analyst, never yields the truth that the students, like analysands in transference, become convinced she must possess. I do not mean the truth of the subject matter of the course, but rather the supposed truth of the lecturer herself and the truth of the students themselves.

The self of the lecturer is split, and Goffman's terms (192–93) describe this split. The part of the lecturer who could be replaced by an actor or a video machine is the "textual self," a talking head presenting verbally a text that could be more conveniently read. Giving voice to this text is another self, the "animator," and the life of this animator remains the unspoken subject of the lecture.

I propose that the desire of the students is for the speech of the animator's self—not the spoken text the animator presents (that is only the price of admission), but the *speech of what animates* that text. For structuralists (if any are left), the subject may be dead, but for students, the key to ideas is in the biography of the thinker. This principle of truth deriving from life experience pervades students' relations not just to those they study but to their teachers.

A student will recall some detail of my life that I have used long ago as an anecdote to illustrate some academic argument. The argument is long forgotten, but the student remembers what I said about myself and wants to fit that detail into a larger pattern. My endless speech in lecture is a sign that such a pattern exists—where else could this speech come from?—but the text that I actually speak in lecture denies access to any truth of that pattern. My lectures implicitly and explicitly hint about me, but my autobiography is never a legitimate topic in any systematic sense.

The lecturer thus incites an interest that he denies, animating not only the lecture but the transference that gives it force. If the lecturer can say all he does about the lecture topic, the student is left to wonder, what could he say about *me*?

Plenitude and Disruption

On the surface, the lecturer presents students with *plenitude*, a speech without end. But that speech eventually turns into an inverted equivalent of the silence of the psychoanalyst. Both the lecturer's speech and the analyst's silence are endless; each can be interrupted, and has to be interrupted, only by the bell at the end of the period. But neither speech nor silence *responds* to its other, at least as that other believes he could be responded to. Listening endlessly to lecture speech that never responds, like speaking endlessly to the unresponsive silence of the analyst, thematizes a lack in those who listen, animating their desire. What this desire is for, insofar as desires are ever *for* anything, is for the subject-presumed-to-know to reveal herself in some exercise of authority. Goffman and Barthes agree that the lecturer must be willing to accept being an authority, which means becoming constructed as a subject-presumed-to-know. Pedagogy seems to begin with how this authority is used, a use that includes its own disruption.

In "The Lecture" as elsewhere, Goffman self-consciously sought to circumscribe his authority. The job of the lecturer, concludes Goffman, is "to stand up and seriously project the assumption that through lecturing, a meaningful picture of some part of the world can be conveyed, and that the talker can have access to a picture worth conveying" (194–95). Goffman's last sentence then subverts the lecturer's claim to authority: "after a speech, the speaker and the audience rightfully return to the flickering, cross-purposed, messy irresolution of the unknowable circumstances" (195). When Goffman throws these unknowable circumstances in his audience's collective face, he goes beyond delimitation of his subject matter. He is challenging each auditor's fantasy of what is desired from "Goffman" the authority, the lecture *persona*.

The essential moment in this circumscription is when the lecturer implicitly asks his students what every psychoanalyst must sooner or later, explicitly or implicitly, ask the analysand: *What do you want from me?* And behind this disruptive question is a more important one: *What should you expect from yourself?*

The pedagogy of the lecture, for which the course content can only be pretext, is imagined by these questions to hinge on self-knowledge. Students, I imagine, ought to come to us for one purpose only: to learn to become editors of their own lives, in Kierkegaard's great metaphor. The essence of what I would call moral education is this capacity for self-reflection: to become moral beings we must see our actions as they are seen by others.

One of the crucial steps in this moral education is finding a proper relation to authorities: a relation that is neither a transference fantasy nor a resistance to any transference. Goffman clearly tells his listeners that they can learn something from him, but they cannot expect that knowledge to clear up their lives. In classroom terms, the student needs to learn that if she sees the professor as either the subject-presumed-to-know or as a windbag who assigns too much reading, both of those are *her* fantasies. If she attends lectures only for information, that is also her loss.

The professorial problem with lecturing is to get beyond fearing reduced images of ourselves in our students' notes and book margins; this fear can be placed under the rubric of counter-transference. The basic problem of university lectures is not grading, or student careerism, or becoming too familiar to your audience. These issues are quite real, but any resolution of them rests on working through a more fundamental recognition of what lecturing is trying to do.

Lecturers must find ways to ask students what they want from us, so that they ask this as a serious moral question *about themselves*. A lecture series must get students to a point of realizing that they *do* want something from us, and then giving them sufficient resources to ask, *on their own*, what this is and why. I should emphasize here that although the teaching relation is a therapeutic one marked by transferences, the teacher is not a therapist. What students do with these issues will be done on their own, the personal relation to the teacher having to remain under cover.

Obviously the moral education I'm talking about cannot be taught but can only be modeled during teaching. Goffman writes about modeling as possibly "the most important thing a speaker does." The model he means is not a model of method, knowledge, or scholarship but rather "a model of how to handle oneself in the matter of one's own claims to position" (192). I have tried to suggest that this position is inevitably that of subject-presumed-to-know. The model Goffman gives us for handling this position is neither by embracing it nor rejecting it, but rather by mindfully displaying its limits and providing openings for students to understand that what they want from the subject-presumed-to-know—this lecturer, you and me—is a fantasy that comes from themselves. When they believe that this fantasy is their own, then they can ask why they are sustaining it.

Using the Teacher

All I can offer is a moral question: What kind of transference relation does our lecturing presuppose, and what do we *do* with this relation?

Our transitive teaching, the stuff we test students on, is largely a cover for something else. This intransitive something else is what I call pedagogy. As pedagogues we must learn to live, as Barthes said, without much knowledge of how our discourse is being received. Unless we can tolerate this lack, we will end up being registrars, sustaining the assumption that grades present a meaningful picture of the world. More pernicious still, we can get stuck in countertransferences, that is, our own need for students' transference fantasies of ourselves as subjects-presumed-to-know. We then act in ways that sustain these fantasies rather than creating openings for them to be relinquished.

As an alternative to this grim prospect, let me return to my lecturing to ill persons and their caregivers. The impact of these lectures is that I can present myself, then and there, as a kind of ego ideal which the audience is already seeking. The lecturer as ego ideal makes himself available as an object of immediate consumption, to be used up fully on the single occasion. The audience's resulting plenitude is their happy illusion of desire being filled: the satisfied sense of having gobbled up a good lecturer.

The ego ideal exists to be introjected—gobbled up—and consumption makes for the immediate emotional gratification of celebrative occasion lectures. But this introjection is only an immature form of real use: an ego ideal is only a primitive version of a transference figure. Real use begins when we have resolved our transferences sufficiently to let the other person *be* other.

I borrow the word "use" from D. W. Winnicott's theory of the baby developing from "relating" to the parent to "using" the parent. In the primitive stage of relation, the infant literally feeds off the mother with no conception of the mother as other. Use begins with a sense of boundaries. The baby still takes from the mother, but a notion of exchange has begun to develop because the mother is beginning to be understood as someone else, not simply an extension of the child's body. Barthes's professor who fears the reduced image of himself in his students' notes can be described as fixated at the level of relation, since he takes that reduced image as true and thus as being, truly, from himself. The student who is caught in an image of the professor as subject-presumed-to-know is fixated at the same level. The difference is that the professor has a moral responsibility to help students to move on, but not *vice versa*.

The resolution of the transference consists of realizing that the transference figure is inedible. In practical terms, the end of transference requires separation; the resolution of the transference dispels the illusion of plenitude at the cost of leaving us alone with lack. Resolving a transference relation necessarily leaves both parties painfully aware of their lack. But this lack prepares for the future *use* of other people, because the other who has been constructed in my fantasies can now *be someone else*.

Lectures as celebrative occasions do not admit the time for otherness to be accepted: it is thus these occasions that seem on reflection to be lacking. Celebrative occasions have their impact by being one-shot affairs, but this is also their limitation. Transferences take time—time to build, and time to resolve. This building and resolution of transferences is the unique possibility of mundane course lectures.

Works Cited

Barthes, Roland. "Writers, Intellectuals, Teachers." *Image-Music-Text*. Trans. Stephen Heath. New York: Hill, 1977. 190–215.

Goffman, Erving. "The Lecture." *Forms of Talk*. Philadelphia: U of Pennsylvania P, 1981. 160–96.

Winnicott, D. W. "On 'The Use of an Object.' " *Psychoanalytic Explorations*. Ed. Clare Winnicott, Ray Shepherd, and Madelaine Davis. Cambridge: Harvard UP, 1989. 217–46.

4 | *Scholae Personae*
Masks for Meaning
Madeleine R. Grumet

A thousand winters
Will strip you bare as death, a thousand summers
Robe you life-green again
—*The Foresters*, Tennyson

Iт's oDD THAT I don't like the term "the personal." In my field, curriculum theory, that's what I'm known for. For twenty years I have drawn on autobiographical accounts of educational experience, reading them through lenses of phenomenological, psychoanalytic, and feminist theory. Related to that work is my effort to study the relationship between reproduction and education and to build discursive bridges between home, where we were children and raise our own children, and school, where we work with other people's children. Nevertheless, throughout these years I have systematically avoided the personal as an emblem for my efforts. Now academics don't often write about the material that we wish to avoid. And unless someone asks us to address these issues that make us anxious or annoyed, we usually don't think about them much at all. They just don't seem to crop up.

By asking me to address the personal in pedagogy Jane Gallop has provoked my resistance, from which her own work supplies relief. Willing to explore her own perplexity and ambivalence she has legitimized mine, and so I will start this discussion turning to the place I would avoid, the thing I would not think about and would not choose to show you, my green robe.

When I think about the personal, I think about my green robe. It's not jade green, although that's what it wants to be as it becomes a robe that I am starting to write about. It begins to lean toward the kind of robe that Joan Didion would write about in "On Keeping a Notebook," with a black satin tuxedo collar and black curlicues embroidered on a slightly iridescent brocade, the kind of robe her aunt Miss Lucy Farnsworth would have brought back from the Orient.

My robe is what some would call kelly green. I don't remember buying it. I could blame it on a relative, but that would be cowardly, and a betrayal. It is warm and thick, orlon probably, often coffee stained, and it is good for writing in on cold Rochester mornings, and afternoons for that matter, if no one drops by. It is not a robe for entertaining.

It can go in the washing machine and dryer, its synthetic fleece indestructible, but it works best when slightly soiled, worn with unwashed hair, a flannel nightgown, clogs, and Gerald's grey socks. When I think about it I remember my body.

It is a green cocoon. After a while words fly out of it.

Maybe if I were younger and thinner, the green robe would be jeans and a sweatshirt. But I grew up in the forties when mothers wore housedresses that were not really robes, but were not really dresses either. You wouldn't wear one to the store, but you were dressed if someone rang the bell. When I would come home from school for lunch, my mother would be wearing a housedress covered with small flowers, and I suspect that even if jeans suited me they would not surround me with morning light and kitchen smells.

When it was my turn to keep house, I would sit at the word processor, in the green robe, until the school bus rolled down the block. Then, as I saw my kids coming up the walk, I'd dash for the shower, protecting them from the sight of my literary decadence, for, unlike my mother, I was not dressed if someone rang the bell.

It is a robe I write in, not about. It is strange to see it move into the yellow letters on my screen.

It is my robe, it has my smell, and as I present it to you [*the robe, please*][1] it becomes my costume. I may never write again.

My ambivalence about this word, "personal," sends me to the OED which reveals the historical incarnations of my present perplexity. Call me the Shirley MacLaine of etymology. "Person" is traced to the Latin verb "personare," to sound through, later falling from act to object as a mask, the thing through which one sounds as in a play: dramatis personae.

That is the first meaning of person, one that the OED admits hasn't made it into English. It offers many more, among them this pair: "The living body of a human being; either a) the actual body as distinct from clothing, etc, or from the mind or soul, or b) the body with its clothing and adornment as presented to the sight of others."

A—flesh or B—fashion?

And so I call this paper "*Scholae Personae*: Masks for Meaning," deliberately choosing fashion over flesh, to argue that the personal is a performance, an appearance contrived for the public, and to argue that these masks enable us to perform the play of pedagogy.

Now that I have opened the door to my pedagogical wardrobe, I propose to recapitulate a series of responses that I have made over the years to one of the most consistent and absorbing problematics in modern pedagogy: what to wear.

Convinced in the mid-seventies that students of education required a greater selection than what was available to them in a field dominated by positivistic social science, behavioral objectives, and standardized tests, I started asking them to write autobiographical narratives of educational experience. Even then I did not refer to these narratives as "personal" writings. Perhaps the avoidance of the personal was merely strategic. In the mid-seventies I was eager to distance this work from humanistic psychology's hip huggers and nehru shirts. And from the start we had to defend this approach from accusations of bourgeois subjectivity levied by colleagues wearing leather jackets that signaled their Marxist and working-class identifications. In 1975, when Bill Pinar and I published *Toward a Poor Curriculum*—a year before the publication of *The Mermaid and the Minotaur*, and two years before Gilligan's 1977 publication of "In a Different Voice" in the *Harvard Educational Review*—the personal still signaled lingerie.

Nevertheless, facing rows of students at Hobart and William Smith Colleges—all of whom wore clothing designed to conceal all ethnic and class stigmata, all attired so that they would look exactly like each other—I asked for autobiographical narratives: seeking the specificity, the material, the lost shoe, the dead rabbit that would return studies of education and them and me to the world.

Single narratives were frightening. Written against the background of a curriculum that disallowed the first-person pronoun, these narratives could take on the status of revelation. But then thrilling disclosures and declarations would slide into a sickening puddle of objectification. Long before postmodernism exposed the pretensions of a unified consciousness, there were Nietzsche and Freud to steer us away from deadly coherence.

James Olney's wonderful 1972 text, *Metaphors of Self*, rescued us and our students from these objectifying sentimentalities by portraying autobiographies as metaphors for the self providing representations of subjectivity for the public world. Olney's autobiographer was hardly static, for he often transformed his own self-understanding through the act of narration, like Sartre, wriggling out of his self-representations as a snake sheds old skins. Rather than the hand-me-down determinism of the Polish playwright Witold Gombrowicz, whose characters' identities and fates are determined by a prop or piece of clothing that accidently touches their person, I chose Sartre's approach, window shopping.

I avoided the personal, just as I avoided "authentic" and "sincere" as descriptors for this prose and for this process, and turned to multiple narratives to invite the range, the contradictions, and all the robes—silk brocade, orlon, rayon (packs well), terry, seersucker, velvet, leather, feather—that students could find for this academic procession.

I would ask the students to write three narratives of educational experience, right at the outset of a course in the philosophy of education. Asking for only two narratives would have invited primordial pairs: mind/body, individual/community, boy/girl, leisure wear/formal dress. Three separate narratives made things hard to match.

I asked students to think of the stories that come to mind when someone says, "That was a really educational experience." I told them that the truth of autobiography was embedded in its detail, not its generalization, and asked them to eschew moralistic propositions. They were instructed to type each narrative and were told that I would read and respond to them and that they would also be duplicated so that other students could read and work with them as well. William Earle's *Autobiographical Consciousness* and Didion provided philosophical and literary frames. At the same time that students were thinking about the stories of their lives and how they would tell them to me, that telling was also being framed as a way of knowing.

Then came the three-week winter break, and I took all the stories home to read. I can still see them, sitting there in the study, next to the computer, waiting for me. I couldn't pick up just one or two and stick them in between trips to the store, or dash off a few before going out to the movies. Each set of three held a green world, thick with vegetation, and the only way I could make my way through it was in my green robe.

Green robed, I would crawl under their leaves, feel the rhythm of their sentences, move to the places they skipped over. A semiotic reading, if you will. I hated entering those texts, giving up my world for theirs, but once I had migrated, I started speaking in their tongue, I became a citizen, started taking notes, started speaking back, asking questions. Like Kristeva's baby I would become mimetic. The echolalia is subtle, but it is there in the style of response that jokes with the jokers, is tentative with the defended, discursive with the loquacious. And then at the end I would surface with a paragraph suggesting the philosophical questions implied in the narratives as well as readings that might inform further pursuit of these issues.

I denied the intimacy of my reading by abstaining from writing on their papers. I would place a number next to the sentence or word to which my comments referred and type them on a separate sheet of paper, sequenced by corresponding numbers. I read them in my green robe, but I typed my responses on the word processor, deliberately interposing the machine, the type of our texts, between our bodies. We made ourselves up in typed face. Masking our handwriting in type endowed our exchange with formality, intended to bring student stories into the legitimated discourse that constituted the knowledge of this philosophy of education course. I do confess that I signed my name, my first name, Madeleine, in black ink, at the bottom of the page. Nevertheless this correspondence was not to be a set of confidences exchanged behind the closed door of the office; in fact, I hardly ever met with students to discuss the narratives, *per se*, but I remember how I felt, handing back the papers after vacation, each with a typed sheet of questions and responses appended. See how much I love you?

As I remember the years of this work it is clear to me how it moved across these spaces, their places and mine, and then dressed itself up to appear in the classroom. If the classroom was my stage, then my study was my green room. The *OED* does not tell us why the color green is used for the place where actors relax, prepare, and gossip before they go on stage, but it does tell us that in a warehouse or factory the green room is used for the reception of goods in a green state: such as cloth fresh from the weaving factory, undried pottery, auto-biographies, etc.

I don't know where the students were or what they wore as they wrote. I do know that the educational experiences they wrote about rarely took place in school. The classroom was our scene. Their stories shifted our view to yet other scenes, and my questions and their reflections often moved beyond the scenes of the narratives to scenes that they disguised or elided, the scenes against the scene, the *obscene*. Herbert Blau suggests that the obscene threatens every scene:

> There is in every performance an aggression against the scene of the perform-ance as a value, a derealization. . . . In the history of theater itself, the scene invariably tends toward fragmentation, closure, loss of outwardness and a sense of infinite behind. . . . The pressure toward a surface makes you wonder what's behind. The scene remains obscene. The obscene submits what should be kept private to public scrutiny. In that act, the value of the private may be reduced. (75)

Behind the scenes, I was raising three children, and raging at my field for refusing to acknowledge the primal scene. At conferences of education research-ers and theorists, children rarely came up. Few admitted to living with children, having children, knowing children, or ever having been children. Nevertheless, so-called reproduction theory was the order of the day. In this tale of procrea-tion, factories and corporations and schools come together to make people in an industrial version of the Immaculate Conception. There was no acknowledg-ment of the possibility that our original experiences of reproduction, of being children, of having children, might influence our relations to other people's children. *Bitter Milk: Women and Teaching* was the book I wrote to portray a dia-lectical relation between reproduction—as we experience it as parents and chil-dren—and education.

Contradictions between the projects of reproduction and the patterns of gender identity provide a space that invites our exploration and transformation. For if the father's project is to claim connection against an epistemological pre-supposition that assumes separation, and if the mother's project is to foster separation against an epistemological presupposition of attachment, then we require a system of schooling where the fleeing mothers and the finding fathers can meet to make the switch.

But what of the teaching mother?

Let me reread my reading of my student's stories, no longer wearing the green robe, but keeping it in view. Here are four stories written by Catherine Fisher. They are my favorite stories, for they are wonderfully economical and full of the world. I am also pleased to read them here as I have read and reread them in other places. Most recently, they were published in an issue of *Liberal Education* where they were read and responded to by teams of liberal arts and science and education faculty from Brooklyn College to demonstrate the ways that autobiographical narratives can be used to ground and frame interdisciplinary discourse in education. Here are Catherine's stories:

Catherine's Stories of Educational Experiences

Story One

There was a woman who lived in my old neighborhood. She had grown-up sons and a dog. I don't remember the dog's name or even that I liked the dog—I just remember it was a blond Pekinese with a pug nose. I used to take the dog for walks. It was something different to do. I never thought the walks were for the dog's benefit; I always knew they were for mine.

One day I decided, after getting permission to walk the dog, to go to Hummels. Hummels was an old, dank store that was full of treasures. It was pretty far away but it was more than the distance that made the walk exciting: Going to Hummels was an adventure because it was in the opposite direction than I usually walked. When I think about this day, I picture myself alone, although I'm positive either my sister Melinda or my friend Donna Baggott was there. Melinda claims it was herself, but I'm still not convinced.

We were about half way to Hummels when I noticed that the leashed Pekinese had slowed down and that his mouth was covered with foamy white stuff. I remember thinking that he must have had milk for breakfast. Within seconds after this thought passed through my head, the dog began rolling around strangely on the grass. I realized something was drastically wrong. Next I remember screaming at the top of my lungs—FASTER, FASTER—to my companion, who was running furiously towards home and was almost out of my sight. A woman appeared. She picked up the dog, placed it on a hill and fanned it with a rug. Her own dogs were standing behind her watching the scene. I went inside the woman's house to call my mom. I had a hard time remembering my phone number, and then my mom could not understand what I was saying—she thought I was telling her I lost my change purse. Within a few minutes my mom and the dog's owner drove up in a car.

The dog was dead. No one yelled at me, but I wasn't consoled, either. I felt really sorry the woman's dog was dead, but I don't think I ever talked to her again.

Story Two

Fourth grade—Girl Scout trip to the Smithsonian. . . . June Smith's mother was the chaperone. We were all gathered around the balcony looking down on the big moving clock. Someone explained, "The pendulum moves as the earth rotates in its axis. . . ." Hmmmmmm, I thought about this, and when I looked up the entire Girl Scout troupe had disappeared. I wasn't particularly concerned, and I found them a while later. I thought the issue was a dead one, but June Smith's mother was mad. As I was getting on the bus to go home, she announced that "Catherine Fisher should not be allowed to go on any more trips because I was careless enough to get lost." I felt betrayed, mad, and helpless, but I said nothing. I knew I could never change her opinion of me.

A few years ago I saw June Smith's mother for the first time since the incident. She recognized me as "the one who got lost in the Smithsonian!" She didn't believe me when I told her my version of the story. Her opinion hadn't changed.

Story Three

One evening when we were very young—young enough for my older brother, younger sister, and myself to fit in a bathtub together—we did just that, we all climbed into the tub and had some fun. Our parents were gone—the grandparents from Texas were staying with us. We filled the tub too high. I remember looking up at the wet ceiling in the room beneath the bathroom. Everyone was mad. They were pointing to the wet spot, telling us to get dressed and come back downstairs to get spanked. We all raced upstairs scared to death. We thought frantically about how we could protect ourselves. We decided to put on as many pair of underwear as we could and hope it wasn't noticed. We raced around the room looking for underwear. The memory ends with the command, "Pull down your pants," and a feeling of inevitability.

Story Four

A big black dog that lived behind our house had caught a baby rabbit. With the help of Mom we somehow got the rabbit away from the dog. We put it in a shoe box and fed it with an eyedropper.

I don't know what I was doing in the dark foyer at night or how the rabbit got on the floor. I stepped on it, though. My mom was there. She took the rabbit upstairs to the lighted kitchen and placed it on the cabinet. Looking up at it, I saw that blood was coming out of its nose—I knew it couldn't live.

I reread the stories; I see the scenes, imagining, remembering scenes behind the scene, our dead hamsters, and the white rabbit we had who died after lapping up the milk from the broken milk bottle. I remember and imagine spankings as well as that photo of my girl scout troop and my mother taken at the Statue of Liberty. I remember what I typed on the page then and there, in my green robe, and what I didn't.

Over and over again the stories portray separations and isolation. "When I think about this day, I picture myself alone." Educational experience is portrayed as the realization of the betrayed and lonely consciousness, suggesting that whatever is shared in common escapes the distinction that makes it memorable. Educational experience differentiates and separates Catherine from her friends Melinda and Donna Baggot, from her mother who cannot understand what she is saying, and from the owner/mother of the dog. In my green robe I remember the repudiations of my children telling the stories of their lives as if they belonged to them alone, the fiction of their singular identities. I am the listening mother. What happened at school today? It was a long time before anybody asked me that question. Eclipsed, at home, the listener, not the storyteller, I point out to Catherine her apparent investment in her narrative solitude.

In my green robe, I read the Smithsonian story as Catherine's complaint against the maternal arrogation. She has moved into space and time, into science. The Girl Scouts (a paramilitary expression of ambivalent female solidarity if there ever was one) leave her alone to contemplate the universe until she is rebuked by June Smith's mother, frozen forever in her characterization as the one who got lost in the Smithsonian. Falsely accused. Years ago I suggested that she read Sartre's *Saint Genet*.

Story three: infantile sexuality overflows all bounds. Brothers and sisters in the bath together, the water overflows the tub, flows through the floor and ceiling below, leaving the stain. As inevitable as the dog's death, as June Smith's mother's indictment, is the humiliation; yet for all its declarations of fear, the tone is playful, for all its sadism, delighted at its exhibitionism. Or at least, that is how it seems to me, reading in the green robe.

Story four returns to death, a struggle of species that makes the shoe box, eyedropper attentions of the would-be savior poignantly insufficient. In this story the observer and putative victim of stories one to three becomes the killer. In my green robe I read it as the killing of her own babiness, a death which even Mom cannot prevent. Life keeps leaking out in these stories, and the knowledge, communication, and plumbing at our disposal are dreadfully inadequate to the task of containment.

What do I write to Catherine? I point out the contradictions, the inconsistencies, and the leaks: the companion that appears and disappears in story one. The shift from third person to first in story three: "Catherine Fisher should not be allowed to go on any more trips because I was careless enough to get lost." And then I leave loss and love to germinate in the deep pockets of the green robe among the chewing gum wrappers and address those themes in the terms of the course. I invite Catherine to think about her stories and to relate them to questions about education. Is education about discovering what knowledge denies? Is rational knowledge the fallacy that permits us to hide from the unavoidable recognition of our own mortality? Where is the lonely cogito of idealism in the compulsive sociability of progressive education? And I do ask her how June Smith's mother learns to see another woman's child as static when her own body must remember the sequence of changes that she has danced with her child. Catherine will choose. I offer more than she can use.

Whatever is too close or too distant is ignored. If she wants to talk to the green robe, she may work with Winnicott's or with Chodorow's texts. Or she may stick to Plato and Dewey or try Norman O. Brown. My hope is that I have met the furry, bloody, sudsy presence of her text with mine, and that I have offered linguistic connections between her world of rabbits and Girl Scouts and the complex contradictions in the work of teaching and education that fascinate me.

Do I work with other people's children to separate from mine or connect to theirs? The green robe is no negligee. I wrap myself as a maternal body as I relinquish my definition to its green indeterminateness, tactile and cozy, rounding off eroticism. Let my children go.

The teaching mother recovers herself and her children in this discourse. Differentiation is not desertion. In Freudian and Lacanian theory separation from the body of the mother is the loss of her. In Lacanian theory the living body and its semiotics are sacrificed to desire and are swallowed into the sign. But Kristeva offers us a sense of the sign that does not entail utter loss of the mother. The mother looks over her shoulder. The baby follows her gaze. The baby is interesting, even fascinating, to the mother, but so is the news, the novel, talking to grown-ups. In Kelly Oliver's reading of Kristeva, access to the symbolic offers a reunion with the maternal body that is experienced as loving something other than itself. My students' stories are interesting to me and so is Kristeva and so is Lacan. The gaze that passes between us includes them. In Oliver's reading the mother's love enacts the transference from the mother's body to the mother's desire. The mother's love provides the needed support for the transference to the site of maternal desire. I am interested in the world. They, sometimes, follow my gaze. They want it because I love it.

With words I am disrobed and articulated. As text, in the typed responses to Catherine and the others, I re-present myself as the object of desire, dressed up in the words of the world. In the mise-en-scène of the classroom, *scholae personae* simultaneously conceals and reveals my leaks, my denied dependencies, my fantasies, my desires. The green robe stays in the green room.

Note

1. Editor's Note: During the conference—"Pedagogy: The Question of the Personal"—at this point in the text, Grumet took her robe out of a shopping bag, hung it up for all to see, and then walked back to the podium to deliver the rest of the paper.

Works Cited

Blau, Herbert. "Letting Be Be the Finale of Seem: The Future of an Illusion." *Performance in Postmodern Culture.* Ed. Michel Benamou and Charles Caramello. Madison, WI: Coda, 1977. 59–77.

Chodorow, Nancy. *The Reproduction of Mothering: Psychoanalysis and the Sociology of Gender.* Berkeley: U of California P, 1978.

Didion, Joan. "On Keeping a Notebook." *Slouching toward Bethlehem.* New York: Dell, 1961. 131–41.

Dinnerstein, Dorothy. *The Mermaid and the Minotaur: Sexual Arrangements and Human Malaise.* New York: Harper, 1976.

Earle, William A. *Autobiographical Consciousness.* Chicago: Quadrangle, 1972.

Gallop, Jane. *The Daughter's Seduction: Feminism and Psychoanalysis.* Ithaca: Cornell UP, 1982.

Gilligan, Carol. *In a Different Voice: Psychological Theory and Women's Development.* Cambridge: Harvard UP, 1982.

Grumet, Madeleine. *Bitter Milk: Women and Teaching.* Amherst: U of Massachusetts P, 1988.

Grumet, Madeleine, and William F. Pinar. *Toward a Poor Curriculum.* Dubuque, IA: Kendall/Hunt, 1976.

Kristeva, Julia. *Tales of Love.* Trans. Leon S. Roudiez. New York: Columbia UP, 1987.

Oliver, Kelly. *Reading Kristeva: Unraveling the Double-Bind.* Bloomington: Indiana UP, 1993.

Olney, James. *Metaphors of Self: The Meaning of Autobiography.* Princeton: Princeton UP, 1972.

5 | Give Me a Girl at an Impressionable Age and She Is Mine for Life
Jean Brodie as Pedagogical Primer

Lynne Joyrich

W HEN, SOMETIME LAST winter, I was asked to come up with a title for my paper on *The Prime of Miss Jean Brodie*, I immediately turned to what, out of a film with a number of remarkable lines, is perhaps the most memorable: Jean's statement, "Give me a girl at an impressionable age, and she is mine for life." The fact that this line stands out so clearly in my memory is not simply due to my own personal obsession with the film (although, as I'll explain shortly, it is certainly not unrelated to that); within the text itself, the sentence is, in fact, repeated twice: once diegetically at the beginning of the film when Jean introduces herself to a new class of girls, and then as a voice-over at the end when the girls from this class (on whom Jean has indeed had a profound influence) graduate. Yet while this double inscription marks the statement as somewhat emblematic (and thus a seemingly perfect choice for my title), its dual referent—both inside and outside the narrative space—also made me a bit hesitant about my appropriation: in *The Prime of Miss Jean Brodie*, the line dividing what's inside or outside the fictional world may be roughly mapped onto the always provisional and fragile line between what's inside or outside the world of the classroom, and I wanted to avoid creating confusion in referencing these spaces in my title. For the impressionable girl I want to discuss is neither simply located in the world of the fiction nor that of the classroom. In other words, I'm not really going to focus on either the ways in which Jean makes an impression on her students or on the ways in which we, as teachers, might make an impression on ours. Rather, to borrow the autobiographical mode that Jean herself often uses, the girl to whom I'm primarily referring is me—one on whom (as both film viewer and critic, student and teacher) Jean Brodie has had an enormous impact.

As I mentioned a moment ago, it would not at all be an exaggeration to say that I've been obsessed with this film. I first remember seeing it on television when I was a student (I think it was my first year in college), and I loved it. At the time, that meant growing to distrust, even despise, Jean while fully identifying with Sandy, the student who rebels against the Brodie regime. I didn't see the film again for quite a while, but I did think about it; frequently, when looking through *TV Guide* to see what old movies were playing, I'd remember the film fondly, almost with longing, and hope for the chance to watch it again. This craving grew into a real fixation—by the time I was in graduate school, the first thing that I'd do when my weekly issue of *TV Guide* arrived was voraciously pore through it, hoping to find a listing for *The Prime of Miss Jean Brodie*, but always emerging disappointed. I called around to local video stores—none of them carried it. When I moved to Milwaukee, I called the video stores here too— again, no luck. In my mind, the film had achieved fantastic proportions—I had never wanted to see a movie as much as I wanted to see this one. Finally, through what was otherwise an unfortunate event, I had my chance: my father had to take some time off because of illness, and he sent me a list of video titles from a library that a friend of his worked at so that I could recommend some things for him to watch. There it was on the list: *The Prime of Miss Jean Brodie*. As might be expected, not only did I recommend it, but I insisted that he get me a copy. When the tape came in the mail, I watched the film . . . and then watched it again . . . and again . . . and again—every night for approximately a month. (In fact, the only time that I've ever resisted viewing the film was when I was getting ready to write—and resisting—this essay!)

Of course, by that time, I was a teacher myself, and so even though my sympathies had not exactly switched, they had become much more complex: I identified not only with Sandy, but with Jean as well. More precisely, I didn't simply identify with any one character in the conflict, perhaps not just in terms of characterization at all. My affect seemed to operate not only within but across these positions—to be based on the poignancy of the division itself. Furthermore, this very division was plural, split between what was inside and out. For in addition to the drama of renunciation and repetition that defines the relations between Sandy and Jean, when I watch the film I also encounter my own double—my past incarnations as viewer, previous identifications I both repeat and disavow. One might say that I reenact the drama of the film in my own (pedagogically informed) spectatorial development.[1] Yet even if this fractured self-reflection helps explain my interest in the film, the sheer scope and intensity of my viewing history makes it difficult to resist questioning the implications of such extreme involvement. What could it possibly mean to develop an obsession with an educational horror story (or perhaps more accurately—a horrific story about education) precisely when I was deciding to become a teacher myself? Was this tale of studious revenge a kind of return of the repressed? I suppose that only my therapist would know the answer to that question for sure. However, if I were to venture a guess in my capacity as cultural analyst instead of scrutinized analysand, I would suggest that it had to do with the very trajectory of recognition, misrecognition, and rerecognition that I've described—that is, with the mobility of identifications, and therefore of knowledges, that the film makes possible.

While my love of this film then exceeds any one topic (indeed, that's the reason for my love of the film), my desire to return to *The Prime of Miss Jean Brodie* here, in the context of a discussion of the theory and practice of pedagogy, is a very particular one: to talk less about the specific issues it depicts and more about the ones that it has led me to consider—which, given my own engagement with the text, tend to focus around questions of spectatorship, identification, and pleasure. In other words, rather than giving a reading of the film's representation of pedagogy as it blurs into both the personal and the political, I am more interested in attempting to give a reading that situates the film itself as pedagogical—in addition, of course, to being both deeply personal (as my own experience demonstrates) and, as I hope to argue, political as well.

What I am suggesting is that *The Prime of Miss Jean Brodie* is not simply a film about education—it is also a film which educates its viewers, which in particular has taught me something about viewing and desire. And this is not simply because of something peculiar to it, because it stands out as a uniquely "good film" (although I believe both that it *is* a good film and that I have learned something specific from its particular textual configuration). Yet the pedagogical process to which I'm referring—the way in which texts may lead to fruitful trains of thought—would be one shared by all media and popular cultural forms. The only thing that might then be peculiar about the case that I am making is this very evaluation (indeed, valuation) of a cinematic text. Within the ongoing debates around cultural literacy, the curriculum, and the politics of education, mass-mediated texts are rarely valued for their pedagogical potential; more often, they have been labeled as the bane of legitimated learning (as threats, according to critics such as Allan Bloom, to literacy, order, and the values of Western civilization).[2]

Jean Brodie, if we entertain viewing her as an educational authority in her own right, might disagree. To the dismay of headmistress Miss Mackay (but prefiguring some of the arguments for bringing "the everyday" into the classroom), Jean inspires her students by the use of popular narrative forms. However highbrow her own tastes, her girls are introduced to art and history through the mediums of romance and gossip (Miss Brodie's "love . . . ly stories" that make lessons "seem like cinema"). But whatever Jean's intentions, popular texts function not simply as inspiration; for (to reverse a turn of phrase from Henry Giroux and Roger Simon), if schools are always "about somebody's story," then we must equally recognize how stories are also always somebody's school (ix). Or to put it in the words of another educational theorist, Elizabeth Ellsworth, "The relation between popular cultural forms and the curriculum becomes even more complex when we recognize that all popular cultural forms are knowledge forms in and of themselves" (48).

Ellsworth, like Giroux and Simon (and the other contributors to their evocative book *Popular Culture, Schooling, and Everyday Life*), is arguing for an expanded notion of pedagogy—one that takes into account the very ways in which knowledges are constructed across daily practices of cultural production, reception, and exchange.[3] While film, television, and other mass cultural texts may then initially appear to lie "outside" the concerns of the present volume, if we think of pedagogy as more than a formal and institutionalized relationship to the profession of teaching, their link to the "inside" becomes more pronounced. In fact, in many ways, mass culture exemplifies the process of double inscription with which I began. That is, in its production of meanings, affective investments, even ways of life, mass culture may be seen as a primary point at which the public meets the private, politics meets pleasure, and pedagogy meets the personal—the point at which, as it is taken up by interlocking systems of exchange (textual, affective, discursive, and commodity), desire itself is disciplined and educated.

These concepts—desire, exchange, the production of meaning—actually point to the way in which I have used *The Prime of Miss Jean Brodie* in my own teaching. For despite the fact that trying to write about it—and therefore make it into a proper academic enterprise—temporarily blocked my ability to find pleasure in the film, I do frequently use it "officially" in the classroom. In fact, I begin my "Women and Film" course with this very text: aside from providing students with an opportunity for a bit of cautious amusement at the thought of dealing with a new class and teacher, the film allows me to introduce a number of important if not founding concerns in feminist film theory. That is, by illustrating the way in which identities are institutionally produced, *The Prime of Miss Jean Brodie* helps expose the operation of historical and representational codes. Gender as a social and cultural construction; the constitution of sexual difference within a regimented order of exchange; the asymmetrical relations that position men and women within the field of vision—all of these issues may be discussed through the use of this film.[4] Indeed, the text may be seen as almost an allegory of the reproduction of sexual identity, of the way in which subjects are systematically en-gendered: in the Marcia Blaine Academy, virtuous young ladies, "their price far above rubies," are churned out according to very precise terms of education and exchange.

Even within the text, Jean refers to the school as an education factory. Furthermore, this factory produces not only gendered subjects but also national and imperial ones. Jean's interpellation of her students as "civilized beings," "Europeans" rather than ignorant and "petty provincials," indicates the way in which the entire system of British schooling was devoted to reproducing an imperialist cultural heritage as well as a system of gendered exchange.

Caught within this structure as it is represented in the text, women's positions are extremely limited (in Jean's words, women's roles are to "serve, suffer, and sacrifice"). They are to be mothers and daughters (dutifully reproducing this imperialist system of social and sexual "intercourse"), wives or mistresses (in other words, either private property—the dismal prospect of marrying Mr. Lowther—or public possessions—"famous for sex"),

Furthermore, whether constructed as private or public property, women are positioned as objects to be seen. Within the diegesis, the emblematic position of painter's model (and the characters' desire to achieve this status) demonstrates how "woman as spectacle" is put into public circulation, but the film also reveals the ways in which "private" moments are also structured according to very conventional visual norms. For example, in the scene depicting the growing romance between Miss Brodie and Mr. Lowther, Mary Macgregor watches Jean and Gordon at the apple tree as if she is viewing a stereotypical scene in a clichéd love story (as, indeed, this scene is both enacted and filmed).

And, at last, composed objects to be seen by all (as they're "painted many times") or else objects seen as ridiculous for their very lack of circulation (the other teachers in the school: the daffy old ladies, sexless spinsters, mannish lesbians).

Refusing all of these options, Jean is left in an impossible position. Wishing to claim desire for herself, transact on her own terms, mediate the look, and take up an active place within history, Jean is bound to dismally fail in all areas: first, she is left with neither sex nor marriage for herself and is further unable to negotiate exchanges down the line (such as her plan to substitute Jenny's body for her own in an affair with Mr. Lloyd); second, rather than determining the image according to the measure of her desire, she can only become a spectacle in other people's eyes (as the sewing teachers say, "She always looks so extreme").

This is only one moment in the film when Jean is marked as spectacle, but there are many others. These produce a variety of effects, either reinforcing or undercutting Jean's power. For example, when the headmistress first accuses Jean of immorality, her response (interpreted as a "tantrum" by Miss Mackay but as "heroic" by Mr. Lowther) leaves them both speechless, demonstrating the power of a deliberate display. On the other hand, in the final showdown between Sandy and Jean, the way in which Jean "always strike[s] attitudes" makes her appear (to Sandy, at least) as a "ridiculous woman," revealing the risk inherent in assuming the position of spectacle. This is not, however, the only risky position: the film also emphasizes the dangers of spectating, most dramatically in the morality story that Jean tells Mary about Peeping Tom, but also in the framing narrative itself (the film's depiction of Jean's and Sandy's desperate attempts to construct themselves as subjects of the gaze).

Finally, removed from all spheres of action, Jean is forced to endlessly remain on the sidelines of the game (or, in deference to both Miss Brodie's feelings about "the team spirit" and the final party scene, perhaps I should say that she's stuck on the edges of the dance).

As she states, prevented from being great herself, Jean Brodie can only strive to "inspire greatness in others." Furthermore, not only must she cede her place in public life, but she must also relinquish possibilities within the private sphere: according to Jean, in dedicating her life to teaching, she has to sacrifice her personal life in order "to consecrate" herself to her girls. This description of renouncing worldly love gives teaching (a profession which is elsewhere in the film described in much more militaristic and/or industrial terms) the aura of a religious calling, thus making it an acceptable arena for female action (like the nunnery that, in the novel, Sandy grows up to join). Nonetheless, women's authorization to lead in even this sphere is vague. As stated by Teddy Lloyd, when it comes to the relations between the sexes, men should be the ones in the tutorial position.

Jean's turn to fascism is then no surprise: What other system so elevates the private to a public function and allows women to enter the stage of history merely by accepting their supposedly "natural" position within relations of exchange (their glorified status as nationalistic bearers of the race or, as in Jean's fantasy of participation, just aesthetic object—"in a crowd of supporters wearing a dress . . . that is right for [her] coloring")?

Jean refuses (or fails at) the role that fascism outlines for women of "reproducing" subjects in the literal sense of sexual reproduction. Yet when it comes to "her girls" (also tellingly referred to as her "brood") she does seem endlessly to strive to reproduce the ideal subject that she herself can never be. In some ways, Teddy Lloyd's paintings concretize this process: he paints a number of the girls (a point highlighted in the book in which he paints them all), but always manages only to reproduce likenesses of Jean.

In an almost perverse reversal of the aims of critical pedagogy, Jean thus steers her students toward actions that can only further enmesh them in dominant relations of power.

This training in fascism may be seen as the distorted inverse of the processes and goals of critical pedagogy in more ways than one: not only is the political activity promoted by Miss Brodie the opposite of the kind of activism engendered by radical educators, but fascism is also one of the few political systems to embrace the pedagogical powers of popular culture (the reliance on theater, radio, cinema, and so on)—again, for opposite ends than those advocated by educators working in the realm of popular culture and critical pedagogy today. I therefore disagree with Giroux and Simon's assertion that the pedagogy of "Hitler's Germany and Mussolini's Italy" consisted solely in restoring a lost classical heritage at the expense of taking mass culture seriously (224). Rather, in these cases of fascism, the two processes coexisted. I would then argue that the use of mass cultural texts does not in and of itself determine a static politics or produce universal ideological implications. Indeed, in both its representation of the girls' developing identifications and its construction of my own, The Prime of Miss Jean Brodie *highlights the multiple divisions that can cut across both politics and pleasures.*

Mary Macgregor, the faithful soldier, provides the most extreme example of this reversal. Mistakenly choosing the surrogate familialism of Jean's *fascisti* over her brother who's enlisted to oppose them, she stupidly goes off to fight in the Spanish civil war.

In addition to the dream of family that most appeals to Mary is fascism's (false) offer of individualism, which seems to be one of the lures for Jean: even as it rallies the masses into unification and homogenization, fascism promotes an image of individual self-fulfillment, promising to break down the division between individual and community, public and private. Of course, this promise is an illusionary one, as is demonstrated in The Prime of Miss Jean Brodie *by the contradictions surrounding Mary Macgregor: Jean claims that Mary's attempted activism on behalf of fascism "illumined" her life, individuating and naming her as a heroine, yet Sandy retorts that Jean's constant reliance on Mary's full name only indicates that she could never remember exactly who Mary was.*

Sandy's homefront battle is less explicitly political, but it directly engages the dynamics of both the personal and pedagogical spheres. As perhaps the true symbolic daughter onto whom the burden falls, her options (particularly in terms of sexual politics) are as dismal as Jean's: marked as the dependable, emotionless "secret service agent," she cannot be a woman, since becoming a woman is defined only according to the most conventional terms (as the object of a man's desire who must take off her glasses in order to get a vision of herself solely through his eyes). Indeed, the film clearly demonstrates (in the cases of both Sandy and Jean) the enormous price women must pay to line up on either side of the spectator/spectacle divide.

Beyond demonstrating the general way in which women are positioned in relations of exchange, The Prime of Miss Jean Brodie *can then also be seen as a drama specifically about gender and the dynamics of vision. I have already noted how Jean is figured both as frustrated spectator and, to an even greater degree, as interrogated spectacle. Yet the film reveals just as much about sexual difference and the look in its portrayal of Sandy. Throughout the film, Sandy moves her glasses on and off, oscillating between her attempts to become first the subject and then the object of the gaze. While the moments of her looking are themselves variously interpreted (Jean describes Sandy both as one who "peers" and therefore makes a rude impression and as one who has great insight and the makings of an excellent spy), the trope of a woman getting rid of her glasses is an overdetermined one in the cinema, signaling the shift in her position and status from threat to containment, usurpation to attraction (Doane, Femmes 26–28). There are a number of examples of this in the film. For instance, Sandy removes and replaces her glasses when she looks at herself in the mirror in Jean's apartment as she considers whether she might have "insight or instinct" (the makings of a lover or not) and again in Teddy's studio as she shifts from the role of model/lover to that of scathing critic. In each case, desirability is associated with the moment the glasses are shorn, and an improper (for a woman) penetrating gaze is associated with the moments when she puts them back on. Yet rather than its stakes being veiled, as is frequently the case in film, the power and pleasure of the gaze in* The Prime of Miss Jean Brodie *is often made quite clear as it is played out explicitly on the terrain of sexuality itself. Think, for example, of the humor in the little girls' first awareness of sex (when they try to imagine Miss Brodie together with her lover Hugh but "can't see it") as compared to the threat later generated by Sandy when she consciously assumes the position of the sexual subject who looks and desires according to her own will (her statement, marked as shocking both inside and outside the diegesis, that neither she nor Jean were interested in Teddy for his mind).*

I have used this film in the classroom to demonstrate precisely these impossible personal and political binds; yet perhaps what I have learned from my own experience with the text is somewhat different. It may be true that Jean and Sandy fail in their attempts to negotiate power and, specifically, positions of viewing that will work for rather than against them.

I'm thinking here both of the play with Sandy's glasses and image and of Jean's attempt to insert herself as a subject of vision and narrative in regard to the slides that she brings to her students at "her own expense"—literally expending herself, since not only can she not see herself as anything other than the prize (instead of the protagonist) of the story, but she is not even able to count in this position very long before being exchanged for another, younger and more desirable version. This slide show scene is another example of a moment when Jean's attempt to assert herself as the subject of the gaze backfires as she becomes instead a scrutinized object. Here, just when she is most caught up in her own inner vision (and when the film itself emphasizes her position as desirer/looker through its lighting and low-angle close-up shot of Jean), there is a sudden shift which reveals her vision to be blurred (the film cuts to an unfocused image of the classroom as Jean mistakes her student's identity). Breaking out of her fantasy, Jean realizes that she has become a fascinating spectacle for her students. I would argue that the poignancy of this moment for the film spectator (particularly the female one) lies in the way it reveals the binds in which women viewers are trapped: the way in which acts of looking may actually work to situate us further on the side of display.[5]

These diegetic struggles may be moving and instructive for viewers, both emotionally and educationally stirring. Yet the poignant exposure of these losses does not have to mean that more satisfying sexual and/or textual negotiations are impossible. As my own retraced pleasure in the film itself demonstrates, the interdynamics and exchanges of cinema (as well as other forms of mass culture) are necessarily more open than that.

What I would like to call "openness," however, may instead appear to be something more disturbingly fragmented. Indeed, the layout of the last few pages makes graphic a bothersome split in my approach to the film. I do not want to present a reading of *The Prime of Miss Jean Brodie* in this essay, yet nonetheless a reading keeps presenting itself. What first began as supplementary notes to a discussion of cinema and pedagogy—the italicized sections of the text—have insistently grown until (as evident from their expansion) they threaten to overtake the entire analysis. It is always a pleasure to talk about this film; clearly, this paper arises from and would theorize that pleasure. Yet my training as a film critic has also made me cautious in this fascination—a fascination with cinema that has (quite literally) been subject to discipline and schooling. In fact, within my discipline, such fascination has been the subject of an academic dispute that is unavoidably central at this time in film studies. I'm referring here to the debates around the politics and pleasures of spectatorship—debates that have tended to harden around polarized terms.[6] I believe that *The Prime of Miss Jean Brodie* has helped me reconsider this dispute, perhaps allowing me to move beyond the usual binary choice of positions: just as my viewing identification is neither exclusively with teacher or student, I hope that my theoretical identification need not be split in a polarized way. Yet the doubling of my text above, the impossibility of choosing either to do a reading or not, signals that I am still working through the difficulties of (understanding) film viewing rather than, in any simple or comfortable way, beyond them.

These difficulties center on questions of viewing and pleasure. On one side of this debate, the position that has come to be known as "screen theory" investigates the ways in which viewer identifications are solicited by textual strategies of address. Interrogating such constructions, screen theory treats pleasure with suspicion, considering it a particularly insidious form of ideological manipulation. In contrast, much of the work carried on under the label of "cultural studies" celebrates pleasure as an empowering and potentially liberating aspect of audience appropriation. Identification, according to this perspective, is more flexible since it is multiply determined—not simply by the text, but by other discursive formations as well. Cultural studies thus explores the diverse ways in which texts might be experienced, often borrowing from ethnographic approaches in order to "read" how various audience groups themselves create spaces for readings.

Spanning both sides of the argument as I attempt to articulate *my* multiple identifications (rooted in my own training as a student and teacher), this essay itself splits into opposing positions—positions which each have unavoidable conceptual and pedagogical tensions. On the one hand, screen theory has been critiqued for its reliance upon ahistorical psychoanalytic models that deny the contingencies of social articulation.[7] Unable to see either how meanings and pleasures are constructed differently across different populations, or indeed how these meanings and pleasures might ever change over time, screen theory may wind up reproducing a particularly reductive understanding of representation, language, and society which belies its basis in more subtle approaches to signification and subjectivity. On the other hand, the cultural studies model can suffer from all of the usual problems that plague ethnographic research: it tends toward a naive positivism, its valorization of experience denies the more complex workings of unconscious desire, and its use of "the people" as informants may enact the same imperialist impulses found in less politically motivated work. While the expressed goal may be one of empowering its otherwise subordinated constituents, cultural studies thus often ends up reiterating the same celebratory rhetoric of dominant media institutions themselves (a rhetoric of demography rather than democracy—that is, the false democracy of the marketplace alone).

When we move from the seemingly open space of this consumer playground to the more disciplined recesses of the schoolyard, we are likely to encounter this same debate, for these arguments in film and television theory have a special relevancy for classroom politics and practices. For example, a challenge to notions of passive spectatorship affirms not only our involvement with cinematic/televisual scenes but also with pedagogical ones (Ellsworth 63). Those interested in a critical pedagogy might then very well turn to the insights of cultural studies, particularly in the light of today's emphases on both media literacy and the politics of cultural diversity. Attuned to the ways in which students form identifications in relation to popular culture and to the ways in which these affective investments might encourage active ideological resistance, educators interested in legitimating the diversity of student experiences have taken up film and television as empowering cultural forms—that is, as texts that seem to authorize student participation and knowledge.[8] Consequently, as if taking a lesson from Jean Brodie herself (here on the root of the word "educa-tion"—from *ex*/out and *duco*/I lead), some teachers use film and TV to lead out what is already there in the students in unexpressed form.

But despite (or perhaps because of) this imagined endorsement from Jean, there are a number of problems with this approach. As Paul Smith has argued, introducing film and television texts to the classroom in this way can lead to an unexamined valorization of media apparatuses and of experience, denying how both are constituted by cultural codes and social regulation (33–34). Taking a position more in line with screen theory, he thus insists that we use our influ-ence to undercut that of mass culture itself. In other words, students will learn to resist the ideological lures of mass culture only if they face resistance to their otherwise uncritical acceptance from those who might teach them a different way to view cultural texts (42–43). This is a crucial pedagogical intervention for, to paraphrase one of my own teachers, the problem with mass culture is less that it excludes disempowered groups than that the pleasure it provides includes us, perhaps to our detriment (as in the case of Jean's students), in a compelling and very effective manner—mollifying and assimilating subjects into an order based on their exploitation (*Camera Obscura* 145). Or again to borrow a turn of phrase from Jean, just as school teachers put old heads on young shoulders, the cinema enlists young bodies for some old and very conventional roles.

This is particularly true for women, the group that serves as linchpin to the systems of both cinematic and larger cultural exchange even as female subjects are radically negated—not only by films but (at least according to attacks on screen theory's pessimism) by many film critics themselves.[9] We see in *The Prime of Miss Jean Brodie* how the pedagogical process of social and cultural reproduc-tion (whether this takes place in the classroom or not) is complemented by that of reproducing gender. Yet there are risks for women in each turn in this dis-pute: not only may we have the most to lose if we should lose sight of the stakes of enlistment and erasure addressed by this debate (thereby maintaining a fa-miliar neglect of women's pleasure), but considering the way in which sexual difference has always been constrained within the rigid parameters of a binary logic, women may also be the most disadvantaged by maintaining the discus-sion within its present polarizing form. In other words, regardless of the par-ticular issues, this very mode of dualistic thinking replicates a structure which feminist critics have tried to disrupt. After all, if there is such an unbridgeable gap either between social subjects and textually inscribed ones or between the methods of analysis brought to bear upon them ("historical/empirical" vs. "tex-tual/theoretical" work), then feminist theory (which seeks to analyze not only Woman's cultural repression but women's historical oppression) would itself be necessarily refused.[10]

However, arguments which attempt to undercut the dualism and break the stranglehold of this polarizing logic may find themselves disrupted and dismantled from within. In other words, that my paper should continue to be torn by this troubling opposition is not (only) a mark of some peculiar personal pathology. For this split in texts and viewers not only defines two different methodological traditions of cultural criticism; it also recurs inside both "camps." That is, the debate over whether the viewer is ideologically manipulated or actively resistant, whether pleasure is suspect or empowering, repeats itself across the range of media theory, creating contradictions not only between but *within* each critical and pedagogical approach to film.

For example, some screen theorists have responded to cultural studies' charges by locating heterogeneity within the psychoanalytic model itself. Emphasizing that identity is never fixed nor fully attained, they have turned to fantasy to conceptualize the fragility and flux of both sexual and textual identifications. According to this theorization, films may stage *mises-en-scène* of desire, but there are multiple slots for the subject within, slots which are not divided by gender even if they are sexually marked.[11]

Consider, for instance, my plural points of identification in regard to The Prime of Miss Jean Brodie, *or indeed, those found in the various fantasy scenes represented in the text itself: the students' collaborative construction of a primal scene between Jean and Mr. Lowther in which they play both roles, and Jean's own shifting identifications when she "projects" (literally and phantasmatically) images from Italy. In imagining a network linking Dante, Beatrice, and a woman whose memory inspired their love, Jean (like her girls) moves across the field of gender in her assumption of positions which are each still coded by the terms of sexual exchange. While not exactly a release from a structure that contains her, this movement nonetheless allows her to participate actively in a fantasy whose valence has therefore been changed—just as my own permutating positions (the divided self-encounters I noted earlier) provide me with an empowering mobile pleasure in regard to the structured fantasy of the film itself.*

Yet while the concept of fantasy may permit film scholars to envision a range of spectatorial positions without accepting reductive models of identificatory roles, this reading of (my) pleasure is still at odds with itself. In what is perhaps an appropriate disciplinary warning from one who happens literally to have been my teacher, Doane cautions feminist theorists that such an approach carries the danger of making its own method obsolete:

> Fantasy theory's desire is to annihilate an identity which has been oppressive—but to annihilate it by fiat, simply declaring it non-operational at the level of an indisputable psychical reality of slippage, splitting, and failure. However, if this is indeed the case, and texts do operate in this manner *vis à vis* their spectators, there is no need for feminist criticism. For feminist criticism must of necessity deal with the constraints and restraints of reading with

respect to sexual identity—in effect, with the question of power and its textual manifestation. It may be true that at the level of the psychical, identity is always ultimately subject to failure, but at the level of the social, and with respect to configurations of power, this is clearly not the case. (*Camera Obscura* 145)

Cultural studies claims to concern itself with exactly this question of power, but basing itself on a belief in empiricism which often replicates a phantasmatic structure, it is not immune to these same epistemological and political binds. In fact, there is an almost uncanny repetition within and across screen and cultural studies: critiquing audience scholars, Patricia Mellencamp makes a point strikingly similar to Doane's but in this case directed to the other side of the theoretical divide:

While "audience" scholars refute their rights of interpretation, speaking in the name of the people and pluralism rather than textual analysis, these scholarly gambits, as valuable as they are if framed by theoretical models, have promulgated a female spectator or viewer outside the containments and contradictions of representation and history. If so many "subversive" readings are available for everyone, with any text, then feminist films and videos addressed to women, by women and about women are hardly necessary, clever readers that "the people" are. The scholar's analysis also becomes unnecessary. (*Camera Obscura* 235)

This expendability of the scholar is due to the very circularity of identifications within the cultural studies construction of pedagogy and knowledge. On the one hand, individuals variously situated within the social field are the objects to be known, but as these differences get diffused onto a general notion of "the people" as a whole, a collective subject is established that both reduces the initial complexity and establishes the masses as "the one[s] supposed to know."

Producing "clever" readings on their own, "the people" themselves would seem to take on the (now dispensable) position of the teacher; however, not always knowing what it is that they say, even this voice of knowledge must be read by an interpreting scholar. While this move seems to safeguard the credentials of the critic, it also has the curious effect of assimilating the ethnographic method into that of the psychoanalytic "talking cure" itself: the empirical viewer, who doesn't know what she knows until her words are interpreted by an analyst, becomes the counterpart of the spectator-subject subjected to the unconscious. Within its own enunciative practices (if not in its theoretical claims), cultural studies might even be said to replicate the processes that it finds most disheartening in screen theory's diagnosis of the spectator. As both described by its critics and acknowledged by some of its practitioners themselves, "it can become an apologetic 'yes, *but* . . . ' discourse that most often proceeds *from* admitting class, racial, and sexual oppressions *to* finding the inevitable saving grace."[12] Paradoxically (but perhaps not unpredictably), this "yes, but" construction—the move from lack to substitution—is a classic example of a fetishistic operation, causing cultural studies to repeat within its own analytic practice one of the defenses over which the dispute initially began: the question of whether or not fetishism is a definitive—and definitively oppressive—structure in viewing.

Although I do not usually do audience research, to the extent that the present paper attempts an ethnography of an audience of one (who happens in this case to be synonymous with the scholar), one might see this split also being played out here.[13] Not only could I certainly be accused of fetishizing this movie, but I too am producing a "yes, *but*...." For, as I noted earlier, while I teach *The Prime of Miss Jean Brodie* in order to illustrate the structures of exchange that help reproduce relations of gender, I would like to believe that I have learned something different from my own multiple encounters with the film. Perhaps it is not surprising that this divide between the subject who recognizes the constraints of ideology and the subject who feels empowered to read against those constraints writes itself here as a split between an "I teach" and an "I believe that I have learned." Yet it is also too easy to oppose pedagogy and pleasure in the way that this implies. For just as my enjoyment of the text itself is trained (culturally, even if not strictly academically, disciplined), so this disciplining elicits the spiraling of power and pleasure that generates the conflicts within cinematic and educational debates.

In making graphic the insistent difficulty of speaking (as both a student and a teacher of film and cultural theory) my fascination with the text, this essay marks the tension and confusion of negotiating these divides. The debates within film theory have made me recognize the problems in either deconstructing or embracing cultural engagement, giving an analytic reading of the film or just declaring my delight. Yet both this reading and statement of enjoyment nonetheless emerge in the (not quite) margins of my text. Given my fractured identifications, it is difficult for me to present them anywhere else. Thus, instead of fully accounting for my interest in Jean as teacher and/or Sandy as student, these identifications are more directly enacted, indeed (in my studied recitation of film debates) acted out. This fragmented construction may, however, hint at precisely the way in which viewers (don't quite) grasp texts.

It's tempting to try to solve the riddle of my extreme engagement with this film—to conclude by somehow summing up what I think I've learned. But if the text has taught me anything, it is the value of keeping my own plural pleasures, knowledges, and history with the film in play, not settling on which identification is the true or "knowing" one, which reading is right. In other words, for me at least, the pedagogical significance of *The Prime of Miss Jean Brodie* does not simply lie in what it says about teaching.

Although it says a lot—about, for example, the pleasures and dangers of personalization, the fascistic potential of even a repudiation of the conservative "transmission and imposition" model of schooling, the authoritarian risks in either side of curriculum debates.[14]

Rather, my experience with the film has acted as a "pedagogical primer" in and of itself. Its fragmentations and divisions, urgency and questions, may point to the very educational value of the struggle—to the way in which we must not dispense with the thorny oppositions repeated across the range of film and cultural theory quite this soon.[15] For rather than simply defining the terms of an impasse, the gap between interpellation and empowerment marks a space that is stimulating rather than defeating, a tension whose productive strain ought not yet be released.

Notes

Thanks to Chris Bratton and Thomas Piontek for their helpful comments and suggestions, to Nicole Cunningham for invaluable discussions and numerous readings, and to Jane Gallop for an astute analysis, discerning editing, and inspired impersonation.

1. In fact, one did: David Crane, in an insightful response to this essay.
2. For critiques of these positions, see Ava Preacher Collins and the essays in Giroux, Simon, and Contributors (particularly those by Giroux and Simon themselves).
3. For these arguments about the relationship between popular culture and pedagogy, see in particular the three essays cowritten by Giroux and Simon.
4. These concepts are all developed through Gayle Rubin's account of the sex/gender system (an account which integrates Claude Lévi-Strauss's theory of the exchange of women together with a psychoanalytic understanding of the reproduction of sexual identity), and Luce Irigaray's discussion of women's resistance to this very system.
5. For related discussions about the emotional charge and ideological implications of another film incorporating diegetic moments of female viewing, see both Kaplan's and William's analyses of *Stella Dallas*.
6. For summaries of these debates and introductions to the positions, see David Morley, "Changing Paradigms"; the chapters in *Channels of Discourse* on psychoanalysis and cultural studies by Sandy Flitterman-Lewis and John Fiske respectively; and *Camera Obscura*'s special issue on "The Spectatrix" (in which the introductory article by Janet Bergstrom and Mary Ann Doane [5–27], the "national survey" report by Laura Mulvey [68–81], and many individual responses address this debate).
7. For critiques of the way in which screen theory conflates the subject interpellated by the text with the subject interpellated into ideology and then collapses both onto a universalizing notion of the unconscious, see Stuart Hall and the articles by Morley.
8. For examples of this approach, see in particular Giroux and the collaborative articles by Giroux and Simon.
9. I'm referring here to the debates specifically within feminist film theory about the possibility of female viewing pleasure, indeed about whether or not "the female spectator" can exist. Laura Mulvey's famous article "Visual Pleasure and Narrative Cinema" initiated this debate. Following up on it were (among others) Mulvey herself ("Afterthoughts"), Doane ("Film and the Masquerade" and "Masquerade Reconsidered," reprinted in *Femmes Fatales*), and Teresa de Lauretis. For either accounts or enactments of

the ensuing disputes, see the debate between E. Ann Kaplan and Linda Williams on *Stella Dallas*; the opposing opinions of Doane and Tania Modleski (particularly in regard to their readings of *Rebecca* [Modleski 1–15 and 43–55; Doane, *Desire* 122–75]); and the various positions outlined in the *Camera Obscura* issue on "The Spectatrix."

10. To investigate the way in which sociopolitical categorizations of gender intersect with linguistic and psychical terms of sexual difference, cultural critics must then dismantle these conceptual oppositions, revealing the correspondences (rather than divisions) between subject and social formations, inside and out. This is probably most obvious in the case of "experience," perhaps the most disputed term of this debate. This cannot be just a matter of prioritizing inner or outer (Jean's "instinct or insight") since, in this polarization, both sides seem to implode from within. "Screen theorists" may be attacked for their abstract notions of signification and the construction of subjectivity, but (like Jean Brodie's take on culture) it is from their own experiences as social and viewing subjects that their theoretical formulations derive. On the other hand, the demand to ground the multiplicity of viewers'/students' "readings" within the variants of experience often proceeds from a neglect of the fact that "reading" (the privileged metaphor for meaning production) is itself a schooled activity—one that (as the film painstakingly demonstrates) must adhere to pedagogical principles and systematic rules.

11. The definition of fantasy as a *mise-en-scène* of desire comes from Laplanche and Pontalis, and has been brought into film studies by Elizabeth Cowie ("Fantasia"). For a discussion of this and related psychoanalytic approaches in regard to the debates over the female spectator, see the *Camera Obscura* responses by (among others) Copjec, Cowie, Creed, Mayne, Penley, Rodowick, and Rose.

12. My discussion of this construction of knowledge and identification is indebted to Meaghan Morris's critique of cultural studies (here quoting from her discussion on 22–25). See also the *Camera Obscura* response by Linda Williams for an acknowledgment of how this strategy functions in her work (333).

13. Charlotte Brunsdon's intriguing discussion of the implications of such autobiographical reflections—her analysis of the effects of treating the scholar as an audience sample—are relevant to my own "ethnography" of the (writing) subject here. Yet Brunsdon claims that this strategy tends to direct scholars away from an investigation of the text and onto a celebration of audiences instead—precisely the opposite of what seems to be happening in this essay. My acknowledgment of my own pleasure in *The Prime of Miss Jean Brodie* leads me away from the theoretical debates on film, viewers, and pedagogy and toward a textual reading that emerges almost unwittingly at the seams of my essay.

14. This is a reference to Giroux and Simon's critique of the conservative pedagogy espoused by people such as Allan Bloom:

> Its goal is a form of education that presupposes moral and social regulation in which the voice of tradition provides the ideological legitimation for a ministry of culture. Its echo is to be found in Hitler's Germany and Mussolini's Italy; its pedagogy is as profoundly reactionary as its ideology and can be summed up simply in these terms: transmission and imposition. (225)

Jean Brodie, objecting to the "transmission and imposition" (or as she terms it, "intrusion") model of schooling in her dispute with Miss Mackay, nonetheless makes no bones about her admiration of fascism, forcing us to realize that the relations between pedagogy and politics are not so clear-cut.

15. For similar arguments in the *Camera Obscura* issue, see (among others) Flitterman-Lewis (158), Patrice Petro (262), and Judith Mayne (232–34).

Works Cited

Allen, Robert C., ed. *Channels of Discourse: Television and Contemporary Criticism.* Chapel Hill: U of North Carolina P, 1977.

Bloom, Allan David. *The Closing of the American Mind: How Higher Education Has Failed Democracy and Impoverished the Souls of Today's Students.* New York: Simon, 1987.

Brunsdon, Charlotte. "Television: Aesthetics and Audiences." Mellencamp 59–72.

Camera Obscura. Special Issue on "The Spectatrix." Ed. Janet Bergstrom and Mary Ann Doane. 20–21 (1989).

Certeau, Michel de. *The Practice of Everyday Life.* Trans. Steven Rendall. Berkeley: U of California P, 1984.

Collins, Ava Preacher. "Loose Canons: Constructing Cultural Traditions Inside and Outside the Academy." Collins, Radner, and Collins 86–102.

Collins, Jim, Hilary Radner, and Ava Preacher Collins, eds. *Film Theory Goes to the Movies.* New York: Routledge, 1993.

Cowie, Elizabeth. "Fantasia." *m/f* 9 (1984): 71–104.

Crane, David. "Only Her Therapist Knows for Sure." ms.

Doane, Mary Ann. *The Desire to Desire: The Woman's Film of the 1940's.* Bloomington: Indiana UP, 1987.

———. *Femmes Fatales: Feminism, Film Theory, Psychoanalysis.* New York: Routledge, 1991.

Ellsworth, Elizabeth. "Educational Media, Ideology, and the Presentation of Knowledge through Popular Cultural Forms." Giroux, Simon, and Contributors 47–66.

Fiske, John. "British Cultural Studies and Television." Allen 254–90.

Flitterman-Lewis, Sandy. "Psychoanalysis, Film, and Television." Allen 172–210.

Giroux, Henry A. "Reclaiming the Social: Pedagogy, Resistance, and Politics in Celluloid Culture." Collins, Radner, and Collins 37–55.

Giroux, Henry A., and Roger I. Simon. "Pedagogy, Popular Culture, and Public Life: An Introduction." Giroux, Simon, and Contributors vii–xii.

———. "Popular Culture as Pedagogy of Pleasure and Meaning." Giroux, Simon, and Contributors 1–30.

———. "Schooling, Popular Culture, and a Pedagogy of Possibility." Giroux, Simon, and Contributors 219–35.

Giroux, Henry A., Roger I. Simon, and Contributors, eds. *Popular Culture, Schooling, and Everyday Life.* New York: Bergin, 1989.

Hall, Stuart. "Recent Developments in Theories of Language and Ideology: A Critical Note." Hall et al. 157–62.

Hall, Stuart, et al., eds. *Culture, Media, Language: Working Papers in Cultural Studies 1972–79.* London: Hutchinson, 1980.

Irigaray, Luce. *This Sex Which Is Not One.* Trans. Catherine Porter. Ithaca: Cornell UP, 1985.

Kaplan, E. Ann. "Ann Kaplan Replies to Linda Williams's 'Something Else Besides a Mother . . .' " *Cinema Journal* 24.2 (1985): 40–43.

———. "The Case of the Missing Mother: Maternal Issues in Vidor's *Stella Dallas.*" *Heresies* 16 (1983): 81–85.

Laplanche, Jean, and Jean-Baptiste Pontalis. *The Language of Psycho-Analysis.* Trans. Donald Nicholson-Smith. New York: Norton, 1973.

Lévi-Strauss, Claude. *The Elementary Structure of Kinship.* Trans. James Harle Bell, John Richard von Sturmer, and Rodney Needham. Boston: Beacon, 1969.

Mellencamp, Patricia, ed. *Logics of Television: Essays in Cultural Criticism.* Bloomington: Indiana UP, 1990.

Modleski, Tania. *The Women Who Knew Too Much: Hitchcock and Feminist Theory*. New York: Methuen, 1988.

Morley, David. "Changing Paradigms in Audience Studies." *Remote Control: Television, Audiences and Cultural Power*. Ed. Ellen Seiter et al. New York: Routledge, 1989. 16–43.

———. "Texts, Readers, Subjects." Hall et al. 163–73.

Morris, Meaghan. "Banality in Cultural Studies." Mellencamp 14–43.

Mulvey, Laura. "Visual Pleasure and Narrative Cinema." *Screen* 16.3 (1975): 6–18.

———. "Afterthoughts on 'Visual Pleasure and Narrative Cinema' Inspired by *Duel in the Sun*." *Framework* 15–17 (1981): 12–15.

The Prime of Miss Jean Brodie. Dir. Ronald Neame. CBS/Fox, 1969.

Rubin, Gayle. "The Traffic in Women: Notes toward a Political Economy of Sex." *Toward an Anthropology of Women*. Ed. Rayna Reiter. New York: Monthly Review, 1975. 157–210.

Smith, Paul. "Pedagogy and the Popular-Cultural-Commodity-Text." Giroux, Simon, and Contributors 31–46.

Spark, Muriel. *The Prime of Miss Jean Brodie*. London: Macmillan, 1961.

Williams, Linda. " 'Something Else Besides a Mother': *Stella Dallas* and the Maternal Melodrama." *Cinema Journal* 24.1 (1984): 2–27.

6 | The Good Teacher, the Good Student

Identifications of a Student Teacher

Chris Amirault

The Good Teacher

THIS ESSAY CONSIDERS my relationship with the best student from my first year of college instruction as a graduate student. I call her my "best student" because she met all of the criteria I have for evaluating what a good student should be. Shannon was in my first- and second-semester writing courses; she took these classes to work on her writing even though she had passed the university's writing competency requirement. She successfully completed all of the course requirements and expectations: she attended virtually every class and handed in all of her assignments on time; she did the readings and the homework and always engaged critically with the topics brought up in discussion; she attended office hours and worked long and hard in and out of class on her papers, trying to make them as strong as they could be. Most important, she seemed to be taking personally the material we discussed. I felt as if I were helping her to develop as a writer, a thinker, an intellectual. She certainly seemed to be learning what I was trying to teach.

During both semesters, she and I met often in office hours to discuss her work. Our meetings in the early spring focused on her revisions to a paper that she planned to enter in an undergraduate essay contest. Though I had given her an A when she first handed in the paper and had at the time recommended that she submit it to this contest, I was never satisfied with her later work on the paper. In fact, it seemed to me that, as she revised it, the paper got worse and not better: the writing got more and more muddy, the focus of the paper more and more blurry. On the day of the contest submission deadline, I found, without any attached note, a copy of her final draft in my mailbox, and in the following days I heard nothing more about it from Shannon when I saw her in class. That was just as well, I thought at the time, for the paper was, in the end, disappointing, not at all indicative of the strong work she had produced all year long. When I received a departmental notice announcing the winners of the contest, Shannon's name wasn't listed, and I wasn't surprised.

A few weeks after I received her final draft in my mailbox, Shannon walked into my office. Seeing her, I expected that she had come to talk about her experience of writing and revising the paper or about specific problems the paper had. However, when she walked in, she announced to me that she had been thinking and that she had realized *why* the paper had turned out so poorly. "I spent all of my time trying to figure out what you wanted me to write, and I couldn't do it," she said. "Only now I realize that what I needed to do was to figure out what *I* wanted to write."

I felt a thrill as she said those words. For the rest of the hour, we energetically discussed my teaching and her learning. We talked about her frustrations with my meticulous close reading and comments, the effects of my eager yet often excessively demanding advice. We talked about how she struggled to revise the paper, to make it clearer and smoother, frequently finding herself overwhelmed by trying to figure out the implications of every comment. As we talked, I reveled in the fact that, somehow, she had come to learn what I most wanted to teach. Somehow, she had learned that what I most wanted as a teacher was for my students to figure out what they most wanted as students. At that moment in which we explored her paper's failure, I was convinced that Shannon was the most successful student I could have.

Shannon's announcement represented the fulfillment of my teacherly desire. Within this fantasy, my fulfillment was achieved by her fulfillment as a student. As she walked out the door, I was convinced that I was a thoroughly good teacher, because I was satisfied only through the satisfaction of my student, who had come to understand what she wanted. Furthermore, by articulating this chain of pedagogical desire and knowledge, Shannon revealed my pedagogical blindspots: I learned that, in my eagerness to suggest improvements to and possibilities for further development in her papers, I had often focused more on my response to the paper as a reader than on her needs as a student learning how to write, and that my careful close reading of individual sentences and paragraphs made it difficult for her to think about revising the paper in holistic terms. Our conversation caused me to rethink my own pedagogical strategies, and in that moment Shannon really taught me something.

Driven by the impulse to reenact this satisfying teaching performance regularly, I set out to understand exactly what had happened in that meeting. Clearly, my pleasure in my student's pleasure is connected to a culturally valorized fantasy that structures most teaching, that of the selfless teacher who teaches "for his students" and not "for himself." By being convinced that I had erased my own narcissistic desires—convinced, that is, that I had in that moment been a perfect teacher—I felt deeply satisfied.

Both my pleasure in my student's pleasure as well as my pleasure in being taught by my student find themselves articulated in certain student-centered pedagogical strategies, ones which, not coincidentally, are valorized in most radical and feminist pedagogy, the very strategies I have taken up in my own teaching. The work of Paolo Freire, in particular, by suggesting such strategies, has provided the foundation for radical pedagogy. His influential *Pedagogy of the Oppressed*, written as a manifesto against teacher-centered teaching and in favor of student-centered teaching, has provided many teachers with a theoretical starting point for rethinking our own teaching. I learned how to teach in an alternative school that valorized the work of Freire and other theorists of radical pedagogy, and my meeting with Shannon seemed to confirm the value of that pedagogy. In contrast to what he refers to as the banking model of education, in which teachers desire to fill empty students with knowledge, Freire constructs a dialectical model of teachers and students who learn from each other as the students move toward attaining freedom. In so doing, the positions of "teacher" and "student" are transformed; Freire renames the newly constructed positions accordingly: "Through dialogue, the teacher-of-the-students and the students-of-the-teacher cease to exist and a new term emerges: teacher-student with student-teachers. The teacher is no longer merely the-one-who-teaches, but one who is himself taught in dialogue with the students, who in turn while being taught also teach" (67).

As we talked, Shannon and I enacted this dialogical model of teaching. No longer a mere teacher, a term that is clearly pejorative in Freire's text, I had become a teacher-student, learning from my student both what her specific concerns were and how I could best respond to them. No longer a mere student, she had become a student-teacher, evaluating her own educational desires and explaining her experience as a student in ways that transformed our teacher/student relation. We were not operating within a banking economy of education and knowledge, but were instead exploring the very nature of our pedagogy, a metacritical maneuver valorized by most radical pedagogies. My partner in this metacriticism had demonstrated that she was my best student-teacher, and she convinced me that, as a result, I must be a good teacher-student. Furthermore, in asserting that she didn't need me, and thus the university, for her to learn, Shannon seemed to resolve the dilemma of the ineradicable, hierarchical authority that structures so much teaching that would otherwise claim to be radical pedagogy. With no little hubris, I felt that the appellation "teacher-student" marked my deft ability to outmaneuver the institutional authority so many teachers strive to dismantle.

Freire's theorization of "teacher-students" and "student-teachers" provided me with a way to understand what happened in my meeting with Shannon; given Freire's authority as a theorist of pedagogy, the understanding felt like a dream come true. This fulfillment is part of what has made Freire's theory so influential, I believe: his pedagogy seems to provide an attainable goal in a context that otherwise thwarts such teacherly desires. It is ironic, in this sense, that Freire is usually taken to provide a student- and not teacher-centered pedagogy, for in this case at least, that very pedagogy provides many teachers with exactly what they want.

The authority given Freire's work in much radical and feminist pedagogy demonstrates that other teachers have come to understand their pedagogy in a similar way, that they too share this fantasy of good teaching. In her article "Feminist Values: Guidelines for Teaching Methodology in Women's Studies," Nancy Schniedewind describes one of the ways in which feminist pedagogy has taken up these issues. Schniedewind's essay first appeared in the journal *Radical Teacher*, and has since been reprinted at least twice, in *Politics of Education: Essays from* Radical Teacher and in *Learning Our Way*, an anthology of feminist pedagogy.[1] The essay's claim to provide "guidelines for teaching methodology" is supported by its publishing history and by the text itself, which offers a model of teaching that has been supported by feminist and radical theorists.

Discussing the question of teacherly authority and its effect on teacher/student relations, Schniedewind writes, "Feminist values argue for replacing hierarchical authority with participatory decision-making. This does not imply structurelessness, but structure that is democratic. In the classroom, it is possible for a teacher to share leadership with both students and other instructors" (13). In my one-on-one meeting with Shannon, it seemed as if we had replaced hierarchy with democracy, teacherly authority with a participatory model of decision-making. I felt as if we were sharing responsibility for our pedagogical relation; in discussing the pedagogy we were creating, simultaneously negotiating criticism of both teacher and student, it seemed as if we had reinvented, and thus reinvested, my authority. By blurring the boundaries of the position of teacher, I seemed better able to teach.

That is, it seemed as if I had gained a more viable authority as a teacher by giving up the hierarchical, institutionalized authority bestowed upon me by the university. Others have recognized a similarly pleasurable and paradoxical effect of such pedagogy on their teaching. For example, in her essay on feminist teaching, Catherine Portuges takes a "pedagogical plunge" by divesting herself of the institutionally authorized objectivity of the teacher and immersing herself as a constructed subject in her teaching. By giving up such authority, however, she learns that, in fact, she has come to gain a new, more genuine authority: "In abandoning the perhaps illusory neutrality of the traditional pedagogical situation, instead of losing what may in fact have been a tenuous 'grip,' I came to acquire a new confidence and authority alongside my students" (193).

By encouraging more group discussion and by inserting her own subjectivity into what had been a seemingly "objective" pedagogy, Portuges discovers that there is new authority available for teachers willing to give up some of their institutional authority. The newly invested authority is not structured hierarchically, with teacher over students, but is distributed across a level space, with teacher "alongside" students—with teacher sitting alongside student during office hours, for example. Like the teacher who teaches better when the position of teacher is blurred, Portuges's "constructed subject" moves away from a stable teacherly position in order to teach better; in giving up this "illusory" position of teacher, she reinvents it, acquiring not only authority but "confidence." This confidence—perhaps hers about herself, perhaps her students' about her—is invested in a newly constructed position that I'll refer to here as "teacher" (in scare quotes), not exactly a teacher yet someone who is still teaching. Even though the position of "teacher" might appear more tenuous at first, for Portuges it provides a "grip" on her teacherly position that might otherwise have been lost.

The "teacher" who critiques the position of teacher is given a privileged if somewhat covert position in much radical and feminist pedagogy. The "teacher" occupies the liminal position between inside and outside of the institution for a pedagogy that wishes to critique the structures the teacher inhabits. This gesture has particular significance for a man teaching through a feminist pedagogy in which the primary hierarchical structure is gender. Such a pedagogy has, for example, helped me think of myself as a good teacher. As someone who tries to attend to gender in my courses and has often looked to feminist pedagogy for help with and justification of my classroom practice, I have felt pleased when I enact feminist pedagogical strategies successfully in my own classroom. This is especially true in my relation to women students like Shannon who seemed to discover their own feminism in my courses. Not only did I become a feminist teacher for these women who were just beginning to critique patriarchy, but as a male feminist teacher, exposing male privilege at work in the texts we read and in the classroom we shared, I performed another deft escape routine. In so doing, I gained new authority as a man teaching within a feminist pedagogy.

Or, as Robert Bezucha puts it in his essay "Feminist Pedagogy as a Subversive Activity," "I became (for myself) a better and (for my students) a more effective teacher after I started to surrender the mantle of 'male' authority in the classroom" (92). Like Portuges and Schniedewind, Bezucha discovers new authority by surrendering authority, but Bezucha clarifies the recipients of this pedagogy's benefits: for himself, he became a "better" teacher; for his students, he became "more effective." Yet unlike Portuges and Schniedewind, who become "teachers" by surrendering their institutional teacherly authority, Bezucha "surrender[s] the mantle of 'male' authority."

Such self-congratulation requires skipping over a nagging question: what should we make of the quotation marks around "male"? In an earlier sentence from the essay that helps to explain this punctuation, Bezucha writes that "the cultural patterns associated with appropriate behavior in public—the prescribed objectivity and impersonal affect of a teacher in a college classroom, for example—are somehow 'male,' even when the instructor is a woman" (81). The gender/sex distinction requires the scare quotes here, which mark that women can, after all, be objective, impersonal, and so on, just like men. However, no such gender/sex distinction is necessary when Bezucha points to " 'male' authority in the classroom"—after all, Bezucha is a man, not a "man." The scare quotes, then, seem to hedge his assertion of surrender, or perhaps his desire to surrender, this male authority, as if he can't bring himself to accept all its baggage. There is something about "male" that, like "teacher," seems better and more stable in this pedagogical narrative—but positing "male" as a liminal position seems more difficult to justify.

As Bezucha's essay leads away from any stable position for this "male" "teacher," it leads toward a happy ending, which would seem to compensate for the increasingly difficult pedagogy the essay attempts to define. As it describes his pedagogical dreams coming true, Bezucha's last paragraph reads:

> There is no doubt in my mind that my experiment with women's history and feminist pedagogy has been worth the effort. It has improved my eligibility really to *teach* students after nearly twenty years in the business. I even got a reward for it. This year, one person concluded her essay by writing, "Not only has the senior seminar helped us understand relationships between theory and practice, it has opened new doors for understanding ourselves via liberation from received ideas." (95)

While the italicization of "teach" recalls the quotation marks I've placed around "teacher," in this final paragraph it doesn't mark a liminal position; instead, the italics emphasize the *real* teaching going on. For this teaching Bezucha receives a "reward," something given by an authority to someone who fulfills the authority's demands; thus the word signals the fantasy of pedagogical reversal. The "reward" is a comment from a student who praises "the senior seminar" for all of the valuable things it has done (explore relationships between theory and practice, liberate people from received ideas). But in doing so, the comment removes the teacher from the scene of teaching; the seminar, not the teacher, is responsible for her learning. This selection from his student essays fulfills Bezucha's teacherly fantasy, removing him from the pedagogical scene. This teacherly position isn't in the margins—it's off the page. Bezucha's "reward" clearly resembles my student's declaration that so pleased me, and in our case, the "received ideas" from which she was liberated were my own.

If, like Bezucha, I had "no doubt in my mind," things might well have ended happily in this essay, too. But I find myself increasingly filled with doubts about this pedagogy that dismantles and reinvents its own authority, structured by a fantasy of teaching for the students and for ourselves, that is fully and doubtlessly attainable.

The Good Student

I felt self-assured and jovial during the week following my meeting with Shannon, convinced of my excellent pedagogy. After years of constant renegotiation and meddling with my teaching, I had finally arrived at a comfortable happy ending, which was just where I like to be. On Friday of that week, Shannon again came to my office hours. Expecting another celebration of our teacher/student relation, I asked her in; once again, she said she had figured something out, and I smiled in anticipation. "I know what I want to be," she announced with confidence. "I want to be a college professor."

I was horrified as she said *those* words. Stunned by her statement, I reacted as if I had done something terribly wrong: far from being a good teacher, I was practicing the *worst* kind of pedagogy, one thoroughly caught up with my own narcissistic reproductive desire, striving to produce little copies of myself in my students. Far from a mutual celebration, the following half-hour was awkward and strained, as I tried desperately to dispel what I read as Shannon's distressing identification with me. Assuming that she wanted to be an English professor like me, I undertook a frenzied attempt to deflect her away from my discipline. I asked her what courses she had taken in other departments; when she listed only two or three, I dutifully explained the disciplinary expectations and epistemological foundations of virtually every department in the university I could think of and encouraged her to investigate each one of them before making any hasty career decisions.

When she left my office, she seemed to be a bit disappointed—probably expecting a different, more enthusiastic response from me than the one she had received. Meanwhile, I felt sick to my stomach, drained of all energy, and utterly confused. Whatever good teaching was, I was suddenly convinced that I *really* wasn't doing it.

I have come to understand my horrified reaction to Shannon's second declaration as a response to its effect on the meaning and value of our earlier scene. Suddenly, it seemed as if the fantastic pedagogy consummated just a week before with this same student was merely a product of my fantasy and nothing else. Shannon's declaration about knowing what she wanted now sounded hollow, a sentiment offered back to the teacher (not to me the "teacher") who asked his "best student" to produce it in the first place, a gesture no more representative of individual thinking or innovative pedagogy than the most formulaic five-paragraph essay. It was, in short, what Pierre Bourdieu and Jean-Claude Passeron call "reproduction," hardly a radical pedagogy from any perspective, yet shown by Bourdieu and Passeron to structure most teaching that would claim that name.

Although their book *Reproduction in Education, Society, and Culture* focuses at length on the institutional and social foundations for this pedagogical reproduction, the student/teacher relationship plays a crucial role, specifically as it is played out between teachers and their "good students." They write:

> As former model pupils who would like to have no pupils except future teachers, teachers are predisposed by their whole training and all their educational experience to play the game of the institution. In addressing himself to the student such as he ought to be, the teacher infallibly discourages the student's temptation to demand the right to be only what he is: the teacher respects, by the credit he gives him, the fictitious student whom a few "gifted pupils," objects of all his care and attention, authorize him to regard as real. (132n7)

In a broad gesture, Bourdieu and Passeron reveal the structure in which the "good student" exists to justify both the teacher, who constructs his or her practice around the fiction of a liberatory pedagogy, and the educational institution itself, which affirms the relation between "good student" and teacher and negates other students' right to be what they are. As the "object of all his care and attention," the "gifted pupil" embodies the teacher's narcissistic desire for reproduction, and at the same time confirms the institutional pedagogy within which both are constructed. Thus, the "good student" is the name of an institutionally constructed position, and the teacher, by speaking to the position where "the student . . . ought to be," can acknowledge only those students who locate themselves there.

Bourdieu and Passeron's discussion troubles the ease with which some pedagogical models define the teacher/student relation, and helps to demonstrate that, in any pedagogy, "good students" are those who are able to locate themselves in the pedagogical position articulated by the teacher's pedagogy. For example, within Freire's model of empowering pedagogy, the good student would be an active learner striving toward a critical conception of the world—but as any teacher who has tried out experimental pedagogies knows, for most students this radical pedagogical position is just as much an imposition as any other. Good students like Shannon, who struggle to locate themselves in the position to which the teacher speaks, make or break any pedagogy. That teachers desire students who will locate themselves in these positions is not a cynical observation; it is an acknowledgment of the narcissistic desire at the heart of most teaching, a desire upon which the authority of educational institutions depends.

Despite the fantasies of many teachers, this institutional authority is far too tenacious to shrug off by a teacher's self-subjection in a classroom; Bourdieu and Passeron's critique shows that a pedagogy that disparages hierarchical, institutionalized authority and dreams of eradicating and celebrating local, intersubjective authority democratically shared with students is only fooling itself.

What's more, only by and through such hierarchical, institutionalized authority are teachers allowed such dreams.[2] After all, as I think most college teachers would agree, a student democracy would most likely demand traditional pedagogy and toss most radical pedagogy with its required risks and experimentation into the trash.

If the "good student" is thus an effect of such institutional authority, it is difficult to establish what a "good student" of radical pedagogy might be. For Bourdieu and Passeron, the radical pedagogical practices at "liberal universities" actually reinforce that authority more effectively than even the most reactionary rule-bound institutions by "more fully mask[ing] the ultimate foundations of [their] pedagogic authority" (66). This directly undermines my stance as a radical "teacher." Reinvesting authority in any university classroom is predicated on existing relations of power that often go unacknowledged, and instructors at "liberal universities," institutions that encourage students to empower themselves, are given the societal and cultural authority that allows such gestures of empowerment. That is to say, while radical fantasies of authority reinvestment may not always proceed through a banking model, they all require some investment capital up front.

Bourdieu and Passeron's critique of the good teacher makes Freire's discussion of the teacher/student relationship seem a bit too simple for its own good. As cited above, Freire writes that "the teacher-of-the-students and the students-of-the-teacher cease to exist and a new term emerges: teacher-student with student-teachers. The teacher is no longer merely the-one-who-teaches, but one who is himself taught in dialogue with the students, who in turn while being taught also teach." Looking more carefully, we can see in this text a tension between, on the one hand, the inevitable desire to conflate teacher and student and, on the other, the ineradicable distinction between the two.

Freire writes that there is only one term ("a new term") emerging here, but the "new term" is in fact two terms: "teacher-student" and "student-teachers." Though the phrase "a new term" contradicts it, the difference between teacher and student is still inscribed in the text, the older and dominant term at the front of each neologism. Freire's claim that "the teacher-of-the-students and the students-of-the-teacher cease to exist" is further troubled by the adverb "merely" in the phrase "no longer merely the-one-who-teaches." Within this narrative, the teacher assumes a dual identity, that of the "teacher" who has divested the position of teacher and taken up a position alongside the students, and that of the person who remains, as ever, the one who teaches. While the desire to divest the position of teacher and its authority through a narrative of empowerment is clear, that desire is contradicted by the insistence of those very positions. Freire's singular "teacher-student" and plural "student-teachers" reveal the impossibility of getting away from demarcated, institutionalized teacher/student power relations: the teacher-student is still the *one* who teaches, even if every once in a while the teacher learns a thing or two from his or her students; the student-teachers are still encouraged by a teacher-student, who thus remains in the privileged position even as he or she encourages them to learn independently and to establish the course of their own curriculum. When Shannon left the room after our first transformative encounter, I remained her teacher and she my student.

In a strangely insistent way, traces of Freire's banking model of the bad teacher seem to linger among the teacher/student relations presented in the essays discussed above. Bezucha's "reward"—his student's statement that the seminar "helped us understand relationships between theory and practice, it has opened new doors for understanding ourselves via liberation from received ideas"—seems to express a contradiction: the notion of liberating oneself from received ideas is, whatever its merits, a received idea. Clearly this student learned what Bezucha wanted to teach her, but how is that different from Freire's construction of the bad teacher? What pleases Bezucha, and what horrifies me, is that our good students have located themselves in the positions to which we speak; that he recognizes his as a "good student" and I recognize mine as a narcissistic projection says more about our own relations to guilt than about the pedagogical structure itself, I expect.

Teachers, Students, and Student Teachers

To negotiate better terms for this dilemma, I want to return to Portuges's article, which has a happy ending that is similar to Bezucha's yet reveals a different way to think this through. Near the end of the essay, she writes that in "abandoning the perhaps illusory neutrality of the traditional pedagogical situation, instead of losing what may in fact have been a tenuous 'grip,' I came to acquire a new confidence and authority alongside my students" (193). Though the rhetoric of the paragraph as a whole implies that this acquisition benefited teacher and student both, Portuges here makes no claim that her students in any way benefited from her "new confidence and authority"; "alongside my students" marks a sharing of space and not of the authority that is supposedly dispersed across that space.

In the essay's final two paragraphs, which follow the above sentence, Portuges sums up the process and effects of her pedagogy by conflating her experiences as a teacher with those of her students. In a key sentence, she writes, "By leaving behind the filmic fathers to whom I had been so attached, my students and I were able to learn from their successors" (193). Portuges narrates her individual subjective relation to the course content by referring to "the filmic fathers to whom I had been so attached," yet goes on to equate her experience with that of her students, writing that "my students and I were able to learn" because of her pedagogy. The rhetorical effect is reinforced by Portuges's choice of pronouns throughout the final paragraphs of the essay, in which the first-person "I" disappears and is replaced by a ubiquitous "we." By the end of the penultimate paragraph, any referential difference between teachers and students is erased, ironically, in a sentence that names that very distinction: "[W]e learned not to equate 'daughter/student' and 'mother/teacher,' for we all, of course, contain elements of both, and represent part of each to ourselves and to each other" (194). By the time the reader reaches the happy ending, Portuges indeed finds herself "alongside her students," but her desire to share that space with students subsumes them in the first-person plural.

In the penultimate sentence of the essay, Portuges writes, "students mirror the separation-individuation stage in differentiating from the blissful state of pre-oedipal fusion with the teacher." Invoking the blissful fusion of students with teacher, Portuges does not mention the blissful fusion of teacher with students in the same paragraph, marked by the subsumption of all students as part of the collective "we." Here is the pleasure and the horror of the pedagogical moment with which I wrangle: what is blissful about this affirming pedagogical structure is not the students' identification with the teacher but rather the teacher's identification with the students.

Bourdieu and Passeron point in this direction by referring to teachers as "former model pupils who would like to have no pupils except future teachers," succinctly naming the interlocked and complementary structures of identification that fuel such pedagogy. While many pedagogical texts discuss identification, they typically do so by stressing the importance of teaching students to identify with others, either other people in their class or characters in literature and other texts. Here and there one finds a mention of students identifying with teachers, but any discussion of the teacher's identification with students is typically absent. Bourdieu and Passeron's formulation is apt, but brief; we clearly need an extended consideration of the complexities of pedagogical identification.

To return to my meetings with Shannon, what had seemed horrific about the second meeting was Shannon's clear identification with me: her declaration that she wanted to be a college professor was seemingly incontrovertible evidence that my best student was merely a reproduction of myself. Through many drafts of this essay and in many conversations about the material in it, I was unable to understand or work through this horror. But one day, more than a year after the experience, while discussing this essay I finally realized that Shannon had simply declared that she wanted to be a college professor. My frantic urgings that she investigate other disciplines had responded to my assumption that she wanted to be an *English* professor. I had responded to my own projection, not to what she had said; no wonder she was confused. My feverish disavowal was in fact trying to deflect not her identification with me but my identification with her.

In the first scene with Shannon, I identified with a student whose desires seemed wholly her own and not at all the product of an identification with the teacher. Here was a student who knows what she wants and can distinguish it from what her teacher wants. Here was a student who was thus beyond the effects of pedagogy, a student who wasn't being taught anything at all but was simply learning on her own, a student without a teacher—a student, I hoped, like me. But as the second scene reveals, my hope was not that she was like me but that I was like her, a "good student." Instead of saving me from my troubling identifications, the second scene revealed my investment in them. I felt horrified recognition when Shannon declared that she wanted to be a "college professor," for, after all, as a graduate student, I want to be a college professor someday too—and, a lot of times, I pretend I already am. Her statement was thus triply horrifying, revealing what I really am (a student), what I desperately hope to be (a real teacher), and what I desperately hope I am not (neither a narcissistic teacher nor a sycophant student).

In her book *Exiles and Communities*, Jo Anne Pagano addresses this conundrum of identification in the training of student teachers. Her description of these students learning to teach presents the personal and psychical dimensions of the interlocking identifications which Bourdieu and Passeron analyze in cultural and social terms. Pagano describes an assignment in an education seminar that asks students to imagine themselves teaching in a specific classroom situation. The assignment generated a familiar narrative:

> Their projections of these scenes disclose two things: a delight in and commitment to their subjects, and total ignorance of the fact that their high school experiences are not representative. Part of the anxiety of teaching begins when one acknowledges difference, when one recognizes one's own unrepresentativeness. The tension is the result of the persistent inclination to assimilate all experiences to one's own.... They imagine their students as themselves, already formed and with their tastes and dispositions. (54)

Pagano's students take as a given that their students are constructed in their image, that their projected fantasy of pedagogy represents a real scene of teaching. Their "good students," then, would necessarily need to conform to this idealized student—would need, that is, to identify with the teacher's construction of the "good student." Instead of emphasizing the need for students to differentiate themselves from the teacher, as Portuges does, Pagano encourages her teachers-to-be to differentiate themselves from their students.

While for Pagano "the anxiety of teaching begins when one acknowledges difference," for me the anxiety of teaching began when I acknowledged, however unconsciously, similarity. My anxiety was connected to blurring the distinction between teacher and student. That confusion is exacerbated because of my own literally liminal position as a student teacher: while a student in a graduate program progressing toward a doctoral degree, I teach two courses of my own. Furthermore, the names "student" and "teacher" mark not only institutional positions but also positions through which I define myself and my successes, positions in which I have a substantial personal investment. I have committed quite a bit of time and energy to being a "good teacher," and have been recognized as such in student evaluations, nominations for teaching awards, and praise from supervisors. What's more, during my years in formal education, I've been called a "good student"—even a "best student"—by some of my teachers, and I have wanted to understand that praise as an evaluation of my performance as a student on its own merits. I liked to think that, far from responding to any particular investment they had in me personally, my teachers were simply good teachers, gratified to see a student coming to understand what it was he desired as a student, coming to realize that what he most wanted was to figure out what he really wanted to say, to think, to understand. They knew how to teach me, and I could learn from that.

This might all sound like reasonable pedagogy, except that it replicates almost exactly the reproduction model Bourdieu and Passeron describe. In order to learn from my teachers, I have had to determine where the teacher believed I "ought to be" and locate myself in that position. But as Bourdieu and Passeron note, that requires teachers who, "as former model pupils who would like to have no pupils except future teachers," have some investment in identifying with me as a student. This is not traditional pedagogy in which a student is supposed to identify with a distant teacher, nor is it a radical student-centered pedagogy in which the teacher is supposed to identify with the student. Rather, it is a pedagogy in which such positions function within a dialectic that recognizes and works the paradox of teacher/student identification.

At the end of the section devoted to her student-teachers, Pagano turns the tables on herself, shifting from a discussion of her students' problems and offering almost perfunctorily: "These are my problems too. Perhaps they were my problems first. In the grammar of human relationships, it is entirely possible that these student teachers are responding to my expression of my desire" (56).

Two pages earlier, Pagano taught us that teachers should recognize their students' difference, but here it appears that she cannot practice what she teaches. This is not, however, a simple contradiction, but rather an instance of the complicated, multigenerational identification described by Bourdieu and Passeron. As she explains the difficulty and necessity of having teachers differentiate between their experience and that of their students, Pagano demonstrates that she cannot prevent herself from identifying with her students, with their anxieties and challenges as teachers-in-training. Yet even if she strives to differentiate her own students from herself, her pedagogy encourages those students to follow her pedagogical model and identify with her as a teacher who doesn't identify with her students.

Pagano's student-teachers return us to Freire's student-teachers. Freire's terms "teacher-student" and "student-teachers" can serve to signal the complex identifications between teacher and student, not the erasure of those positions. Pedagogy, whatever else it might mean, requires a dialectical movement between the positions of teacher and student, recognizing both positions as fully inhabitable, mutually reinforcing, valuable, and real.

Rereading Freire's terms in this way would mean learning from Freire dialectically instead of being faithful to his original intention—instead of being "filled" with "the content of his narration." Ironically, Freire's *Pedagogy of the Oppressed* has often been oppressive for this reader, primarily because it refuses to give up the banking model in its own textual pedagogy: the text deposits Freire's experience in a reader presumed to be empty. Yet, however oppressive it might have felt, Freire's book has managed to teach a lot of people, myself included.

This same irony haunts most writing about pedagogy, the rhetoric of which so often seems to contradict its theoretical implications. Like Pagano and Freire, pedagogical writers both present a model of good teaching and inevitably contradict it, at least in their textual practice. I believe such contradictions are unquestionably valuable. For example, I'm convinced that my critique of my relation with Shannon is on target, that my pedagogy has more to do with my investments and identifications than with anything else. Yet I'm similarly convinced that most of the claims of the first part of this essay are true: that in fact Shannon was my best student, that she learned something valuable from me, and that she managed to teach me something about my pedagogy. To deny that real teaching and real learning took place between Shannon and me would be to deny the possibility of pedagogy.

Notes

1. The article first appeared in *Radical Teacher* 18 (1981), was reprinted as "Feminist Values: Guidelines for a Teaching Methodology in Women's Studies" in Charlotte Bunch and Sandra Pollack, eds., *Learning Our Way* (Trumansburg, NY: Crossing, 1983) 261–71, and again reprinted in Susan Gushee O'Malley, Robert C. Rosen, and Leonard Vogt, eds., *Politics of Education: Essays from* Radical Teacher (Albany: SUNY P, 1990) 11–21, under its original title. I am unable to account for the appearance and subsequent disappearance of the indefinite article over the years, though I am fascinated with it.

2. Linda Brodkey, writing on teachers and students in her "The Literacy Letters" project, points out that attempts to equalize authority and establish more "personal" relations between teacher and student ignore the structures within which such relations can be established in the first place. "Many teachers . . . attempt to relinquish their control by staging opportunities for students to take the privileged subject position in, say, group discussions or collaborative assignments that grant them, at least temporarily, a measure of control over educational discursive practice. Attempts to transform classroom discussions into conversations between peers are thwarted to the extent that teachers fail to re-

alize that their interpersonal relationships with students, as well as their institutional ones, are constituted by educational discourse. While the power of a discourse is not absolute, neither is it vulnerable to change by individuals who ignore its power" (129). Like the interpersonal relations Brodkey describes, this pedagogy cannot help but reproduce the very system it fights if it fails to acknowledge that it obtains its authority to engage in the fight from the system itself.

Works Cited

Bezucha, Robert. "Feminist Pedagogy as a Subversive Activity." *Gendered Subjects: The Dynamics of Feminist Teaching*. Culley and Portuges 81–95.

Bourdieu, Pierre, and Jean-Claude Passeron. *Reproduction in Education, Society, and Culture*. Trans. Richard Nice. London: Sage, 1970.

Brodkey, Linda. "On the Subjects of Class and Gender in 'The Literacy Letters.' " *College English* 51.2 (1989): 125–41.

Culley, Margo, and Catherine Portuges, eds. *Gendered Subjects: The Dynamics of Feminist Teaching*. Boston: Routledge, 1985.

Freire, Paolo. *Pedagogy of the Oppressed*. Trans. Myra Bergman Ramos. New York: Continuum, 1990.

Pagano, Jo Anne. *Exiles and Communities*. Albany: SUNY P, 1990.

Portuges, Catherine. "The Spectacle of Gender: Cinema and Psyche." Culley and Portuges 183–94.

Schniedewind, Nancy. "Feminist Values: Guidelines for Teaching Methodology in Women's Studies." *Politics of Education: Essays from Radical Teacher*. Ed. Susan Gushee O'Malley, Robert C. Rosen, and Leonard Vogt. Albany: SUNY P, 1990. 11–21.

7 | The Teacher's Breasts

Jane Gallop

IF THE ADJECTIVE "personal," elevated to substantive status, has here become a central focus for pedagogical theory, it is singularly due to the thinking and working of something called "feminist teaching." Feminists teaching and feminists talking about teaching have not only challenged the exclusion of the personal from the academic but have gone so far as to insist that the proper measure of learning is personal. Even a cursory glance at feminist writing on pedagogy will yield a continual and widespread affirmation of "the personal," as content, style, and method of pedagogy.

I have chosen to consider feminist pedagogy for the obvious reason that "the personal" is writ large there. But I'd like to take another look at feminist pedagogy for the perhaps more surprising reason that—despite all the validation, legitimation, affirmation, and celebration—in fact "the personal" remains a "question" there, a knotted, thorny, troubling question.

The editors of the best-known collection of essays on feminist teaching tell us that one theme that recurs throughout the collection is, as they put it, "the transforming power of the personal as the subject and method of feminist education" (Culley and Portuges 5). This 1985 anthology, *Gendered Subjects* (regrettably now out of print in the U.S.), is a fair representation of the range and issues of feminist pedagogy, offering an opportunity to examine what Margo Culley and Catherine Portuges, the editors, locate as a "recurrent theme"—"the transforming power of the personal."

The subtitle to *Gendered Subjects* is *The Dynamics of Feminist Teaching*. "Dynamics" may imply "transforming power," but it also suggests that this anthology is primarily concerned not with feminist curriculum but with classroom dynamics and teacher/student relations. Feminist consideration of "the personal," in this volume as elsewhere, often refers to the inclusion of personal experience in class discussion and academic work. But the subtitle suggests that the emphasis here is on "the personal" not as pedagogical content but as "dynamic," on the teaching relation as enacted between persons. Although the term "gendered subjects" probably can include the gendering of subject matter, the title most likely implies that what characterizes "the dynamics of feminist teaching" is that students and teachers are themselves subject to gender and gendered subjectivities.

As might be expected, central to the volume is women teaching women. This relation is very much gendered, that is, thought according to models which characterize women precisely in contradistinction to men. These models tend to follow a strong psychoanalytic bent, particularly in the direction of the Chodorowian object-relations theory that had such currency in feminist academic discourse in the early 1980s. The teacher/student relation is again and again understood through analogy with the mother/daughter relation. Culley and Portuges tell us that the collection originated in a paper entitled "The Politics of Nurturance" which they, along with three other colleagues, wrote in 1979. "The Politics of Nurturance" is now the anthology's opening chapter, and "nurturance" is a key concept in *The Dynamics of Feminist Teaching*.

Although pedagogy between women both predominates and offers the book its theoretical paradigm, there are other gendered subjects in *Gendered Subjects*. Three of the essays are written by men (see Bezucha, Snoek, and Schilb). Since the model for good or feminist teaching in this volume is a nurturance which does not transcend gender to something like "parenting" but remains tied to "mothering," these men teaching are in a difficult position. All three reflect explicitly on the contradictions of feminist teaching by a man; in this context, they necessarily experience themselves as subject to gender; in this context, men teaching are aware that they cannot avoid the effects of gender upon their relations with students.

Although the *theoretical* pieces, such as "The Politics of Nurturance," are written as if all students were female,[1] in the volume's *experiential* tales of teaching, male students keep showing up. And making trouble.[2] Female *and* male teachers tend to respond to male students with fantasies not of nurturance but of discipline.

Each of these genderings of the pedagogical relation specifically and profoundly inflects the question of authority. The woman-to-woman paradigm shows the teacher giving up her authority and its association with distantiation in favor of blurring the boundaries between teachers and students. Maleness in either teacher or student affects this paradigmatic blurring of authority. The male teacher can't seem to get rid of his authority, particularly in the eyes of his female students, but he sure would like to. And the male student challenges the teacher's authority, particularly the female teacher's. However much the teacher might dream of divesting her- or himself of authority so as to get closer to the female student, she or he clearly does not want it taken away by the insubordinate male student. These structures are crude and schematic, but . . . as with most of the workings of gender and/or authority, the crude and schematic is usually all too apt.

Speaking of the crude and schematic: these genderings of the pedagogical relation likewise inflect the question of sex. The female/female relation is explicitly celebrated as "erotic."[3] It would seem, however, that "erotic" is not quite a synonym for sexual here, since the question of actual sexual relations is almost never posed. The single exception is the one out lesbian article which treats sexual relations, real and fantasmatic, between female teachers and students as a problem (McDaniel 130–35). The contrast between this singular article—subtitled "My Life as the Only Lesbian Professor"—and the rest of the volume suggests that the unproblematic celebration of female/female eroticism may itself be the site of unsuspected heterosexist presumption. The "only lesbian" essay aside, the female/female "erotic" shares in the general fluid boundaries of a maternalized femininity, a hyper-feminine gendering of sexuality.

In marked contrast with the rosy "eroticism" of all-female pedagogy, relations between male teachers and female students are sexualized as harassment. *Gendered Subjects*—true to its name—always explicitly genders sexual harassment: as Adrienne Rich puts it, "Sexual advances toward female students by male professors" (26). And, as for male *students*. . . . In the dynamics of gendered teaching, they pose a sexual question, if not a paradigmatic threat. They can neither be subsumed in the maternal desexualized erotic nor made to fit the sexual harassment case.

Around 1985, around the country, women's studies was expanding and/or being transformed into gender studies. The anthology *Gendered Subjects* partakes of that moment. Structures which applied to women alone are being expanded and/or transformed to include men as explicitly gendered. In this case, feminist teaching is no longer woman-to-woman, but gendered teacher/gendered student. The woman-to-woman model imagined feminist teaching as a safe space. When feminist teaching comes to mean the recognition that all pedagogical subjects are gendered, there is a real sense of loss in giving up the notion of that idealized safe space, but there is also, I would suggest, a substantial theoretical gain. *Gendered Subjects*, the book, entitles that gain, saying up front that feminist teaching is a dynamic between gendered subjects. Since, in fact, *all* teaching takes place between gendered subjects, then feminist pedagogy can help us to see these gendered relations largely underrecognized in pedagogical theory.

I would like now to turn to a particularly dramatic scene of gendered pedagogy in *Gendered Subjects*. Helene Keyssar's contribution to the volume is an account of a feminist theater production course she taught. She gives her essay the ambiguous and evocative title "Staging the Feminist Classroom." I take my cue from Keyssar's title to read her essay as a representation of "*the* feminist classroom," and to make connections between the story she tells of what happened in the classroom and the play the class actually stages.

Keyssar's pedagogical style and principles seem fairly typical of the volume. For example, explaining why, rather than assigning a script, she has the class as a whole choose the play they will perform, she tells us: "Although I knew that this would . . . minimize my control, I did so precisely to undermine my authority." She would like to "counter" her students' "perception" that she is the teacher and the director (110–11).

The script they choose is Susan Miller's "Cross Country," a play with a classic seventies feminist protagonist who leaves her marriage for a more risky and fulfilling autonomy. This particular feminist heroine, named Perry, not only leaves her husband but also, in the same self-liberating gesture, leaves her job as a college teacher. The simultaneity of these two gestures suggests that, like marriage, teaching constrains women.

Keyssar's pedagogical principles are straight out of the women's studies tradition, but—like many who promoted the move from women's to gender studies—she believes feminist teaching should not be restricted to women: "I made it clear that men were welcome in the course. . . . I wanted to make clear my own conviction that feminism was . . . not just . . . about women. . . . The presence of men in the class would make certain kinds of talk more problematic, but that kind of problematizing seemed valuable" (110).

As expected, "the presence of men in the class" does indeed cause problems. The most dramatic moment in Keyssar's essay is an example of "that kind of problematizing" and provides a "valuable" lesson, for the class, the teacher, and then for the reader of *Gendered Subjects*. Keyssar's essay analyzes the moment for its theoretical implications, and I would like here to continue that teaching, finding the incident particularly dense with implications for feminist pedagogy.

Keyssar specifically locates the scene within the larger drama of male students becoming explicitly and uncomfortably gendered in and by the feminist classroom: "the men in the class . . . were growing increasingly silent during class discussions. . . . they showed a sense of being seen as the enemy" (117–18). Keyssar concludes her framing of the incident: "their strongest feelings were the displeasure of exclusion from a group in which they wanted to be full members" (118). This phrasing ("strongest feelings," "displeasure of exclusion," "in which they wanted to be full members") begins to suggest a scenario of frustrated penetration, as the students' maleness becomes increasingly salient.

Keyssar goes on: "These half-hidden tensions exploded unexpectedly in the context of a scene in which Perry asserts her power" (118). This "scene in which Perry asserts her power" is a scene in the play between Perry as teacher and a male student. Unlike Keyssar, the feminist teacher who works to undermine her own authority, the protagonist, a feminist teacher from another genre, is "assert[ing] her power."

In the scene being rehearsed by Keyssar's class, Perry "asserts her power" by refusing to do her teacherly duties. She is behaving erratically, and, most important, refusing to take the term papers the students have just written for her. A crowd of students stands outside her office, shocked and confused by her unteacherly behavior. They choose a male student as their representative to go in and find out why she won't accept the papers. She tells him she likes his smile and insists he call her by her first name, then flippantly suggests that the students should rewrite and improve the papers she has not even looked at. He protests—"don't jack us off"—and she puts her arms around his neck and kisses him. "Now get the hell out of here," she says and kisses him again. And then once more, still telling him to go. The scene concludes with these stage directions: "He goes. But not without first touching her breasts" (Miller 56–57; recounted in Keyssar 118).

Perry here is a bad teacher. She is putting herself, her wishes and needs, before the needs of the students. Keyssar recounts this scene in detail, on her way to talking about an incident that happened during rehearsals. The scene produces interesting disruptions and reverberations when introduced into Keyssar's classroom, effects we will consider shortly. The scene likewise produces disruptive reverberations when rehearsed by Keyssar in the context of *Gendered Subjects*. Recounting this scene, Keyssar brings into the anthology, into the discourse on feminist teaching, something otherwise absent: the feminist as bad teacher.

The heroine who stops being "good," stops catering to the needs of others, Perry comes from a long line of bad-girl feminists. Along with this "liberated woman," feminism has also always included a good womanly image, championing heavily gendered superior female values. For example (and it always is the primary one): nurturance. These two images have jostled each other across the range of feminist thought and activities: sometimes in conflict, sometimes in alliance, less frequently in dialectical interaction. Most of the debates in feminist theory as well as many of the fights in feminist organization can, at least in part, be understood as playing out the confrontation between bad-girl and good-girl feminism.

Feminist pedagogy, however, has been an exception. In the discourse of feminist teaching, the bad girl has been at best an object, at worst invisible, never a speaking subject. Although feminist pedagogy has sometimes promoted the bad-girl student, feminists as teachers have almost always spoken from the place of the good woman. Perhaps because teaching itself has been associated, since the common school movement of the early nineteenth century, with traditional "good" femininity, that is, with selfless, sexless nurturance.[4] By retelling the scene in Perry's office, Keyssar casts the "bad girl" in the role of teacher on the stage of feminist pedagogy.

In bad-girl tradition, Perry pursues the sexual experimentation that two decades ago was sometimes mistaken for women's liberation. And one of her adventures, central to the play Keyssar's class chooses yet never mentioned by Keyssar, is a love affair with a female student. In fact, the term-paper-refusal, office-kiss scene occurs right after the student she is sleeping with leaves town in the middle of the term because the student can't cope with the affair. The bad-teacher scene anthologized in *Gendered Subjects* is linked to a worse-teacher scene. Bringing Susan Miller's sexualized teacher into the anthology, Keyssar provides a faint echo to Judith McDaniel who, as the volume's "only lesbian professor," brings sexual trouble into the eroticized feminine space of nurturance.

Perry's affair with her student is never mentioned in *Gendered Subjects*. The bad-teacher scene that explicitly troubles Keyssar's feminist classroom is not woman-to-woman but female teacher/male student. And Keyssar focuses not on the bad teacher but on the problem student, the recalcitrant male student. Not the one in the play who touches the teacher's breasts, but the one in Keyssar's class who plays the one in the play . . . and who touches the teacher's breasts . . . wrong.

"Instead of approaching Perry hesitantly and literally touching her breasts, the man playing the student strode towards her and fiercely, with overt erotic impulse, grabbed and held each of her breasts" (118). I don't know what Keyssar's phrase "literally touching" literally means, but it suggests that when the script says "touching her breasts," the sense should be self-evident, "literal," not a matter for interpretation. And thus the interpretation by the so-called man playing the student would be particularly egregious. Keyssar tells it as if everyone else could see immediately how it should have been done, and the error thus could only be some sort of acting-out: "unless he were extraordinarily violent or crazy, the young man would no more grab her breasts and caress them than he would disfigure a painting in a museum" (119).

I will return later to the analogy between the teacher's breasts and a painting in a museum. For now I want to follow the classroom drama of the problematic male student. At first merely unruly, when corrected he becomes obstinate: "The man playing the role of the male student insisted on the correctness of his initial interpretation, essentially on grounds that 'no man would do otherwise.' . . . Hours of talk seemed only to plunge us deeper into a mire of misunderstanding and, even when I violated one of my own cardinal rules and demonstrated the kind of touch most of us felt appropriate to the moment, the actor responded with a different, but even more eroticized, gesture than previously" (119).

Keyssar repeatedly refers to the culprit as "the man playing the student." He is, of course, also, among other things, the student playing the man in the scene, but she does not call him that. Her phrasing suggests that he is really a man but is only pretending to be a student. A real student would be too intimidated by a teacher to respond sexually. His "overtly erotic" gesture belies the role he is playing and reveals his true identity: " 'no man would do otherwise.' "

Given the setting of this confrontation in a general drama of male students in the feminist classroom, we might take this phrase "the man playing the student" to bespeak the contradiction posed by any male student, particularly for the female teacher. The contradiction, here played out around the question of sex, entails the question of authority. While the teacher has authority over the student, the *female* teacher has no authority over the man. What the student in the play does by touching the teacher's breasts, the student in the real classroom does by not accepting the teacher's interpretation of what would be appropriate student behavior.

Can a man be a student or, to the extent he is a man, is he only always playing a student, a fiction that is belied whenever he shows he is really a man? Is the student role itself, finally if only ever implicitly, gendered female? And maybe not just in feminist pedagogy?

"By reversing the rules of both student-teacher and male-female games," Keyssar writes, "Perry had made herself mysterious and impenetrable . . . the young man would no more grab her breasts . . . than he would disfigure a painting in a museum" (119). By being sexually aggressive, Perry is "reversing the rules of male-female games," making herself, so to speak, "impenetrable." But as for "student-teacher games": this scene of Perry "asserting her power" may be breaking the rules, but is hardly a reversal of the teacher-student relation.

This sentence marks a point of confusion where "Staging the Feminist Classroom" is explicitly trying to think the gender relation ("male-female games") and the pedagogical relation ("student-teacher games") at the same time. The pairs are ordered so that student lines up with male, teacher with female. This is not the order of theoretical models of hierarchy, authority, and polarity,[5] but rather comes from the actual relations at play, in the scene and in the classroom. Those relations are already, from the point of view of theoretical models, reversed. The encounter of female teacher and male student troubles any simple superimposition of these two sometimes analogous "games."

When the man plays the student and the woman plays teacher, gender rules may be reversed, but pedagogical rules are broken. Perry breaks those rules by being seductive and irresponsible toward her student. She has already broken what McDaniel in *Gendered Subjects* calls "Rule Number One: teachers do not become [sexually] involved with students" (133). And, in the context of Perry's unruly behavior, Keyssar too, in *her* encounter with the stubbornly male-gendered student, finds herself breaking rules: "I violated one of my own cardinal rules and demonstrated the kind of touch most of us felt appropriate."

Whereas McDaniel's Rule Number One explicitly concerns sex, Keyssar's "cardinal rule" concerns authority. Presumably it forbids her from showing students what to do, rather than letting them figure it out, in keeping with her general style of teaching and directing. Yet, faced with a "man" in place of a student, she finds herself assuming the position of authority she has worked so hard to avoid. Keyssar describes Perry's scene with the male student as "asserting her power" and, although we might want to question that characterization of Perry, the phrase does very aptly describe Keyssar's response to *her* male student. Perry and Keyssar, in very different ways, both end up treating the male student as a man rather than a student: Perry by flirting rather than caring, Keyssar by trying to overcome rather than empower.

The man playing a student drives Keyssar to lay bare the authority that as a feminist teacher she has been underplaying. To her consternation, her authority does not put him in his place as a student: "even when I violated one of my own cardinal rules . . . the actor responded with a[n] . . . even more eroticized gesture." To Keyssar's surprise, asserting her authority makes the male student more not less recalcitrant, and more not less sexual.

Keyssar gradually comes to understand that "he could not project anything but aggression in response to a woman's exhibition of power" (119). The conflict is resolved when the feminist class recognizes the male student's gender: "we assumed . . . that the man could leap into the role of the sexually exploited person—but everything in his experience refuted the possibility of such a role for a man. . . . All of our attempts to 'enlighten' the male actor had been based on accounts by women of incidents in which men in positions of power had made sexual approaches to them. . . . We had asked the actor to think of himself in that moment as a woman, but . . . he had to conjure up a world in which women had power and used it. . . . Once we were able to admit the complexity of his task, the actor was freed to attempt affable imitation of what he thought we wanted, and that, in the end, was better than where we had begun" (119–20).

"In the end, better than where we had begun": the "kind of problematizing" produced by "the presence of men in the class" proves "valuable" as the incident ends happily. They were trying to fit the man into a women's studies model— "we had asked the actor to think of himself . . . as a woman"—but are forced to move beyond that model to a gendered pedagogy. Once they recognize that he is a man, he is able to "play" a student.

Despite this neat resolution of the conflict, a couple of questions about the incident remain, questions that are central for feminist pedagogy, at least as represented in this 1985 anthology grappling with feminist teaching beyond the all-feminine classroom. The first question involves pronouns, identities, individuals, and collectives; the second will return us to the teacher's breasts.

In the passage just quoted, you might have noticed that Keyssar consistently uses a first-person-plural pronoun. The conflict is represented as between the class as a whole ("we") and the man: "he" is the problem, the singular which must be resolved back into the ensemble.[6] At the moment that she breaks her cardinal rule, however, she uses a first-person-singular pronoun. His obstinate singularity forces hers, pushes her into the role of teacher and breaks the illusion that she is just part of the ensemble.

This staging of the classroom as "we vs. he" resonates with Keyssar's interpretation of the teacher-student scene in the play. Although otherwise quite complete, her account of the scene leaves one significant detail out. Miller's script tells us that the student entering Perry's office is the elected representative of the crowd of students outside the door. In the play, it is the male student who can oppose the teacher with a "we." Keyssar never mentions his representative status, introducing him only as "one male student who assertively enters her office," thus constructing him as different from the rest of the students, positioning him as she does the student in her class. The juxtaposition of the scene in Perry's office and the drama in Keyssar's classroom poses the question: Who can speak for the class and who stands apart from the pedagogical "we," the male student or the female teacher? Keyssar's interpretation tends toward embodying difference in the male student.

I see here the work of the Chodorowian model of gender that subtends the volume as a whole. In that model, individuation is itself gendered male. Although the many feminist theorists who have contributed to the gendering of distinction vs. togetherness undoubtedly intended to be descriptive, gendered descriptions seem unable to avoid powerful prescriptive effect.

The maternalized model of femininity might also be at work in Keyssar's interpretation of the teacher's breasts. In order to demonstrate the correct approach to the teacher, Keyssar has recourse to a surprising analogy: "the young man would no more grab her breasts and caress them than he would disfigure a painting in a museum. He might, however, fleetingly touch a painting—or a breast—to test its reality and to determine limits" (119). What she first refers to as a "literal" touch is here, by means of the figure of the painting, specified as "fleeting." And as Keyssar is finally able, by analogy, to articulate her interpretation, the breasts become singular: "fleetingly touch a painting—or *a* breast."

As Keyssar imagines it, the only appropriate way to touch the teacher's breasts is to touch the teacher's *breast*. The problem is that Miller's script specifies the plural. Not only is it much harder to imagine a fleeting touch of *both* breasts but, beyond the problem of physical interpretation, it seems to me that the difference between breast and breasts is precisely the difference between a symbolic and a sexual interpretation. The difference between the breast and the breasts might function like the infamous phallus/penis relation.[7]

In the context of feminist pedagogy, it might also signify the difference between the good teacher and the bad. There is one other breast in *Gendered Subjects*, precisely one and not two. "The Politics of Nurturance" suggests that the woman teacher "purveys the maternal breast" (16). The breast—singular, symbolic, and maternal—is precisely the imaginary organ of nurturance, what the good feminist teacher proffers to her daughter-students. Refusing to nurture, Perry, the bad, sexual teacher, brings into the discourse of feminist pedagogy not the breast, which is already appropriately there, but the breasts.

Like a painting in a museum, the breast is idealized, decontextualized, and removed from history. It belongs to the infantile misperception of the mother, when the infant takes the breast for part of his body, before he perceives the mother as a separate person. The pre-Oedipal fantasies that underpin the teacher as nurturing mother lead teachers such as Keyssar to submerge her subjectivity in the cozy "we" of the feminist classroom.

Gendered Subjects repeatedly and invaluably stages the confrontation of this dream of the feminist classroom with the question of gender. The incident I have considered is no doubt the most dramatic example but is otherwise not unrepresentative. The bad-girl feminist teacher and the male student who rubs his teacher the wrong way disrupt the idyllic hyper-feminine space of a gender-appropriate feminist classroom.

Keyssar states that she welcomes men into the feminist classroom, knowing they will disrupt the feminine, knowing they will cause problems, but wagering that the "problematizing" will be valuable. I share Keyssar's belief in the value of that disruption. I see it as part of a theoretical move frequently staged in this anthology. Beginning with a model of maternal pedagogy, *Gendered Subjects* repeatedly calls that model into question—sometimes theoretically, sometimes anecdotally, sometimes unwittingly, sometimes directly. A maternal pedagogy might appear utopic, but it is also subject to traditionally gendered prescription. While feminist teaching based in appropriate feminine behavior has been implicitly defined by gender, feminist pedagogy can teach us to analyze effects of gender in our pedagogical practice rather than just acting them out.[8]

Notes

1. Or add "and men" in parenthesis, a gesture which suggests an inclusion that would change nothing.
2. For example, see Culley 213–14 and Bezucha 88–89.
3. See, for example, "The Politics of Nurturance" 17–19. For a similar celebration of the erotics of feminist pedagogy, see Grumet.
4. See, for example, Grumet 38–39, 54–55, 83.
5. Compare Culley 211: "the male as teacher, female as student model."
6. This last word is meant to resonate with the title of Keyssar's course: Feminist Theater Ensemble.
7. I am indebted to Fran Bartkowski for this association, which she offered me in August 1992.
8. A similar argument about the implicit gendering of feminist pedagogy is made in *Gendered Subjects* by Friedman. See, for example, 206.

Works Cited

Bezucha, Robert J. "Feminist Pedagogy as a Subversive Activity." *Gendered Subjects* 81–95.
Culley, Margo. "Anger and Authority in the Introductory Women's Studies Classroom." *Gendered Subjects* 209–18.
Culley, Margo, Arlyn Diamond, Lee Edwards, Sara Lennox, and Catherine Portuges. "The Politics of Nurturance." *Gendered Subjects* 11–20.

Culley, Margo, and Catherine Portuges. Introduction. *Gendered Subjects* 1–8.

Friedman, Susan Stanford. "Authority in the Feminist Classroom: A Contradiction in Terms?" *Gendered Subjects* 203–208.

Gendered Subjects: The Dynamics of Feminist Teaching. Ed. Margo Culley and Catherine Portuges. Boston: Routledge, 1985.

Grumet, Madeleine. *Bitter Milk: Women and Teaching*. Amherst: U of Massachusetts P, 1988.

Keyssar, Helene. "Staging the Feminist Classroom." *Gendered Subjects* 108–24.

McDaniel, Judith. "Is There Room for Me in the Closet? Or, My Life as the Only Lesbian Professor." *Gendered Subjects* 130–35.

Miller, Susan. "Cross Country." *West Coast Plays* 1 (1977): 41–80.

Rich, Adrienne. "Taking Women Students Seriously." *Gendered Subjects* 21–28.

Schilb, John. "Pedagogy of the Oppressors?" *Gendered Subjects* 253–64.

Snoek, Diedrick. "A Male Feminist in a Women's College Classroom." *Gendered Subjects* 136–43.

8 | Face to Face with Alterity
Postmodern Jewish Identity and the Eros of Pedagogy

Roger I. Simon

> The project of history is not to reify identity but to understand its production as . . . [a] process . . . subject to redefinition, resistance, and change.
> —Joan Scott

> How do we negotiate between my history and yours? . . . It is necessary to assert our dense particularities, our lived and imagined differences; but could we afford to leave untheorized the question of how our differences are intertwined and, indeed, hierarchically organized?
> —S. P. Mohanty

IN RECENT TIMES, many of us working and studying in educational institutions have been acting on what S. P. Mohanty describes as the necessity "to assert our dense particularities" (13) in both curriculum formation and the practices of pedagogy. This activity has often been mistakenly read as rooted in a politics of positive recognition, based on the assumption that the public assertion of the collective history to which one belongs is supposed to serve as a corrective to some felt deficit in self-esteem. However, the articulation of identities in a pedagogical encounter cannot be reduced to a personal desire for cultural acknowledgment. What's at stake must be written in different terms.

The challenge issued by the assertion of historical particularities is to rethink how that difference will be deployed, rendered, and positioned in regard to both the substance and process of learning. As a "place" of meeting and an act of provocation, teaching is an occasion where one may come face to face with difference. It is a place where one is constantly confronted with the incommensurability of that which cannot be reduced to a version of oneself. It is also the occasion on which such alterity can be returned. Written this way, the assertion of particularities becomes a fundamental challenge to the nature of our participation in pedagogy.

After sketching what it means for me to teach from an overt, specific, and non-essentialized identity position, what I call "teaching as a Jew," I shall attempt to theorize how such a practice shifts my relationships with students. Focusing on my teaching in a doctoral program, I will spend a good deal of time laying out my understanding of the circulation of signification and eros structuring graduate faculty/student relationships. Since this aspect of doctoral education has been remarkably under-theorized, this section of the essay may be of independent interest as part of the attempt to clarify the intertwining of emotion and desire in institutionalized practices of teaching and learning. While my text weaves through a variety of themes and concerns, its basic ground is how one might rethink education within a yet-to-be-achieved postcolonial frame where the embrace of alterity defines the very condition for achieving knowledge.

To "Teach as a Jew": A Postmodern View

On Saturday mornings during the Spanish Inquisition, diligent priests would climb to the roof of a town's highest building to see if smoke was issuing from the chimneys of the houses of those Jews who had professed their conversion to Christianity. If a home was without chimney smoke, the inhabitants would be subject to detention and torture in an attempt to provoke an admission that they were observing the Jewish Sabbath. Such suspicions were not always unfounded. Indeed there were Jews who, while submitting to the discipline imposed on public life and outwardly conforming to the cultural genocide initiated by church and state, did preserve their faith and those Jewish practices that could be maintained in secret.

Over five hundred years later secrets are still being kept although clearly on different terms. For the most part Jews have accepted their civic integration into Euro-American nation-states on terms which have regulated the separation of public performance and private commitments (Mendes-Flor and Reinharz 103–39). The majority of Jewish academics have been educated in public institutions of higher learning where they have acquiesced to an implicit rule that, even if some aspects of their cultural and spiritual commitments inform their work, these were not to be made evident or topical in their writing or teaching.

While opportunities for Jews to enter university teaching have been (and perhaps in some regions continue to be) restricted, my purpose here is not to argue that, as university teachers, Jews are presently forced to disavow or suppress a public assertion of their categorical distinctiveness.[1] While Jews do participate in the freedom to publicly affirm their collective affiliations, such freedoms should not be taken for granted. What must be recognized is that the *social forms*[2] which have defined university teaching have proscribed the manner in which, *performatively*, Jewish academics have felt it appropriate to be Jews. Within Jewish studies programs or disciplinary-based courses that include content pertaining to aspects of Jewish history, culture, or theology, the conventions of teaching as a Jew are still proscribed. This proscription is in part enforced through the suppression of the relation of pedagogy and "the personal." This suppression has been the result of a strategic embrace of notions of objectivity borrowed from traditional disciplinary studies and seen as necessary for achieving academic legitimacy. There are, of course, many questions that one might ask regarding this proscription. My concern in this paper is to begin to explore the consequences for pedagogical relationships when such proscriptions are transgressed.

As someone engaged in university teaching as well as attempts to theorize its practice, I am putting this issue on the agenda because of its intimate connection to one aspect of "the personal" in pedagogy: *the exploration of the difference that difference makes for the complex dynamics of pedagogy*. My concern is not with absence or presence, not an analysis of the structures which limit or encourage the assertion of Jewish identities in university-teaching relationships. Rather my question is: as the proscription on the performance of a university teacher's Jewish identity is transgressed, what does this transgression block or mobilize (and in each case, for whom) in pedagogical relationships? While my concern is specifically with the transgression of proscriptions placed on Jewish identities, such issues of course are not limited to Jews. Thus I anticipate these issues might be extended to other performative identifications which have been historically rendered marginal, "othered" in relation to an institutionally normalized "mainstream," yet, when embodied, powerful in informing the reciprocal investments between teacher and students.

These are not parochial pursuits. They are tied to a political project whose task is the elaboration (as a necessary condition of justice) of what it might mean to live and work ethically within the embrace of heteronomy (Certeau 177), a problem that I see as central to late-twentieth-century North America. This project challenges us as university teachers and students on the ground of our own participation in pedagogical relationships. It has led me to explore the implications of teaching from an identity position which—by its very practice—raises the problem of difference and community, at least within the institution in which I spend most of my time.

I am trying to conceptualize a form of pedagogical practice which might break with a totalizing and synoptic thought that reduces the other to the same (or apprehends the other in reference to the same). Extrapolating from Levinas, I imagine breaking totality through an excess of specificity, causing us to face an other which refracts categories.[3] From within this political project, it is important to work out what it means to "teach as a Jew" in a way that not only transgresses normalized notions of difference but as well refracts the categories through which I am apprehended.

But once uttered, this phrase "to teach as a Jew" is too problematic to leave unattended, even for a moment. To say I am a Jew is to set myself apart.[4] This is not a quasi-ontological separation, a reduction into some sort of essence that can be distilled from the "Jewish experience." I assert no quintessential history or tradition on which to found an identity (which is not to deny either history or tradition). The mark of difference in my practice is not dependent on the incorporation of Yiddish or Hebrew expressions that purport to situate me in some notion of collective thought (unwilling as I am to forsake my appropriation of these languages). I speak here as a Jew without claiming any authority to speak for Jews. My figure (heterosexual male, Askenazi, North American diasporic) is not to be taken as a metonym, a representational trope in which the voice of the Jew is reduced to my voice.

As Judith Butler points out, the material or linguistic assertion of identity is not a question of offering an adequate representation of a preconstituted group; it is rather the performative invocation of an identity.[5] Such invocations not only are intended to resist the threat of erasure or marginalization; they are also occasions for the enunciation and enactment of the desire for recognition, affiliation, and commitment. Never innocent, such invocations should not be taken for granted. It is important to think about the invocation of identities as a strategic provision: a valuable articulation which—at the moment its value is recognized—is subject to an interrogation of the exclusionary operations which produce its identity-terms.

I am aware of this as I publicly "cite" myself as a Jew in my writing and teaching.[6] This is not a matter of being a Jewish teacher as identified by a particular set of multicultural interests, memories, investments, and affiliations placed easily within the mosaic of differences which constitute the nation-states of North America. Teaching as a Jew is *not* a matter of simply being seen as Jewish, as one might mark specific individuals as Greek, Mohawk, or Japanese. Such categorical renderings both totalize differences and block the provocation of facing up to the experience of alterity. As Sylvia Wynter has brilliantly pointed out, "multicultural difference" renders ethnicity generic and thus fails to disturb the presumption of a universal episteme within which an integrated public culture is possible.

Citing myself as a Jew in the context of my pedagogy requires something other than a display of the trappings which others could interpret as an affirmation of ethno-cultural membership. Rather than essentially given just by "being" a Jew, teaching as a Jew takes work; it is constantly being achieved. In my embodied presence as a male diasporic, post-holocaust Jew, I must produce myself by engaging with the *texts* which I take as constituent of *a* "tradition" that itself must be held for interrogation as to its exclusions. Provisionally, these texts are situated in a threefold structure which varies as Jewish identities proliferate.[7] The first element in this structure is the study of theological texts (Torah in its broadest sense) raising questions concerning one's obligations to God and to the diversity of life which shares (but currently not on equal terms) our fragile biosphere. The second element includes historical and literary texts whose study elicits partial perspectives on the diversity of Jewish communal life and the continual struggle for a Jewish existence, a standpoint that poses questions as to the significance of such narratives for *me* (recognizing that my questions will differ from those of Jews situated otherwise). The third element includes the contemporary social text of Jewish life with its complex relations in which Jews are positioned and position others, both encouraging and, at times, severely limiting possibilities.

The productive engagement with these texts ought to display this productivity so that as a Jew one can never be reduced to one's Jewishness nor accept a rendering of one's self within another's version of what constitutes Jewish characteristics. This engagement constitutes what I mean by postmodern Jewish identity, a practice through which a Jew makes evident the constructedness of her or his identity. "Teaching as a Jew" in this context means that the traces of one's engagement with Torah, history, and the social text of one's times would be apparent in the face of one's pedagogical presence.

While there are dangers to such a practice which I will discuss later on, what interests me here is the degree of Jewish specificity required in order to "teach as a Jew," a specificity which would transgress what has been normalized as an acceptable display of Jewish identity in one's pedagogy. "Teaching as a Jew" does not necessarily imply teaching about Jews or exclusively for Jews. I am arguing that "teaching as a Jew" denotes a pedagogical condition, initiated by my specificity as an embodied Jew, which enhances the achievement of knowledge through the interactive return of difference in the dynamics of teaching and learning.

It is to the potential consequences of such a practice that I now wish to turn. I must, however, first develop a picture of some of the core dynamics which structure doctoral education, specifically the circulation of signification and eros which regulates how students and faculty relate to each other. I will then go on to consider how this circulation might be rearticulated by the postmodern practice I have called "teaching as a Jew."

Signification and Eros in Doctoral Study

I focus on doctoral education because this takes up the majority of the time I devote to teaching at the Ontario Institute for Studies in Education, the graduate school of education of the University of Toronto. In 1991–92 it consisted of approximately 150 faculty with an enrollment of 2,331 graduate students, 868 of which were in Ph.D. or Ed.D. programs. I therefore regularly teach doctoral seminars and supervise the dissertation work of a large number of students.

I think there is something unique in pedagogical relations with doctoral students. Such relations often seem to generate intense intellectual and emotional dynamics which shape the contexts in which such teaching takes place:

courses, dissertation committee meetings, office meetings, hallway and cafeteria conversations, written responses to student work, conversations with students in pubs or at parties. These contexts make possible a degree of intimacy in faculty-student relationships which is quite distinct from the forms of interaction which structure, for example, undergraduate education.

This distinctive intimacy is often the locus of a complex circuit of signification and eros that conditions the work of teaching and learning. This circulation incorporates but is not fully accounted for by classical notions of transference and counter-transference. It is a dynamic wherein the acts of each party in the pedagogical relation are structured by how each "reads" and "invests in" the other as the locus of ambitions, aspirations, fears, and anxieties. These actions incorporate, if not presume, a hoped-for intellectual and emotional return. This circulation operates both in fantasies and in fact to define a set of possible complicities among people whose learning is conditioned by the play of desire between them.

This desire is not a free-floating abstraction; rather it is a distinctly intersubjective affective force that enters into history as communication addressed to an other. It is an insistent affect, a demand directed toward the *embodied* presence of an other who holds the possibility of providing pleasure to the degree that she or he responds to this demand. I am convinced that the desires mobilized in pedagogical relationships, with their experiences of pleasure and pain,[8] have been important aspects of university-based teaching and learning.

Reactions of colleagues to an earlier draft of this essay elicited a variety of cautions and objections to introducing the notion of desire and erotics into a discussion of pedagogy.[9] Some thought the word "desire" too overdetermined with connotations of sexuality, suggesting instead concepts such as affinity, preference, or expectation. However these terms seem inadequate to underscore the promise of pleasure in teaching/learning relationships. Others thought it dangerous to discuss desires because to do so introduces a terminology that might, given a restricted reading, too easily be misconstrued as providing a possible excuse for sexual assault or harassment. This is admittedly a potential danger; however, I cannot see how we will confront the problems of abuse and harassment without discussing the desires for pleasure which operate in education.

Additional objections came from colleagues who denied the importance of such issues on the basis that erotics and desire were not a part of *their* doctoral education. I am not here claiming that all educational experiences include such dynamics, only that there are structural reasons why such emotional tendencies ought to be taken seriously. Less helpful were suggestions that professors who talk about student desires directed toward their teachers are engaged in a fantasy in which they think their students have "the hots" for them or, at the very least, are engaged in an obsessive fantasy about their importance in their students' lives. More helpful were suggestions that my discussion be balanced by recognizing that cohorts of graduate students who support each other cognitively and emotionally can decenter and displace the singular importance of faculty in the institutional lives of students.

This essay, however, will explore only a specific set of dynamics between teachers and students. A more extensive treatment of these concerns would trace the erotic character of university pedagogy to the institutional histories which have established and continue to reproduce the feudal-like economy in which symbolic and material capital are dispensed, and filiation and fidelity returned. While the following discussion will be rather abstract, these structures are not lived abstractly. Embodied differently in relation to factors such as age, gender, sexuality, or racialization, these structures are manifest in such recognizable forms as sexual desire, respect, affection, deep admiration, projection of parental or progenitive figures, and the sublation of institutional hierarchy in the quest for personal intimacy. My concern here is specifically with those structures of desire traceable to the institutionally structured *situation* of doctoral education. Although other desires might be both mobilized and projected in such encounters, I am not attempting to account for the entire range of attraction or repulsion among professors and graduate students. Additionally, in positing structures of desire *in general*, structures that are felt and understood differently by different people, I am not excluding the possibility of desires specific to sex/gender identities.

I want briefly and speculatively to acknowledge four aspects of the complex range of desires which often eroticize students in the eyes of faculty. In the first instance I may constitute my teaching as an act of love, as a "gift," structured by my desire to arouse and instruct the desire of others (Gallop; Simon, "Pedagogy"). The fulfillment of this desire often requires the return of love, at least through a student's acknowledgment of the act of giving and the value of the gift. When this value is constituted in my students' desire for me, it renders the "gift" of pedagogy a form of seduction.

In the second instance, my teaching may be structured within a desire to provide myself with a "love object" who is a reflection of myself. The degree of narcissism I require at specific times will mediate my response to students who quote or cite my publications, appropriate my vocabulary in an act of intellectual identification, and, more generally, display the marks of a student experiencing what is sometimes called an "academic epiphany."[10]

A third instance appears when my teaching is structured by my desire for an intellectual partner; particularly if the institution I work in provides little opportunity for the gratifications possible in collegiality. This form of desire acknowledges my pleasure in intellection; it does not require either an amorous return of my pedagogical gifts nor a presence in which I can recognize myself as my own love-object. What is instead required is a partner in pedagogy who is prepared to take me seriously and provide a sense of engagement, one who will construct with me the sensuousness of the "academic dance."

In the fourth instance, my teaching may be structured by desire for solidarity, for a partner in whom I can see how my work might continue to inform *and* be informed by something beyond the boundaries of my own work. This requires students who embrace a political or cultural community of which I am a member and who can be addressed within a collective project and commitment.

Although such speculations only scratch the surface of professorial desires implicated in the intimate conversations of doctoral education, I wish now to move to the other pole of the circuit and consider more extensively what structures student desires for faculty. The following comments would not presume I have the right to represent the interests and consciousness of others. This is an indignity I wish to avoid (Owens 259–61). Yet in attempting to write about the dynamics of teacher/student relationships, I will draw on conversations with students and observations made during my years studying and teaching in universities. Since I wish to speak about students, the following comments might be read by some as speaking on behalf of students. Since I cannot completely avoid this,[11] I want to stress that my primary concern is not whether the following remarks "get it right" so much as whether they open up a discussion too long ignored. I hope this text will be read as an invitation for students and teachers to continue the conversation about the affective framing of doctoral education.

To begin, I want to acknowledge a two-part problem many of my doctoral students face. At OISE 60 percent of the doctoral students are over the age of thirty-five, and approximately 70 percent of all students are women. Most are returning to school after a period of paid employment or unpaid work in the home. They hope a doctoral degree will not only deepen their understanding of issues that are important to them but will also provide the opportunity for an academic career. In this context, they are not only developing a sophisticated analytic ability, but many must also confront and rearticulate their personal identities and commitments. Thus, for many students graduate study can become a period of personal transition, a time of displacement and contradiction when one may become temporarily unintelligible to oneself.

This sense of displacement and contradiction is heightened if students encounter a form of teaching which minimizes the provision of information and rejects knowledge as a simple addition to one's intellectual deposit. Instead, doctoral students may encounter readings and discussion intended to probe understanding, interrogate assumptions, and explore the very conditions of learning. As Frigga Haug suggests, these students are often compelled to embrace learning as a conflictual and uncomfortable process of unlearning that involves abandoning a safe position. This may be risky, particularly when one's convictions or experiences are challenged. This combined uncertainty produced by the transitional demands of graduate school and the challenges of an unsettling pedagogy can make graduate education a severe personal trauma.

Given that many doctoral students are redefining their identities, it is not surprising that the faculty students choose to work with often become personally quite significant. Questions pertaining to professional life that a student might discuss with a dissertation director often lead to serious personal questions such as "who am I?" "what are my commitments?" and "how should I act in the world?" Such questions require a framework within which to respond, a framework with a moral dimension that will be supported in their encounters with faculty.

Compounding these issues of identity displacement and reformation are the effects of the structural dependencies initiated by the institutionalized relations of power in traditional university education. These power relations structure dependencies on faculty that are not only psychological but professional, related to prospects for one's survival in a program and likelihood of completing the degree. Such dependencies can include forming a thesis committee, obtaining letters of recommendation, earning good marks, eliciting faculty help in mediating administrative conflicts, getting approval for course selections, even receiving faculty-approved access to computer accounts or special library holdings.

These factors set the conditions for a highly invested relationship with faculty in which a professor's speech (what's said and not said), writing (what's written and not written), and actions (what's done and not done) are made to bear considerable intellectual and affective weight. Students use accounts of professorial speech, writing, and action to produce a series of overdetermined and affect-laden *image-texts* which help them choose who they might study with.

These image-texts are often traded in pubs, cafeterias, hallways, and student offices.[12] They include intellectual and interpersonal aspects of faculty work as well as elements of one's public institutional persona and personal style. These might encompass what a professor said in class or wrote in a publication; a position a professor took at a departmental meeting; information about a professor's willingness to accept certain lines of argument in class discussion or written assignments; information about the support a professor gives students with their theses; observations on the quality and quantity of time a professor devotes to interactions with particular students; and whether or not a professor is known to be homophobic, anti-Semitic, racist, or sexist. As well as such concerns, image-texts often include readings of professorial hairstyles, clothes, vehicles, and preferences in regard to books, films, music, and sports, as well as what students know of a professor's past and present "personal" life. Observed contradictions between the established image-text of a professor and specific actions that might be seen as inconsistent with that text, especially contradictions between publicly professed positions and privately indulged in behavior, are of particular interest.

The fascination of many graduate students with faculty image-texts is not to be misconstrued as idle curiosity. Image-texts matter a great deal in providing a concrete (although at times inaccurate) basis for predicting whom students can communicate with and who would be likely to support their work. However, given the difficult identity questions initiated by entrance into graduate school (questions which continually seem to beg for resolution), these faculty image-texts also become important resources for identification and the focus of student desires within the intimate pedagogy of doctoral education.

It is in this context that elements of the image-texts of faculty are eroticized, interpreted as constitutive aspects of a body responsive to student desires. "Eroticized" does not here mean constituted as a source of sexual gratification. This may be one embodied form of eroticization but it is certainly not the only one possible. Rather what is signaled by this term is a cathexis which produces the teacher as a source of possible pleasure. As a teacher, it is important to acknowledge one's eroticization, to realize that one's actions matter to students. Indeed, to act responsibly in such a situation may be to seek supportively to lessen the degree of cathexis. The substance of the eroticization of faculty is, in part, articulated in Shoshana Felman's groundbreaking work on the importance of Lacan's theoretical writing for questions of pedagogy, through which one might posit a dimension of a student's desire for a professor as a demand for "the subject-presumed-to-know." Faculty image-texts that promise a response to this desire quite sensibly become a locus of attraction.[13] This attraction is doubled if a student believes that recognition by a professor embodying valued image-text characteristics would serve to confer on that student a degree of academic credibility, authorizing his or her "right" to a position in a particular graduate program.

There are, however, additional image-text characteristics whose interpretation can lead to the eroticization of a particular professor, characteristics which would respond to desires other than the "knowledge" which some students long for. One such desire is for an engagement with a professor who knows how to know, who doesn't teach concepts and skills but rather the condition that makes it possible to learn concepts and skills. This professor conveys how she or he learns and in the process learning is achieved dialogically. Such a professor will be eroticized by students who wish for a pedagogical partner on these terms.

Another student desire is the wish for a discursive environment in which one feels intellectually and emotionally at home (for example, feminism, queer theory, postcolonial studies).[14] While such environments are often produced among students, at times a student feels that she or he might experience "home" with a particular faculty member, thus eroticizing that professor. Students may also desire the figure of a professor who hopes, who provides an image-text which does not read as a testimony to the cynicism and despair that sometimes pervades academic life, but rather evinces a sense of joy, purpose, and possibility in intellectual work.

Such desires do not, of course, exhaust the range of ways in which faculty image-texts are read. I have simply tried to illustrate how particular faculty are eroticized for particular students and to acknowledge that this eroticization structures conversations within doctoral education. The context for learning will be erotic, where education has been historically and institutionally framed to proceed through intimate interaction and structural dependencies. With so much invested in professor/student relationships, it is no wonder that doctoral seminars and student/faculty conferences are often emotionally intense experiences.

Face to Face with Alterity

Every faculty member with substantial investments in doctoral education has to confront this erotic structure. However, a professor believing that "for teaching to be realized, for knowledge to be learned, the position of alterity is indispensable" (Felman 83) confronts a specific challenge. From a position of alterity one can return a difference that is essential to an educational dialogue. This difference, instead of something to be "acquired" by a student (where it would be repeated as, for example, "Simon's position"), must be used in a pedagogical exchange that enhances both student and teacher learning.[15] Nevertheless, the return of difference is not always appreciated, as it may frustrate student desires and lead to a de-eroticization of a faculty image-text.

This leads me back to my earlier starting point: What is the difference my difference makes if I face my students embodied in a practice in which I "teach as a Jew"? What erotics are possibly blocked or opened up and with which students? And what are the implications for rearticulating the terms on which education might take place?

Remembering that teaching is a situated, embodied act, I recognize that to "teach as a Jew," my Jewish body will have to be *seen* more clearly, more concretely. This will not mean simply marking my body so it can be recognized as Jewish (for example by wearing a *kippah*), which by itself would only invite the imposition of predetermined meanings.[16] It will, however, mean refusing to leave my difference at the door. Neither an "ethnic" recovery nor testimony, such pedagogy will challenge students to forego closure on their conceptions of Jewish identity while I visibly produce myself as a Jew through an engagement with contemporary, historical, and traditional "texts" which inform Jewish life. It will require that I teach how I read these texts against the grain of contemporary predicaments, forming dialectical constellations between various Jewish perspectives and the postcolonial aspirations of a diasporic world (Simon, "Remembrance").

I have little doubt such a pedagogical practice would influence the image-texts that are written about me as a faculty member. As these image-texts intersect with student desires, one of the first questions asked might be, "Who is this body for?" "Is Simon doing this because he wishes to work more extensively with Jewish students?" Given the way identity politics has been assumed to manifest a particularism of interest, my body in its Jewish specificity may be seen as speaking less invitingly to non-Jewish students. In other words, my particularity becomes an "othering" behavior which functions to exclude participation in a conversation.

This leads to a possible second question: "Why does Simon need to constantly refer to things Jewish?" "Is he having an identity crisis?" This question makes sense only because of the absence of reference to Jews and Jewish perspectives in the "normal" course of university teaching. It signals that a degree of Jewish topicality may be tolerated, but that there are limits; thus one can transgress boundaries of acceptable educational discourse by inserting too much Jewish particularity. This question as to "why the need to refer to things Jewish" mis-recognizes and personalizes the political project of "teaching as a Jew," missing the challenge of learning in heteronomic relationships.

In the secular environment of the university in which I teach, a third question is likely to be asked: "Is Simon really serious about theological questions?" "Why does he keep kosher?" "Does he actually go to synagogue on Saturdays?" As with all image-text questions, these are not idle concerns. Students who view theological matters as irrelevant to their lives (as most of my doctoral students do) are suspicious of any attempts to engage them in a serious consideration of what such perspectives have to offer. Being seen as "overly religious" is not likely to be eroticized except by those few students with similar sensibilities. In this terrain, too, the boundaries of educational discourse are policed.

Then there is the symptomatic question: "What are Simon's views on the Palestinians?" While this question may be motivated by a curiosity to hear my views on the Israeli-Palestinian conflict, it often contains an additional hidden dimension. It can be meant as a "test item": as an attempt to uncover a "blind spot," the limits to one's progressivism. However, in certain contexts, the question may signal even more: a rearticulation of the "conceptual Jew," that representational practice which constructs a notion of who "the Jew" is, unrelated to specific interactions between Jews and others, but intimately tied to the self-identification practices of the people rendering the representation.[17] While the attributions accorded the conceptual Jew have shifted historically, as Pierre Andre Taguieff suggests,[18] in the late twentieth century "the Jew" is increasingly presumed to be implicated, through assumed support for Zionism, in imperialism and racism. For students committed to struggles against racism and colonialism, this current abstraction of Jewish identity may become a vehicle with which to measure my Jewish body for the way it fits this rearticulated conceptual Jew. This operation is objectionable in several respects: it de-links struggles of anti-Semitism and anti-racism; in its demand that I be accountable for Israeli state policies, it reconstitutes anti-Semitism itself on new ground; finally, it suppresses the possibility that one can critique Israeli government policy without aligning oneself with the struggle to eliminate Israel as a "cancerous growth" on the body-politic.

At stake in all these questions are the limits that "teaching as a Jew" sets on the eros that might be mobilized in the context of my teaching. Such practices might be eroticized by Jewish students[19] and non-Jews who accept the attractions of heteronomy. Because I define my project as "teaching as a Jew" without necessarily teaching about Jews or specifically for Jews, the above questions must be worked through beyond the attitude of tolerance.

Conclusion

I have attempted to clarify some of the implications of a pedagogical practice which, at root, is a form of cultural politics. This politics is founded on three assumptions. First, it is strategically necessary at this time to engage in a politics of presence which challenges the operative categories of the conceptual Jew. There is no such thing as "the Jewish body," but there are many different kinds of Jewish bodies, all of which must be seen. This presentationism is to be undertaken in part as a strategic form of resistance to the increasing threat of anti-Semitism. However, it is also addressed to members of "the Jewish community" who wish to erase the sight of specific Jewish bodies which transgress the "normalized" performance of one's Jewish identity. This corporal diversity and specificity demands recognition of the multiplicity of Jews that exist in order to resist attempts at closure on the question "what is a Jew?"

Second, I am assuming that the display of how I perform/cite my Jewish identity through my engagement with a structure which provides the basis for such activity will help rupture totalizing categories in which knowledge of an other is reduced to the terms on which one is intelligible to oneself. In the wake of this rupture stands the possibility of relationships which are never totalized but always in a situation of excess. This is why the face-to-face encounter matters. The alterity that is incarnated in the face of the other is an alterity that subjective consciousness cannot easily grasp, since it permanently contests the prerogatives of consciousness to "give meaning" (Handelman 253).

It is important to recognize, however, that manifesting alterity may require giving up the "pass" which has permitted movement through social space. Undoubtedly, giving up this pass can mean subjection to malevolent judgment and abuse. The hope, of course, is that the pedagogical encounter with difference, on different terms, will reveal the inadequacy of the categories used to understand another, since such abstractions will always be inadequate to material presence in its fullness. While this sentiment betrays a considerable and perhaps naive idealism, it does envision what pedagogical relationships might look like in settings where, as students and teachers, we would exercise agency and responsibility.

Third and finally, neither self-affirmation nor toleration is the logos of this project to "teach as a Jew." I do not need such a practice to "feel good about myself," and I consider toleration a trap. Toleration is a position which secures the normal which, Deborah Britzman emphasizes, always reconstitutes an *us/them.* "Teaching as a Jew" attempts to disrupt this normality, to initiate a transgression which can mobilize practices which might displace the norm. Such attempts ask what practices would displace normalizing, static, or universalizing identities so that teachers and students might become partners in interrogating what can be known beyond that which is taken to constitute the other.

Notes

I wish to thank Deborah Britzman, Michael Chervin, Helen Harper, Robert Morgan, Alice Pitt, Bonny Peirce, David Purpel, Sharon Rosenberg, Arleen Schenke, Bart Simon, and Handel Wright, all of whom generously offered helpful comments on various versions of this essay. Jane Gallop's incisive and extensive editorial suggestions much improved the presentation of ideas. Many thanks Jane. An initial draft was presented at the conference "Pedagogy: The Question of the Personal," Center for Twentieth Century Studies, University of Wisconsin-Milwaukee, April 1993.

1. For Jews marked within other practices of discrimination, the basis of restriction has been multiple. For instance, Jewish women have been excluded based on both gender and Jewish identifications. Structures of multiple restriction have also been faced by gay and lesbian Jews as well as Jews currently marked as "not white" within the racialized social formations of North America.

2. Social forms describe certain ways of doing things that become the taken-for-granted, "goes without saying" options for constituting daily life. These forms are discursively regulated and materially encouraged, constituting institutionalized practices which secure particular sets of collective interests. See Corrigan.

3. Emmanuel Levinas: "The void that breaks the totality can be maintained against an inevitably totalizing and synoptic thought only if thought finds itself *faced* with an other refractory to categories" (40). Levinas's notion of "face" has received extensive discussion. For a recent and valuable addition to this commentary see Handelman. The concept of "face" is inter-textually referenced throughout this essay. Along with Handelman, James Ponet, and others, my grasp of this term is influenced by but not reduced to its association with the connotative meanings of the biblical Hebrew word *"panim."*

4. "To set my self apart." Simple words which are inadequate in the face of the enormity of violence which Jewish life has been subjected to during the last 2,000 years. This "setting apart" has never been a neutral process and the terms on which it has been accomplished have rarely been defined solely by Jews.

5. Comments by Judith Butler in the context of conference discussion reprinted in special issue of *October.*

6. Butler: "[I]t seems important to me to rethink performativity, as Derrida suggests, as citationality, for the invocation of identity is always a reinvocation . . . and there is promise in the iterability of the signifier. . . . I do not profess a subject who generates its performances. . . . what I did suggest was that it is only through the citing of a norm, a citing which instantiates and institutes the norm, that a subject is produced" (110–12).

7. In offering a structure, I am admittedly setting limits on the range of possible resignifications that might be attached to the term "Jew." I nonetheless offer this as a strategic intervention.

8. I refer here specifically to that pain, associated with teaching and learning, which I take to be centrally connected to the existence of desire. To the extent that the possibility of pleasure in learning is present as either an aspiration or expectation, its mitigation can lead to anger, hurt, frustration, and disaffection.

9. One objectionable objection evoked the specter of Nazi propaganda in my conjunction of the figure of the Jew and a language which uses the terms "eros" and "desire." In my view, this response is malicious in citing an anti-Semitic trope and revisiting it on me, rendering my text as an agent of its reproduction. This tactic will be familiar to those readers who remember how, at the turn of the twentieth century, Freud and other psychoanalysts were attacked for disseminating a "perverse Jewish science."

10. While I generally believe that students should be challenged in such manifestations, it is also important to recognize that initial attempts at working with a new discourse may require a certain stage of "trying on" a language in order to attempt to understand it.

11. A more divergent form for presenting issues such as those raised in this essay would be a paper written multiply by teachers and students which attempts to encode the tensions of teaching-learning situations in the very form and substance of the writing. For an example see Lewis and Simon.

12. In one U.S. university, graduate students have organized an internal departmental e-mail conference to exchange information about courses and stories about professors.

13. As Felman (84–86) makes clear, the subject-presumed-to-know elicits transference which may vastly complicate the demands placed on faculty. This includes aspects of resistance as well as attraction. The dynamics of transference may, at times, indeed play a significant structural function in the intimate conversation that is doctoral education. To avoid overly complicating this section of my essay I will not discuss this here. I will just mention that the eroticization of specific image-texts is tied to transference as aspects of image-texts and the situation of institutional learning elicit specific forms of projection.

14. The notion of "home" has been criticized by Bernice Reagon as referencing a homogenized environment, constituted outside of the difficulties of coalition building and working across differences. However, such critiques in no way diminish the necessity of recognizing the desire for affirmative affiliation and a temporary respite from the challenges of contestation and cooperation in order to rethink past practices and reconstitute identities and future directions.

15. An extended account of learning within the return of difference would have to discuss this return as originating in both the teacher and student. Handelman's reading of Levinas points in a helpful direction. "Language is address, appeal to, and welcome of the other as Other and not the other as representation or category determined by my concepts. In this sense, language maintains the other and approaches the other as *teacher*. . . . This is not the kind of Socratic teaching which is a remembering of what is already in the self, but a teaching coming from the 'exterior,' from what is outside the self and its concepts, from an other that is separated and foreign, from the 'infinity' of the Other, a 'traumatism of astonishment' " (221).

16. I am speaking quite personally here in full awareness that other Jewish bodies have been involuntary marked by a range of stereotypical physical characteristics. See for example Gilman.

17. For a detailed, historical discussion see Bauman 38–60.

18. As discussed in Zipes.

19. While not reducing all Jewish students into a categorical assertion, my experience has been that my explicit stance of "teaching as a Jew" provides a locus of affiliation for those Jews who are struggling with questions of identity and/or who are open to interrogating the relation between their own Jewish specificities and their academic work.

Works Cited

Bauman, Zygmunt. *Modernity and the Holocaust.* Ithaca: Cornell UP, 1989.

Britzman, Deborah. "Is There a Queer Pedagogy? Or Stop Being Straight!" Ontario Institute for Studies in Education. Toronto, Feb. 1993.

Butler, Judith. "Discussion." *October* 61 (Summer 1992): 108–20.

Certeau, Michel de. *Heterologies: Discourse on the Other.* Trans. Brian Massumi. Minneapolis: U of Minnesota P, 1986.

Corrigan, Philip. *Social Forms/Human Capacities: Essays in Authority and Difference.* London: Routledge, 1990.

Felman, Shoshana. *Jacques Lacan and the Adventure of Insight: Psychoanalysis in Contemporary Culture.* Cambridge: Harvard UP, 1987.

Gallop, Jane. "The Student Body." *Thinking through the Body.* New York: Columbia UP, 1988. 41–54.

Gilman, Sander. *The Jew's Body.* New York: Routledge, 1991.

Handelman, Susan A. *Fragments of Redemption: Jewish Thought and Literary Theory in Benjamin, Scholem, and Levinas.* Bloomington: Indiana UP, 1991.

Haug, Frigga. Lecture. Ontario Institute for Studies in Education. Toronto, Dec. 1992.

Levinas, Emmanuel. *Totality and Infinity.* Pittsburgh: Duquesne UP, 1969.

Lewis, Magda, and Roger Simon. "A Discourse Not Intended for Her: Learning and Teaching within Patriarchy." *Harvard Educational Review* 56.4 (1986): 457–72.

Mendes-Flor, Paul R., and Jehuda Reinharz. *The Jew in the Modern World: A Documentary History.* New York: Oxford UP, 1990.

Mohanty, S. P. "Us and Them: On the Philosophical Bases of Political Criticism." *Yale Journal of Criticism* 2.2 (1989): 1–31.

Owens, Craig. "The Indignity of Speaking for Others: An Imaginary Interview." *Beyond Recognition: Representation, Power and Culture.* Berkeley: U of California P, 1992. 259–62.

Reagon, Bernice Johnson. "Coalition Politics: Turning the Century." *Home Girls: A Black Feminist Anthology.* Ed. Barbara Smith. New York: Kitchen Table-Women of Color, 1983. 356–68.

Scott, Joan W. "Multiculturalism and the Politics of Identity." *October* 61 (Summer 1992): 12–19.

Simon, Roger I. *Teaching against the Grain: Texts for a Pedagogy of Possibility.* New York: Bergin, 1992.

Wynter, Sylvia. "America as a 'World': A Black Studies Perspective and 'Cultural Model' Framework." Stanford U, 1990 MS.

Zipes, Jack. *The Operated Jew: Two Tales of Anti-Semitism.* New York: Routledge, 1991.

9 | On Waking Up One Morning and Discovering We Are Them

Naomi Scheman

I.

I SUPPOSE IT was inevitable. If you're talking about the personal these days, the erotic is on the scene—if not by its explicit presence, then by its conspicuous absence. And if the scene is the pedagogical, the site of instruction, of knowledge and self-knowledge, the language of psychoanalysis presents itself, bidden or not. And once you're on the terrain of transference and counter-transference, there it is: students in love with (or at least drawn to) teachers, and vice versa. A distaste for psychoanalysis, or even for modernity, won't help, either: for those more classically inclined, the Platonic route takes us to the same destination.

Not that teacher/student erotic encounters, fantasized or otherwise, don't happen. But something about their unquestioned centrality in our discussions throughout the conference troubled me, and I couldn't quite tell why. Of course, there are all the reasons to be wary about potential and actual abuses of power and trust, but those seem taken care of (in theory, at least) by the psychoanalytic model, since sex between analyst and analysand is more strictly forbidden than sex between teacher and student (in theory, at least).

Then, speaking from the floor, Patsy Schweickart told a story. At the age of ten she asked herself one day, with no sense of anxiety, only puzzlement: "What are parents *for*?" In retrospect she takes her question to be both a tribute to her parents—a reflection of their having instilled in her a sense of security and agency that left their role invisible—and a model of what she hopes to be, as a teacher, in her students' lives. Now, at some point, an analysand might calmly and bemusedly wonder (it might, perhaps, even be a sign of successful termination), "What was my analyst for?," but certainly not in the midst of transference.

When Patsy told her story, with its moral, my unease suddenly made sense: all the talk of student-teacher eroticism had no connection at all with my experience, as a student or as a teacher. Not that I didn't find classrooms sexy. At least since graduate school[1] I have found them very sexy indeed, but the eroticism I found there was among the students, a site totally occluded by the psychoanalytic model, where all one's "siblings" are, however vividly, only imagined.

My graduate school experience was as positive as that of any other woman

I know, something for which I have Barnard and my teachers there, Sue Larson and Mary Mothersill, largely to thank. Had I come to Harvard needing to be assured that I had what it took, that I could plausibly aspire to becoming a philosopher, I would have been dependent on my teachers' good opinion in a way that I suspect might well have precluded my getting it. As it was, not only did I feel confident that I could aspire to being a philosopher, I took myself already to be one. Freed of an anxious dependency on my teachers, I reveled in the comradeship of my peers. We used to joke, in fact, that the best thing the faculty had done was to admit all of us, leaving us for the most part in each other's hands: *that's* what *they* were for. (Or so it seemed: as with Patsy's parents, there was a lot more to it than that.)

One of the best parts of my experience of those days was the permeability of the boundaries between the sorts of relationships we had with each other. It was, I think, essential to the permeability in particular between the sexual and the intellectual that we met each other on terms of equality. Between teacher and student, inequality is unavoidable, even if it is not a defining part of the erotic equation (and we might doubt that that could ever be the case; certainly the transference model would lead one to be skeptical, as would by now commonsense feminist reflections on the social construction of desire). It may have taken chutzpa for me to have known then that I was a philosopher, but it would have been madness to have thought myself the intellectual peer of my teachers. But it was not madness—it ought not even to have taken chutzpa, though perhaps, sadly, for a woman it did—to think myself the intellectual peer of my fellow students.

Equality between women and men was and is a rare thing, and usually sex messes it up. Part of why I remember those days as utopian is that I don't think that happened. (This is, of course, fertile ground for self-deception, but after twenty-five years, a feminist consciousness verging on the fanatical, and a reasonably successful career, I haven't had to reconsider. I do, however, need to be careful. I know that for all sorts of reasons my experience was far more positive than that of most women, there or elsewhere, then or at any other time. Even more problematically, there were ways in which my choices—both that I had them and how I made them—were the cause of pain to other women. So I can't generalize and I shouldn't romanticize what it was like. But, having said that, I do still believe that what I lived was a utopian possibility—that is, that its value did not depend on my carelessness about it, nor on its rareness.)

I see the same spirit among the students I work with today, though, so far as I can tell, they act it out with less abandon than we did—a not uncommon difference between the seventies and the nineties. The major difference, though, is the open and pervasive lesbian eroticism among them, characterized by a playful inclusiveness that embraces the heterosexual women students who are unthreatened by it.

It also embraces me. In the early days of the pioneering feminist graduate students in my department I was in a frequent panic about boundaries. It seemed that they needed me far too much, needed my support, my good opinion, my honest and tough criticism, my attention, and my care. All of the above, all of the time. If, for example, the criticism threatened to weaken the support, there was nowhere else for them to get it, no one I could take turns with. (I'm sure I'm exaggerating, and I probably did then, but I'm quite certain not only of my own anxieties, but also of corresponding ones on their part, even if mine outstripped theirs.) And playful friendship, let alone anything hinting of the erotic, scared the hell out of me.

I'm no more likely now than I would have been then to have a sexual relationship with a student I work with, but playful, even erotically tinged, friendship is one of the blessings to me of the flourishing of the graduate student community. The particularities of my relationship to any one of them are mediated, buffered, by my relationship to them as a group and by their relationships with each other. I attend and host potlucks, get teased, go dancing at the country and western bar (taking turns leading when we two-step), join in celebrating their commitments and their children. Neither they nor I forget that I'm not one of them, that I have power they rely on and a position they aspire to, that they, just as did their predecessors, depend on me for tough criticism as well as support. But moving into and out of different roles, meeting different needs, is far less awkward when they and I know that they have each other and when the less formal, more friend-like interactions between us are for the most part communal.[2]

Part of what I'm negotiating in these relationships is my transformation from sixties student radical to full professor. It is a point of honor to belong to the group dubbed by Roger Kimball "tenured radicals." However uncomplimentarily he meant the term, it is for me, as for many others, a matter of intellectual as well as political integrity to retain a right to the "radical" in light of the safety from personal consequence implied by the "tenured." That is, of course, not an easy thing to do. Although I don't worry about inappropriately using the students I work with to satisfy my erotic needs, I do worry about inappropriately using them to satisfy my need to appear to myself and others as genuinely radical, as not having sold out, not having accepted the implicit bribes that went along with my academic success, able to be counted on if need be to bite the hands that feed me, even as I'm on friendly, first-name terms with many of the people whose hands they are.

In my own case, I was out of the country from the summer of 1968 to the fall of 1969, and when I returned, my political home, Students for a Democratic Society, had dissolved, many of its members going into the Weather Underground. I wouldn't have known how to follow them had I wanted to, and I couldn't quite bring myself to want to, though I have never been confident about why I didn't. I had, for what seemed to me irrelevant reasons, not been at Columbia when my comrades had gotten beaten in the police riot, and I could point to no differences between us prior to that year's events that gave me any confidence that I'd not have joined in their despairing exit from being the good children that most of us were: we really did think (for what it's worth, I still do think) that we were saving what was best in universities and in American society from evil people who were selling us all down the river for their sick dreams of unlimited power and monetary gain.

But, as I said, I didn't know where the others were; besides, graduate school beckoned, and I did love philosophy, and Cambridge was a heady and delicious place to be. From such desiderata, helped along by cowardice and inertia, are life choices made. Now, twenty-five years later, I'm trying to give an accounting of myself not only to the idealistic adolescent I was but to the political activist I might have become. And the temptation is to turn to my students and say, "I did it for you, because I think that you matter, that it's just not true that the real world starts where the campus ends; because I think that your lives are real lives, and making a difference to them is making a difference in the real world; because what we do together can be radically transformative, not only of you but of the other lives you touch. Please reassure me that I haven't been coopted, that you don't see me either as an irrelevant relic of a failed radicalism or, perhaps worse, as just another liberal infatuated with radical chic. Tell me that I haven't become one of 'them.' "

It's too much to ask. But, worse, it's the wrong sort of thing to ask. It's asking, in part, to be accepted as one of them, to be granted, not visiting privileges in the community they've created, but full membership. And finally, it's incoherent: it's asking to be absolved in the wielding of power I fully intend (and they need me) to go on wielding, asking to be granted the magical combination of knowledge and innocence, power and purity. (In different but related contexts, I think something like this is what white or heterosexual women often ask, with equal inappropriateness and incoherence, of women of color or lesbians. An important difference is that it's at least arguable that, unlike racist or heterosexist privilege, the privileges of academic positions do not always and only serve to advantage those who have them at the expense of those who don't.)

The knowledge and power of which I want to be absolved are, of course, exactly those that students are in school in part to acquire: they are apprenticing for the position of privilege I am finding so compromising. All very well for me to voice my discomfort with the apparatus of academia: I have tenure. The situation is infinitely riskier for those who want to join me there and whose ability to do so can be threatened by their adopting stances that might not only lose them favor with those whose favor they need but, perhaps even more important, cynically alienate them from a discipline and a form of life they want to inhabit, however critically.

II.

When I was in fourth grade a paper I wrote on evolution was turned into the class play, and I got to narrate, as Father Time. I had even then a loud voice and the ability to project to the back of the school auditorium. When, on the day of performance, I was outfitted with a microphone, no one told me I could let it do that work for me, and my voice reverberated down the halls. I didn't know how to modulate it under conditions of institutionally sanctioned amplification, and, nearly forty years later, I still don't quite have the knack.

It's a tricky situation. The school provided the microphone and, so long as I boomed out the lines I was supposed to say, my voice got picked up and carried. But had I decided to deviate from the script (I wrote it, after all, so why not?) and called for a schoolyard insurrection, I'd have had the plug pulled on me pretty quickly. I have now, of course, a great deal more scope for deviating from the script (academic freedom doesn't afford much protection to fourth graders), but it would be foolhardy, especially in the face of the efforts of wealthy right-wing foundations and the academics they fund, not to worry about the health of the relatively friendly environment on which I have come to depend. My own job may be safe, but the conditions that make it possible to do what I take to be the real work of that job are much less clearly so: an institutionally validated women's studies department and feminist research center, a philosophy department receptive to feminist students, and a university receptive to adult students with work, community, and family responsibilities; and some degree of institutional commitment to multiculturalism and to gay/lesbian/bisexual studies.

But it is, I find, psychologically easier to focus on the threats to my privilege than on its reality. Even if the microphone can be yanked, the fact is that at the moment it's plugged in, and I have to learn how to speak through it. I have to learn, for example, how to allow for the difference in the weight my words carry. I learned to speak in public with the bravado of the rebel, confident that whatever I said would be filtered through heads cooler, more pragmatic, more conservative than my own before anything was actually done. For the most part, of course, this "confidence" was a cause of anger or despair, since it meant that what finally made it through all those filters would be such a faint whisper as to make little or no difference to the goings-on that had elicited the rebellious words. By contrast, my words today have acquired at least considerable perlocutionary, and in some cases illocutionary, force.[3] I am in a position to make things happen.

From such a position, naughtiness can be at best unseemly and at worst irresponsible. I'm a great believer in naughtiness (having exhibited far too little of it as a child), in part because it helps to keep rules and those who make and enforce them on their toes and a little off their guard. Like the three-year-old's constant demands to know "why," naughtiness presses the limits of the otherwise taken-for-granted, as puns and other verbal wordplay press the limits of intelligibility. Discovering what we can get away with is a good way of figuring out why some things are required or forbidden, of uncovering the hidden stakes behind the rules.

As Barnard prepared me for Harvard in large measure by making me unneedy of the approval of my teachers there, so Harvard similarly prepared me for the world I moved into as a junior faculty member. Confident, not to say arrogant, I adopted a stance of naughty irreverence toward the subject of philosophy, playfully tweaking the nose of this character who worried about the reality of the world beyond that nose, not to mention of the nose itself. The first time I tried it, it didn't work: I found myself among excessively solemn canonical loyalists, and I lost my job. But in the far friendlier environment of the University of Minnesota, I was tolerated, even encouraged. I was, I at least like to think, seriously naughty, responsibly transgressive.[4] But then I got promoted to full professor.

Not that I didn't think about it. Part of me was more than happy to stay junior to most of my colleagues—securely tenured, but still somehow a kid. But the role was fitting me less and less well. Not only did I want the respect that came with being seen as what a German colleague once referred to as "internationally reputated," but it did neither feminist philosophy as a field nor the colleagues and students who relied on me for letters of recommendation any good for me to seem to be stalled in the middle ranks. I managed, in fact, nearly to convince myself that I was giving up the psychic freedom of my less-than-fully-senior status for the greater good.

As noble a gesture as this was, the reality is that, in a world filled with injustice, I've succeeded. Leaving aside the more global examples of oppression and exploitation, the academic world nourishes some and starves out others in ways that are hardly models of fairness. I had, ironically, made my career by crafting a critique of that unfairness. So promotion was a replay of the anxieties of tenure: Whom had I betrayed for this to happen? What had I done wrong to be so rewarded? What Faustian bargain had I struck, and when and how was my soul to be collected? Or had it already been, and was I even now doing the devil's work?

The devil? Just whom did I have in mind? The distance between me and those I might be tempted to demonize, at least in the academic arena, had disconcertingly shrunk. And then there's the pesky question of that microphone. The amplifier to which it's hooked up has been getting stronger and stronger, and I have no intention of pulling the plug myself. (I have no illusions about who would grab it if I did: as we've learned in other arenas, simply dumping privilege, even if one can actually do it, does no one one cares about any good.) I can try to use my access to it to give a boost to other voices, but I can't turn it over entirely (for one, if I seriously tried to do that, the plug would be pulled: that we play gatekeeper is one of the nastier bargains radical academics have to strike), and to the extent that it is mine to turn over, that's part of the problem.

These conundrums notwithstanding, there is a lot those of us with access to the various apparatuses of voice-amplification can and should do to democratize that access. But my concern here is how to think in a politically responsible way about my voice when I'm at the mike, and in particular when it's directed to students (rather than on the one hand to administrators or on the other to feminists and others outside the academy whose ally I would be).

One of the ironies in my relationship to students doing feminist work is that insofar as I see them as colleagues—insofar, for example, as I see their work not as student exercises but as contributions to projects we jointly care about—I see myself not only as their teacher but, like them, as a contributor to those projects. That is, I don't, as it were, see myself, like Patsy's parents, as invisible, nor can I bring myself to hope that they will. The question about what I'm for is answered in part by my producing, as they do, some of the work that we care about. And, especially in a field as new and as small as feminist philosophy, some of my work will be among the work that constitutes the subject matter of our discussions, the syllabi of our courses. The very strength of their community and the delights of my participation in it become part of the problem: I want to be visible to them, but it's hard to find the ground between invisibility and being the center of attention.

III.

When I was an undergraduate my teachers seemed socially quite distant. (After I got to graduate school it seemed silly to continue to call my undergraduate professors "Miss Larson" and "Miss Mothersill," but I didn't find it easy to switch to "Sue" and "Mary," even though by then the norms had shifted and that's what their current undergraduate students called them.) Thus the seriousness with which they took me philosophically seemed comfortably subjunctive: they were treating me as if I were a philosopher, a colleague, a peer—when obviously I wasn't. It seemed to be how they taught, with a confident expectation that I would grow into the status subjunctively conferred.

In graduate school the matter was somewhat different. Especially in philosophy there's little reason to be in graduate school if one doesn't aspire to becoming one's teachers' colleague, so being treated that way (the subjunctive being replaced by the future indicative) is simply being treated decently, that is, not as though one's admission were thought to be a mistake. But in my experience, first names or no, the distance remained; it seemed not so much relational (a matter of our roles as teacher and student) as relative (a matter of age and status).[5]

Certainly when Harvard began hiring people for nonrenewable three-year positions ("folding chairs"), those faculty members were much closer to the graduate students: they were younger than some of us, some of them didn't have their Ph.D.s yet, and our community was much easier to feel a part of than that of the senior faculty. On those terms, I am long overdue for a change of status, but the reality is that I feel more, not less, a part of the graduate student community than I did before. Part of it is that, unlike my peers in graduate school, who were nearly all in their mid-twenties, the graduate students at Minnesota are of a range of ages, many of them having returned to graduate school after having done other things: like many of the undergraduates there, they are adults, with adult lives and concerns, not in the extended adolescence continuous schooling can prolong.

But their not all being half my age, though it no doubt helps me to feel a part of their community, doesn't explain why I need to. That, I think, goes back to the tenured radical stuff, to my neither wanting nor being able to be in the position either of relatively out-of-the-fray nurturing teacher or of *éminence grise*. If their community is where the action is, it's where I feel the need to be. It would be against my politics (not to mention demonstrably false) to think that the action wasn't there, that they were only in training to do someday what I do now. The irony is that my taking them in this way seriously raises my stakes in their acknowledging me, makes me less willing to recede into the background, to leave a puzzle about what I'm for. I'm reminded uncomfortably of parents who are trying too hard to be their children's friend to be their parent: Is this less a problem in very large families with secure, happy siblings? I don't know.

I have a different sort of concern with women students, especially feminists, who don't find feminist philosophy to be what they choose to do, either because something else simply interests them more or because they find the arguments about the relevance of gender to (at least) most of philosophy unconvincing. Since I used to be in their position, hooked on epistemology and metaphysics, which I confidently believed had nothing to do with gender or with anything else political, I feel I know something of what it's like. But that feeling is an illusion. For one thing, it's hardly helpful to convey the impression (and hard to avoid doing so) that, since I was once where they are, they will someday, when they learn better, be where I am. For another, the center of gravity has markedly shifted. Back when I believed that gender was irrelevant to epistemology and metaphysics, hardly anyone in the Anglo-American philosophical world believed anything else. Today, although most of that world still thinks of epistemology and metaphysics in apolitical terms, there is a strong and vocal feminist presence that both asserts otherwise and claims to have been oppressed by the dominant views. That latter claim is an especially problematic one: it can be unbearable to find out that something one loves has been used as a club (in both senses of the word) to terrorize and ostracize people one cares for and identifies with.

Without the microphone, when I was just shouting into the wind, I could be confident (again, it usually felt more like despair) that no one was going to be seriously affected by anything I said. Now, both because of the force of my words, published or spoken, and because of the size and vigor of the community I helped to form and continue to mentor, women I care about—students I would like to be able to teach—are hurt by what they perceive to be the distance between who they take themselves to be and a picture of women that they find in those words and in that community. If it were a picture I thought were somehow false, I could work to correct it, but that's not the problem. It needn't be false to be problematically coercive, and I don't know what to do about that.

Part of the problem is something that comes up in a number of diverse contexts, namely, a disparity between privilege as it exists within a group and as it exists in the world around the group. One of the points of separatism is in fact to create such disparities, to create contexts in which an identity that is marginal or oppressed in the world at large is central, and in which those whose identity it is have the power to decide how things will go on. Such disparities can cause problems, especially if the group is not strictly separatist, allowing or even welcoming members who choose to ally with, though they don't share, the identity in question (or if the identity that becomes central is a subset of the one around which the group formed, as a feminist group can come to have lesbians as its most central members). The central group members will typically be exceedingly aware of the marginality of the identity that brought them together: the outside world will loom as the frame within which they defend, usually perilously, their space. The others will typically be far less aware of the salience of their privilege in the outside world (it's likely to be relatively invisible to them) and much more aware of their own marginality and lack of privilege within the group.

The problem is particularly acute when central group members are not the only ones to feel marginalized or oppressed by the rest of the world. One doesn't have to be a feminist philosopher or even a feminist (though it helps) to feel marginalized and oppressed by the world of academic philosophy: being a woman is enough. And communities of feminist philosophers are natural places to turn for support, especially when, as in my department or in the Society for Women in Philosophy, such communities are strong and vibrant. But for good reason those communities are likely to have at their centers strong counter-identities that may feel to some more marginalizing than welcoming, be that lesbian or a radically feminist stance toward philosophy.

Like the problems confronting "tenured radicals," these are problems of success—success at changing parts of the world when most of it remains untransformed. I have solutions for none of these problems. My hope is that in raising them I have done something more than whine about things that only the overprivileged have the time for. I do, when it comes down to it, believe that teachers and students inhabit the real world and that what we do with each other matters, and that doing it responsibly is neither easy nor trivial. So the something more I hope to have done is to have contributed to that work by sketching not just a self-portrait but a picture in which some of you will find yourselves—with whatever mixture of relief or discomfort—and others of you will find people whose exasperating behavior may seem a little less opaque.[6]

Notes

1. I was an undergraduate at Barnard, and the experience made me an ardent advocate of women's colleges. But the feminism of Barnard when I was there (I graduated with my class in 1968, but I left the year before, when I married a Columbia student and followed him to MIT) was of an earlier era: there was nothing to hold me back, after class, from immersion in politics and romance on the other side of Broadway. And in those days of official homophobia and silent closets, the last thing I associated with women's spaces, be they dormitories or classrooms, was eroticism.

2. The other thing that helps is that over the years they have taught several of my colleagues how to be good teachers for them, so, for example, mine is not the only faculty criticism they can trust nor the only faculty support they can count on.

3. The terms are J. L. Austin's. "Perlocutionary force" refers to the effects one's words can have, for example, to frighten or to persuade. "Illocutionary force" refers to what it is that one's words directly, performatively, do, as when one promises, asks or answers a question, or, with the authority of office, brings it about that, say, a syllabus is laid down, a policy is enacted, or a grade is assigned. See J. L. Austin, *How to Do Things with Words* (Oxford: Clarendon, 1962) 98–107.

4. Issues of seriousness and responsibility, naughtiness and playfulness have concerned me since I was a child, when I resolved to become an adult, but never a grown-up. Adulthood meant taking oneself and others seriously, being responsible; being grown-up meant solemnity and the loss of playfulness. I have never, by the way, understood why not taking oneself seriously is meant to be a virtue: However could one trust people who failed to take themselves seriously? (If taking oneself seriously seems to require a suspect metaphysics of selfhood, the problem ought to be with that seeming. The idea that any notion of selfhood that allows for taking oneself seriously is suspect accounts for why so many of the rest of us find certain postmodernists untrustworthy.)

5. I'm quite certain that the difference is not one of relative eminence but of the differences in my status and between the two schools. It was a commonplace for Harvard undergraduates to complain that the faculty didn't seem to pay much attention to them, presumably because they were paying attention to the graduate students. The graduate students knew better. There were and are excellent and dedicated teachers at Harvard,

including in the philosophy department, but it's not the ethos of the place: another undergraduate commonplace mirrors the perception I shared with my fellow graduate students—that most of one's education comes from other students. Barnard was, and I assume still is, very much a teaching college, however eminent its faculty.

6. My thanks to Jane Gallop and to Kathleen Woodward and the Center for Twentieth Century Studies at the University of Wisconsin-Milwaukee for the conference on "Pedagogy: The Question of the Personal" that helped to shape my reflection on the topics of this essay. (That reflection took shape in a somewhat different form on the occasion of my writing the introductory essay to a collection of my papers, published in 1993 by Routledge under the title *Engenderings: Constructions of Knowledge, Authority, and Privilege.*) Thanks to Jane also for her urging that I write up what I said at the conference. Writing in this way "for Jane" is a fascinatingly disconcerting experience, rather as though my editorial superego has been unceremoniously turfed from its office by my id, which has taken up residence there, its feet up on the desk. This essay is also marked by a degree of expansive and reflective distance. I am writing from the charmed space of the Society for the Humanities at Cornell, a place of many temptations and few obligations: it precisely does not "concentrate the mind." My tenure here also allows me the opportunity to explore some of these issues in conversation with, as it were, surrogate colleagues and students, as one can more easily explore familial tangles with someone *else's* parents or siblings. But my greatest debt is to the members of SOΦIA, back home in Minnesota, as well as to other philosophy and women's studies students there, equally for inspiration and for critique.

10 | Taking Multiculturalism Personally
Ethnos and Ethos in the Classroom
Gregory Jay

I.

SINCE ITS BEGINNING in the 1970s, the movement known as multiculturalism has taken two distinct directions. On the one hand, multiculturalism celebrates the diversity of cultural groups. Sometimes called ethnic revitalization, this multiculturalism seeks to preserve the cultural practices of specific groups and to resist the homogeneity of assimilation. It sees the identities of individuals as primarily cultural, determined by their membership in a group, and not as the expression of a unique self-consciousness. Oriented by identity politics, this multiculturalism rejects the individualistic model of personhood and instead stresses the analysis of communal expressive traditions. The forms and values of these traditions, in turn, become the focus of curriculum reform. Pedagogy is responsible for developing a competence in the student, such that he or she can understand various cultures and appreciate their achievements. This competence may even lead to the student's choosing to join in that culture's practices, though this may be seen as a social faux pas and as a violation of the decorum of essentialism. For marginalized groups, an appreciation of their culture can improve student performance and so reverse the effects of bigotry and discrimination.

On the other hand, multiculturalism grows out of the political movements of the 1960s—such as the struggles of women, the poor and working classes, people of color, and gay men and lesbians. This multiculturalism is oppositional rather than pluralist. It is less interested in celebrating difference than in resisting oppression. Sometimes called radical, critical, or strong multiculturalism, this branch of the movement targets the unequal distribution of power in society. Rather than accepting the borders between cultural groups, it insists on analyzing how cultural divisions are constructed historically through racist policies or other institutionalizations of oppression.

Radical multiculturalism would not be satisfied with teaching the appreciation of African American cultural forms but would look critically at why African Americans so often sing the blues. This multiculturalism implies a global, often Neomarxist, reading of the specific class relations between dominant and subordinate groups. In some cases, these critics move away from the focus on culture, rejecting it as an ideological distraction from the material conditions and political arrangements determining the shape of subjectivities. Returns to economic or political determinism, however, are no more satisfying than models that examine culture only as a set of aesthetic practices. As Cameron McCarthy argues, we need "an alternative formulation that attempts to avoid privileging either 'cultural values' or 'economic structures' as 'the' exclusive or unitary source of racial inequality in schooling" (5).

What strikes me, especially in the context of this volume, is the common assumption of both multiculturalisms when it comes to the personal: identity in each case is defined and determined by culture. In contrast, any reference to persons or individuals, then, tends to sound like a throwback to the discredited discourse of Enlightenment liberalism, whose image of the universal man turned out to be the reflection of a few European and American white guys. I think we need an alternative formulation that avoids privileging either the social constructionist or liberal pluralist accounts of personhood in a multicultural society.

It is often said, sometimes with a conspiratorial spin, that the white masters of poststructuralism promoted the disappearance of the subject and the author at the very moment when the disenfranchised were finally gaining power and voice (see Gates). Though I grant that this may not be entirely a coincidence, I would point out that in their own critiques the liberation movements also replaced personal identity with cultural subjectivities. Social constructionism goes hand in hand with multiculturalism, as both see the individual as the expression of the cultural practices of socio-historical groups. The poststructuralist cry that "language speaks man" finds an eerie echo in the articulations of how race and ethnicity, sexuality and gender, class and nation speak the person.

Yet multiculturalism and the liberation movements often associated with it continue to exhibit discomfort about replacing persons with subject positions. The experience, the literature, and the theorizing on multiculturalism insistently bring out the stubborn tensions between persons and positions. For example, as I live it, cultural identity is not a matter of choosing between a personal essence and a social construction. These are hypothetical entities in dialectical relationship to one another, and the shape their conversation takes over time constitutes the character of my person. Agency is one metaphor to name this dialectic. Agency appears in the way I take a social construction personally, as my duty, my responsibility, my ethos, my law, my enemy, or my love. Agency also names the tendency of cultural practices to become reified and bureaucratized, to become agencies in the institutional sense. These agencies can make people their instrumental agents, robbing them of their persons in the process of making them their subjects.

I think there could be something healthy about insisting on the difference between persons and cultural identities. The difference between me and my cultural identity creates opportunities for change. Taking these opportunities as occasions for agency, I also end up taking some responsibility for what happens as a result. If my cultural identity and I were the same, and if I imagined that identity as homogeneous and univocal, then my actions and beliefs would follow in strict accord. I would be on automatic, so to speak. Of course the multiplicity of my cultural identities, and their lack of any totalizing framework, ensures that this never occurs. My positions, by virtue of race or class or gender or sexual orientation or age or nation or political ideology or professional vocation, include many contradictions, making me usually the dominant, sometimes the marginalized, and quite often just the muddled one in the middle.

Negotiating the internal conflict of cultural identities requires as much or more energy and theoretical savvy as negotiating the differences between social groups or cultural formations. These groups and formations are not grounded in singular essences; they are coalitions and affiliations whose appearance of identity comes into being through history, strategy, and struggle. Categories such as "heterosexual" or "white" or "Jewish American" or "middle class" are not natural or divine divisions but rather the products of history. This does not make them false, unimportant, or unnecessary, but it does mean that we must accept some responsibility for them, whether we wish to advocate or deconstruct them. The solidity of these categories remains fragile and transient, as the history of these and other group formations demonstrates. What we have learned from Foucault and others about the "invention" of "homosexuality" as an identity category may be applied to the history of words like "white" and "middle class" as well. Such words not only name but help shape the groups to which they are attached. Like any name or noun, these categorical labels generalize at the expense of particular differences that are forgotten in the process. As McCarthy notes, "An essentialist approach to race typically ignores or flattens out the differences within minority groups while at the same time insulating the problem of race inequality from issues of class and sexual oppression" (118).

The differences between the Dutch, German, English, French, Swiss, Russian, and Italian are forgotten, largely for political reasons, when the category of "white" subsumes them all. Likewise the category "middle class" obscures the real differences between men and women, gays and straights, and whites and blacks who share an otherwise common socioeconomic bracket. The differences within particular categories are suspended, then, when the identity of the group gets constructed, and these suspended differences are always potentially the sources of fracture and realignment as subjects respond to new claims on their passions and allegiances. "Person" is another name for the individual who is the remainder of this process, the leftover when totality fails, or the agent who negotiates the new contract.

There's always something a bit suspect about the plea not to "take it personally." In the case of multiculturalism, the plea would seem especially odd, given the roots of multiculturalism in the grounds of identity politics. But is a cultural identity personal? The problem of taking multiculturalism personally comes back to this puzzling question. I want to dwell for a moment on the possibility that identity and the personal are not the same thing. If they were, how could an individual experience the crisis of wondering whether to take being black or white, gay or straight, Christian or Muslim personally? To pose cultural identity in the form of a question, as something that someone can choose to take or reject, already introduces an element of agency, freedom, or voluntarism that strict essentialists or determinists reject. Personally, I think the resilience of the idiomatic question testifies to a practical belief that agency is both real and desirable, even if this means being vulnerable to ideological manipulation and one's own naïveté. While multiculturalism should continue to advocate an antiracist, postcolonial, and resistant politics of the marginalized, multiculturalism should also lead to a horizon of ethical questions that cannot be entirely subordinated to identity politics or the analysis of ideology and political economy.

Within the practices of education, multiculturalism assumes some degree of personal agency in its teachers and students. Teachers are expected to take multiculturalism seriously, if not personally, and to change their syllabi, their classroom behavior, and their administrative goals. Students are expected to consider the possibility that the cultural values and practices of their group may be either the ideological mask of a will to power or the encoded expression of a people's resistance, outrage, and pride. Whether in the case of teachers or students, multiculturalism opens a gap between personal selfhood and cultural identity, and this is to the good.

II.

Me, I got a late start taking multiculturalism personally. It was the early 1980s. I was teaching survey courses in American literature and had begun to introduce culturally diverse works into the canon of my syllabus, partly in response to the racial makeup of my classes at the University of Alabama (see Jay). Being from a suburb in Los Angeles and having spent the previous eight years in relatively elite institutions of higher education, I wasn't accustomed to much in the way of racial diversity. The course tried to represent the heterogeneous groups who have given their radically different answers to Crèvecoeur's famous question, "What is an American?" As the list of categories multiplied—Native American, African American, Asian American, Polish American, Irish American, Jewish American—I felt left out. Who were *my* people? More uncomfortably, what was I doing trying to represent the Other anyway? Couldn't they speak for themselves? What was my ethical relation to this professional and pedagogical practice? Given the manifest failure of the institution to provide the marginalized with access to speech or representation, what was my responsibility? According to some of my African American students, my responsibility certainly did not include designating them as the spokespersons for the race. The job of analyzing and denouncing racism in a classroom dominated by whites was, for them, the white man's job, since he'd invented race in the first place.

Identity politics and its discontents started following me home at night. Child of a secular Jewish father and a lapsed Mormon mother, I found myself puzzling over my own cultural identity. Did I have a race or ethnicity? A gender or a sexual orientation? A class or a nationality? Was my cultural identity singular or plural? And was it something I got by inheritance and imposition, or something I could choose and alter at my will? Perhaps most important, why hadn't I worried about all of this before? Who was I that I hadn't had a cultural identity crisis? Why had I so suddenly become a white man? Was it only because I now lived in Alabama? Or had I been an invisible man to myself for all the years before?

Of course I had had lots of identity crises before, but not ones that turned so specifically on how cultural categories determined experiences of identity. Being a child of the radical 1960s, I had long since taken it for granted that my primary social identity was that of an oppositional intellectual. Hadn't I chosen a marginal and unprofitable major in college? Hadn't I consciously rejected materialism and sought higher values in art and philosophy? Hadn't I, to my father's bewilderment, decided to teach literature as a career and ended up in Tuscaloosa, Alabama? Even if I had become a professional, I could take some pride in being relatively ill-paid, unrespected, uninfluential, and routinely alienated. I thought of the cultural politics of my identity in conventional terms, positioning myself as the enemy of variously named forces of right-wing evil. Surely the night-riders of the Klan and I had nothing in common and could never be identified with each other. Of course I clung stubbornly to the utopian dream of my own person, not recognizing how I too wore the white sheet wherever I walked.

After writing an essay on American literature and multiculturalism, I decided to design a course called "Fictions of Multiculturalism," which I now offer regularly at UW-Milwaukee. The readings include modern prose fiction texts by a culturally diverse group of writers as well as critical and theoretical essays in multiculturalism. Institutionally, the course fulfills my university's new "cultural diversity" requirement, so the enrollment includes people from a variety of majors. Fortunately, it has also drawn a culturally diverse student population, at least relatively speaking, as mine is a predominantly white working-class school.

In its design, syllabus, and classroom approach, the course intends to ask students both to take responsibility for their own cultural identities and to practice forming relationships with people who do not share their subject position, values, skin color, religion, etc. In the multicultural classroom, the authority of one person's experience quickly runs up against that of someone else, so that the limits of such authority may be usefully marked and analyzed. Clashes of cultural identity do not always yield to a happy pluralism, however, or cheerful tolerance. On the contrary, the differences between cultural groups are often fundamental, sometimes deadly, and are better brought into the open than repressed (at least in the classroom). Multicultural pedagogy inevitably confronts the problem of how a social structure can successfully accommodate persons who find the beliefs or truths of others to be unacceptable and intolerable.

To get my students to take multiculturalism personally, I first assign them to write an analysis of their own cultural identity, which, it turns out, is very different from writing a personal essay expressing one's self. We use this paper and the first few readings to explore what a cultural identity might be, where you might get one, and how you might feel about the ones you have or the ones that others have. The notion of "cultural identity" strikes many of the students as strange. In the context of American individualism, the concept of cultural identity seems anomalous: identity is supposed to be personal, idiosyncratic, something that you don't share with anyone else. Seeing one's *self* as a cultural identity tends to erode the feeling of uniqueness so prized in American culture.

This gets us to the paradox which the assignment aims to bring to the surface. Dominant American culture defines the person as essentially private and thus by definition as lacking a cultural identity. A cultural identity would be a restraint on individual freedom, a straitjacket of convention, a prescription of inauthenticity. A cultural identity would limit what the person wore, ate, said, kissed, worshiped, wrote, bought, or sold. Modern entrepreneurial individualism, or consumer identity, considers cultural practices as strictly commodities, as entirely relative to the fundamental project of the self's acquisitive freedom.

It is no surprise, then, that many of my puzzled students end up writing essays about how they do not have a cultural identity. Some proudly announce that they are "just Americans," while others more wistfully describe themselves as "merely normal." This perception of the self as "American" and "normal" usually involves an implicit or explicit comparison to people whom the student identifies as having a cultural identity. These people with cultural identities are usually African, Native, or Asian Americans. They are described as having special cultural characteristics, unique food and music, strange languages, different beliefs. And, not incidentally, their skin is usually darker.

Of course the lost students I am describing are the descendants of European immigrants, especially those in the third and fourth generations. They are most likely to see themselves as the norm and to see other groups as special, particular, or deviant. Having lost many of the ethnic characteristics that differentiated the quite diverse European populations who settled and assimilated in the United States, these students have also assimilated the notion that freeing one's self of cultural peculiarities is essential to becoming a normal, prosperous American. They do not see their own clothes, food, beliefs, values, or music as constituting a distinctive culture, just as they do not see themselves as having a cultural rather than individual identity. As you might expect, the exceptions are children of first- or second-generation immigrants whose families and neighborhoods have consciously preserved linguistic, religious, culinary, and social practices identified with the "old country."

Students from non-European backgrounds have much less trouble with the assignment, since they are accustomed to being seen, and seeing themselves, as having a cultural identity that is "different." While these students never fit into neat boxes, and while their personal experiences and senses of identity vary enormously, almost all share a daily consciousness of having to negotiate between their sense of being a person and their sense of belonging to a group. Their person, they feel, is often not identifiable with the symbolic figures that populate the hegemonic culture. They rarely see people like themselves on TV, except perhaps during the local news. On the other hand, persons who see themselves as very similar to the dominant cultural imaginary do not experience themselves as having a cultural identity, since in their eyes they are not different. The universalization of their cultural presuppositions whitewashes them, allowing them to mistake the cultural for the personal, and making them invisible to themselves.

I should note how gender skews this pedagogical exercise. As you might guess, many women define their cultural identity in terms of their gender. They discuss how important their condition or experience of gender has been in shaping their ideas, feelings, and values. This assertion tends to come more strongly from self-identified feminists, but it also comes from many women of various political stripes. In two semesters that included over seventy students, I never had a male student write about the importance of gender to his cultural identity. Just as the children of European immigrants tend not to see their skin as having color or their values as being culturally specific, men tend to dissociate their gender from their individuality. I found this pattern extraordinary, knowing as I do how much time men spend talking about and asserting their masculinity. Yet, probably in part because of the nature of the course and the presumed values of the instructor, none of the men wrote about how growing up male had affected their identity.

The results in the area of sexual orientation were similar. Given the prejudice against homosexuality in our society, it is understandable that only one person explicitly identified herself as lesbian through the assignment. (One other discussed her recent exploration of bisexuality.) And why should a gay or lesbian student come out to classmates? Is it any of their business? Is sexual orientation a private, personal identity rather than a social or cultural identity? Here the ethical puzzles for the instructor are daunting. On the one hand I want

to make my classroom a place that supports the expression of marginalized subjectivities, and I want that expression to alter the prejudices of other students.
On the other hand, what right have I to make the sexual orientation of my students a matter of pedagogical manipulation? Is this the business of the professor? Can the professor, given his business, avoid professing biases and values in
regards to sexuality or race or other social divisions merely by remaining silent
upon them? And who is to say that sexual orientation is an "identity" waiting
to "come out" anyway? Clearly the puzzles here are different than in the cases
of race and gender, where the body usually gives the subject's identity away
without their being able to choose whether to "come out." Yet even then, my
ethical dilemma seems different in dealing with subjects depending on whether
their position is privileged or subordinated. Rightly or wrongly, I have not felt
much restraint about putting the race of white people or the sexuality of men
before the class as a subject for critique, and I regularly push students in these
categories to a more public reckoning with the relationship between their personal and their group identities. The results of the initial assignment, in any
case, give us a chance to analyze which kinds of identity seem to have ready
access to public representation, and what particular problems people face when
speaking about different identity positions.

One consequence of the assignment was to drive a wedge between race and
culture. The students who felt they did not have a common culture belonged to
the category that race discourse dubs "white." I have argued that this feeling
was in part ideologically motivated, a blind spot of privilege and hegemony. But
I also want to argue that in a way these students are right. Strictly speaking,
there is no such thing as white culture. Culture makes sense when talking about
ethnic groups and geographic populations, but it makes less sense when oriented solely by skin pigmentation. Historically, the term "white" was invented
in the seventeenth and eighteenth centuries to provide Europeans, especially
Europeans settling in the American colonies, with a word for their difference
from Africans and Native Americans. As the scholarship of Afrocentrism demonstrates, the term "white" stands for a politically constructed group, grounded
in a mythical Greco-Roman classicism.

"White" designates the supposed common culture binding diverse European immigrants. Since their ethnic and national groups do not constitute a
common culture, historiography had to invent one for them to help justify the
project of colonialism and the institution of slavery. White is a political category,
not a cultural one. What holds white people together is not a common language,
religion, cuisine, literature, or philosophy, but rather a political arrangement
that distributes power and resources by skin color. No wonder my students were
confused. To be a white person is to have certain advantages, socially and politically and economically, but being white does not provide you with a culture.

There is, I think, an American culture, but it is not defined by ethnic groups or racial distinctions. Rather it is grounded in economic individualism, wedded to the practice of consumption, and hostile to the traditional constraints of cultural systems whenever these inhibit the workings of the marketplace. In this capitalist metaculture, cultural beliefs and practices are not traditions that constrain and guide behavior but commodities that may be deployed in order to create effects of pleasure, knowledge, profit, and power. Hence the much observed phenomenon of the postmodern subject, a person whose cultural identity is essentially and repeatedly decentered.

III.

Though multiculturalism begins in identity politics—in the conflation of personal and cultural identity—it should not end there. Taking multiculturalism personally is a way to move in, through, and beyond identity politics, while respecting the conditions that make those politics a recurrent necessity. We may want to challenge the centrality of "identity" itself in arguments about culture, for example, by considering the difference between "having" an identity and living by an ethos.

While a first step may be to recognize and respect someone else's difference from me, that realization still tends to leave me in the privileged position: I have the luxury to decide to be tolerant and liberal. The structure of superiority is left intact. The sense of my own settled and unquestioned identity is also left intact, while all the "otherness" is projected onto someone else. The next step, and it is an ethical as well as political step, is to see my own subjectivity *from the other's point of view.* The exploration of otherness and cultural identity should achieve a sense of *my own* strangeness, my own otherness, and of the history of how my assumed mode of being came into being historically. I could have been someone other than I think I am. And maybe I am.

I am thus proposing a pedagogy of disorientation as a complement to calls to restructure the educational institution from the other's point of view. McCarthy cites Bob Connell's contention that we ought to "bring the uninstitutionalized experiences of marginalized minorities and working-class women and men 'to the center' of the organization and arrangement of the school curriculum." This suggests that "a political and ethical principle of positive social justice should inform the selection of knowledge in the school curriculum" (132). I take McCarthy's "ethical" as an injunction to subscribe to a principle larger than our own self-interest. I hold my cultural identity and its practices to the standard of justice, and ask how my mode of being affects the lives of others.

Taking multiculturalism personally will not, in the end, provide you with an identity, or resolve the hostilities between races, or diffuse tribal warfare, or remedy those inequalities inherent to multinational capitalism. But the often surprising kinds of personal and cultural identifications facilitated by the multicultural-literature classroom produce antiessentialist affiliations, as students make connections across the insulating boundaries we have taught them to respect. This does not mean harmonious understanding or celebrations of ethnic pluralism, however; more likely it involves bringing cultural and personal conflicts into the open. The classroom will need an ethical discourse for handling these conflicts, just as it will need a political analysis for understanding their material conditions and consequences.

Thus politics can also be understood in terms of how the person negotiates the space between identity and community. A relentless critique of every student and teacher's bad faith is contemptuous of the ideal of community. Unlike critique, politics as a social enterprise requires that persons form communities based on a mutual recognition of common interests, which must be understood in part by testing discourses against persons and ideas against experiences.

So I resist the movement toward "depersonalization" among some advocates of oppositional pedagogy. According to Donald Morton, for example, "persons" must be "distinguished from their 'discourses' " so that those discourses can be effectively critiqued (82). This distinction removes the critique of discourses from the realm of the ethical, where relationships between persons require attitudes such as tolerance, respect, responsibility, sympathy, justice, and humility. Most students will not readily perceive a distinction between the professor's contempt for their discourse and contempt for their persons. I do not think we can remedy the past injustice, which dismissed people's discourse because of their bodies, by returning to an ideal wherein discourses are evaluated without reference to the bodies that produce them. If multiculturalism has a central lesson, it is to teach us to respect this embodied character of cultural production.

Treating persons as only discourses would apply poststructuralist theory to pedagogy in a manner that is both theoretically reductive and strategically harmful. Depersonalizing critique and pedagogy would underestimate the emotional and idiosyncratic ties that individuals have to knowledge and power (see Worsham). The connection of persons to discourses is an ethical one and cannot be reduced to ideology. The person takes responsibility for negotiating the relationship between discourses (or institutions) and the experience of the individual. An ethic is precisely a set of principles that is not coincident with the person, but rather something he or she embodies only individually and imperfectly.

I believe that ethical imperatives inform political change, since concepts of justice and of rights include a moral dimension. Self-interest and the acquisition (or resistance) to power cannot found a community or a political philosophy; the former cannot do justice to social relationships involving conflicting self-interests, and power without a concept of the good is only instrumental and thus nihilistic. Social inequalities will not be alleviated without structural changes in the government and the economy, to be sure, but these cannot be motivated or justified without recourse to moral arguments about the evils of unbridled self-interest and the irresponsibility of the will to power. Demonstrating these points will involve careful historical argument about the particulars of a social legacy, as well as scrupulous theoretical debate about what constitutes the good, universally and in a given instance.

A discourse on ethics can strengthen the process of creating mechanisms that do justice to the competing claims of different cultural groups. It can also make for affiliations between individuals who in their everyday lives often differ with each other, and themselves. The importance of this ethical moment needs to be reasserted and restored in the current climate, where "the political" (often vaguely if at all theorized) reigns. In the agency and decisions of the ethical subject, the competing demands between the universal and the particular seek their only practical justice. The ethnic and the ethical will have to recognize each other in this territory or institution of competing demands. To get beyond the accusations and scapegoating and name-calling, we need to acknowledge the mutual dependence of our ethical and political persons. Unless we can believe in our responsibility to each other, we may be in store for an endless history of self-righteous violence.

Works Consulted

Aufderheide, Patricia, ed. *Beyond P.C.: Toward a Politics of Understanding.* St. Paul: Graywolf, 1992.

Banks, James A., and James Lynch, eds. *Multicultural Education in Western Societies.* New York: Holt, 1986.

Berman, Paul, ed. *Debating P.C.* New York: Laurel, 1992.

Brown, Wesley, and Amy Ling, eds. *Imagining America: Stories from the Promised Land. A Multicultural Anthology of American Fiction.* New York: Persea, 1991.

Chicago Cultural Studies Group. "Critical Multiculturalism." *Critical Inquiry* 18 (1992): 530–55.

Epstein, Barbara. " 'Political Correctness' and Collective Powerlessness." *Socialist Review* 91.3–4 (1991): 13–35. Rpt. Aufderheide 148–54.

Erickson, Peter. "What Multiculturalism Means." *Transition* 55 (1992): 105–14.

Escoffier, Jeffrey. "The Limits of Multiculturalism." *Socialist Review* 91.3–4 (1991): 61–73.

Gates, Henry Louis, Jr. "The Master's Pieces: On Canon Formation and the African-American Tradition." Smith and Gless 89–112.

Giroux, Henry. "Post-Colonial Ruptures and Democratic Possibilities: Multiculturalism as Anti-Racist Pedagogy." *Cultural Critique* 21 (1992): 5–40.

Graff, Gerald. *Beyond the Culture Wars: How Teaching the Conflicts Can Revitalize American Education.* New York: Norton, 1992.

Guttman, Amy. *Democratic Education.* Princeton: Princeton UP, 1987.

Harpham, Geoffrey. *Getting It Right: Language, Literature, and Ethics.* Chicago: U of Chicago P, 1992.

James, Alan, and Robert Jeffcoate, eds. *The School in the Multicultural Society.* New York: Harper, 1981.

Jay, Gregory. "The End of 'American' Literature: Toward a Multicultural Practice." *College English* 53.3 (1991): 264–81. (See also the critiques of this essay, and my response, in *College English* 54.2 [1992]: 220–24.)

Lauter, Paul. *Canons and Contexts*. New York: Oxford UP, 1991.

McCarthy, Cameron. *Race and Curriculum: Social Inequality and the Theories and Politics of Difference in Contemporary Research on Schooling*. London: Falmer, 1990.

Mitchell, W. J. T. "Postcolonial Culture, Postimperial Criticism." *Transition* 56 (1992): 11–19.

Morton, Donald, and Mas'ud Zavarzadeh, eds. *Theory/Pedagogy/Politics: Texts for Change*. Urbana: U of Illinois P, 1991.

Ravitch, Diane. "Multiculturalism: E Pluribus Plures." *American Scholar* (1990): 337–54. Rpt. Berman 271–99.

Rich, Adrienne. *Blood, Bread, and Poetry: Selected Prose, 1979–1985*. New York: Norton, 1986.

———. *Your Native Land, Your Life*. New York: Norton, 1986.

Rorty, Richard. "The Priority of Democracy to Philosophy." *Reading Rorty: Critical Responses to "Philosophy and the Mirror of Nature" and (Beyond)*. Ed. Alan R. Malachowski. New York: Blackwell, 1990. 279–302.

Said, Edward. "The Politics of Knowledge." *Raritan* 41.1 (1991): 17–31. Rpt. Berman 172–89.

Schweickart, Patrocinio. "Engendering Critical Discourse." *The Current in Criticism: Essays on the Present and Future of Criticism*. Ed. Clayton Koelb and Victor Lokke. West Lafayette, IN: Purdue UP, 1988. 295–317.

Smith, Barbara Herrnstein, and Darryl Gless, eds. *The Politics of Liberal Education*. Durham: Duke UP, 1991.

Taylor, Charles. *Multiculturalism and "The Politics of Recognition."* With commentary by Amy Gutmann, ed., and Steven C. Rockefeller, Michael Walzer, and Susan Wolf. Princeton: Princeton UP, 1992.

Worsham, Lynn. "Emotion and Pedagogic Violence." *Discourse* 15.2 (1992–93): 119–48.

11 | Disinfecting Dialogues

Cheryl Johnson

WHEN I PROPOSED the title of my essay to Jane, I think she realized that without a subtitle (one of those "colon +" constructions) I would have too much liberty to do what I want to do. And she was right: I wanted enough space to manipulate those two words in any fashion I could. I soon realized that I had every intention of making this essay an example of what I have come to understand about the nature of the conversation between me and, not only my students, but also in many instances my colleagues. It is a conversation, a dialogue, marked by the desire for cleanliness—for no odors, no germs; it is a sanitized, deodorized, bleached (no pun intended) interaction which keeps the very "funkiness" of racism and sexism temporarily at bay and simultaneously denies my students access to an inverted sense of "funkiness"—an intimate, engaging cultural "immersion" into the smells, textures, and rhythms of African American culture through its literature. I planned to give such a presentation, to use the kind of language we academics are so enamored of, in order to trick and tease your sensibilities into believing that I will have given you my thoughts on how my personal "location" questions my pedagogy and vice versa—how pedagogy questions my personal. In other words, by engaging in my own version of academic signifying, an unholy union of academic and vernacular language, I hoped to escape or subvert the expressed interest/focus of this conference—to examine the personal. For me, examining the personal involves telling the personal, and I'm not ready to do that yet. If I were like Janie in Zora Neale Hurston's *Their Eyes Were Watching God*, I could maybe put "mah tongue . . . in mah friend's mouf" (6)—tell my story to someone else who would be responsible for its retelling. At this point in my life, in my career as an academic, in my status as a black womanist intellectual, I can identify more with Sethe in Toni Morrison's *Beloved*: "[This] is not a story to pass on" (275). At least, not yet.

In previous drafts of this essay, I had pulled out masks that even I didn't know I had. There was the "She's really smart" mask and the "She is quite witty" mask. I did not spend too much time with the "She is theoretical" mask but thought about the "Oh, I didn't know she was Afrocentric" mask. Any one of them placed carefully over my face at any time of my presentation was designed to manipulate your perception of me in such a way that you, the audience, would displace your uneasy feelings which said "She isn't talking about the personal and the pedagogical." Even later, over coffee, or at the conference's cocktail party, you would not approach me and say "I really liked your talk, but, really, you were out of place here, you didn't after all discuss the topic." You see, I would have disinfected my talk in such a way as both to disinfect and infect you; in other words, you will have been infected with the germ of cleanliness, of sanitation. Your language to me would be so shining bright, so unsmudged . . . nevertheless, we will have an old cloth available, just in case we missed an infected spot, or to quickly wipe away one which inadvertently appeared.

So, why the frank admissions? On one hand, my state of mind is akin to that of the nameless narrator in Ralph Ellison's *Invisible Man*, who says in the epilogue, "I whipped it all but the mind, the mind. And the mind that has conceived a plan of living must never lose sight of the chaos against which that pattern was conceived" (580). By accepting an invitation to present a paper at this conference, I, unwittingly, mentally positioned myself within the chaos of that intractable triangle or trinity of race, gender, and pedagogy, because the process of thinking about my place in academia has forced me to step outside of my own subjectivity and subjectively subject myself to scrutiny. And, although I can only partly investigate that subjectivity, I will, at least, put the masks aside and share some of my thoughts on this subject. Another reason is the coordinator of this conference; she would, over coffee or Maker's Mark, say, "Now, Cheryl—" and I would feel the mask shift. So, I will give her partly what she wants.

What I will focus on is the "why" part of disinfecting dialogues instead of how. Why would a black womanist intellectual professor locate a safe and sterile site for the discussion of African American literature, criticism, and culture? Why does she deliberately disobey her ancestors' call for her to assume the role of intellectual griot—the oral storyteller of history and culture—because such "telling" preserves historical memory and cultural identity. And, finally, why do her students join her in this bleached place armed with their bottles of ammonia and paper towels so that they can help keep this dialogue safe? Please be forewarned, however, that even as I put my masks away, that something of the trickster still informs my consciousness here; I am merely slouching toward the personal.

I. The Body as Text

In Rey Chow's discussion of the "politics" of Asian literature in universities, she refers to the "terms of reference" students of Asian literature bring to their reading of this literature (31). These terms of reference, even if they are informed by stereotypes, ruptures, and displacements of the Asian subject and literature, nevertheless facilitate the students' ideological construction and experience of the literature. In other words, students come to the classroom equipped with their own cultural codes, which they impose on the text. I would like to take Chow's observation further—to suggest that students bring their "terms of reference" about the professor to the classroom also, and their "reading" of the professor's body provides another textual consideration concomitant to the literary text.

To illustrate this phenomenon, I will provide an example in which I compare my experiences in the classroom with what I think might be the experience of an imaginary other—a white male professor. I am fully aware that I am engaging in the old binary opposition game, but aside from the fact that such use reveals my enslavement to Western modes of thinking, it is also an easy way for me to make my point. Race and gender clearly separate me from my imaginary other, and those differences are then read by the students we encounter. I am also interested in the ways in which the "other" professor and I intersect—ways which are not so easily discernable. For instance, we both may share a commitment to academic and intellectual integrity, and I will have noticed that this professor's scholarship and teaching, marked by sincerity and authenticity, are both enviable and righteous. Further, we share similar concerns about American literature, the so-called canon, and we talk and write (well, he does) about these issues with both passion and compassion. In other words, this guy is no Allan Bloom. Because of the ways in which we interact, I am concerned about the opposition embedded in words like "white," "male," and "other"; thus, I would like to "name" this fictitious professor and vocally mark the ways in which we interact by giving him the first letter of my last name, producing a Professor J. Now, this fictitious Professor J. teaches African American literature courses, even ones which could be especially painful, like the literature of the nineteenth century which, of course, includes slave narratives and other writings about that "peculiar institution." This course may be painful to a man like Professor J. He and his students read about the horrors of slavery, the social Darwinism which offered scientific evidence/convenient excuses for slavery's existence, the religious hypocrisy which essentially stated "and God created you people to serve us, but He will greet you at the back door to heaven," and the Southern economic system which was constructed on the backs of black men and women (and they still did not get their forty acres and not one mule). Even as he provides all of this and more to his students, he is painfully aware that his body, white and male, is a historical referent of the slaveowner. And even if he were to say to his students on the first day, upon entering the classroom, "Not my ancestors; I've checked," the awareness of his privileged status, both historically and nowadays, is clear to both himself and his students. This Professor J. also knows that he need not reserve two minutes at the beginning of class to strike his right breast with his left hand, repeat *mea culpa* three times, and say, "Forgive me, class, I am a walking personification of the sins of my fathers." The reality is that his personal history, whatever it may be (unless we discover a Paul de Man-like past lurking in his background) will not problematize his presence in the classroom or his teaching of African American literature. OK, maybe everyone will not love him, but, generally, his presence cannot be disputed because academic history grants him an inalienable right to be there. The fact that his pedagogy intellectually rights or lefts the sins of his fathers certainly accredits his role. In "Feminism, Voice, and the Pedagogical Unconscious," Laurie Finke chastises "some feminists [who] write about pedagogy as if they believe that the classroom is a universal and ahistorical space, rather than a local and particular space embedded within a specific institutional culture that serves a range of disciplinary and institutional objectives" (8). Traditionally, the rightful occupant of the local and particular space has been white and male—not a brown-drenched signifier of difference.

On the other hand, the combination of this brownness with material representations of femaleness disrupts traditional notions about who occupies the position of authority and power in the classroom. Students must find other "terms of reference" to displace their culturally learned assumptions about black women. Those assumptions are ones which positioned black women in demeaning or subservient roles; as professor, she assumes an inverted position, one of power and authority. One manifestation of students' dis-ease with the black female professor is their hesitancy, sometimes downright fear, of engaging in dialogue with her about African American literature and culture. Some rhetoricians have discussed the need to orient students to academic discourse; the same can be said about cultural discourse. Students are quick to realize, however, that the patience that may be granted them as they learn one discourse may not be extended to them as they struggle to gain access to the other. In other words, they struggle with the possibility of insulting, with language, the person who stands in front of them with the right answers and a grade book. The result is either silence or language which is so neutral, so bland, that it disinfects the very subjects under discussion. The racial/gendered professor, cognizant of the students' fears and struggle, may respond with similar language as she fears the prospect of alienating them from any interaction with the literature. So, a kind of mutual cleansing takes place; no funkiness here.

II. The Crisis of the Colored/Negro/Black/African American Intellectual

By using the various names which either have been given to African Americans or the names in which they have renamed themselves, I am not suggesting a sequence or chronology here. Instead, I want to argue that although each new name was an attempt to bestow an identity—a diversion from a previously assumed identity—in actuality each name represents a desire for unity amid disunity. The latest name, appropriate though it may be, semantically registers this disunity: African American—a hybrid of two cultures, but the union is tenuous at best—always shifting, unstable. The space between the two words both alienates one identity from the other and also allows for some breathing room with a view of the other side as the two sides define and redefine each other. For the colored/negro/black/African American intellectual, the renaming has not concomitantly refigured her role in academia or her community. She remains marginalized from both.

One of the earliest investigations into the place of the African American intellectual is Harold Cruse's *The Crisis of the Negro Intellectual*, published in 1967. Beginning with the Harlem Renaissance and ending with the Black Arts Movement, this book analyzes the peculiar crisis of black intellectuals—the perils of being in both the white and black worlds and the absolute necessity for doing so. The following quotation from *The Crisis* opens Cornel West's 1991 exploration of this issue in his essay "The Dilemma of the Black Intellectual":

> The peculiarities of the American social structure and the position of the intellectual class within it, make the functional role of the Negro intellectual a special one. The Negro intellectual must deal intimately with the white power structure and cultural apparatus, and the inner realities of the black world at one and the same time. But in order to function successfully in this role, he has to be acutely aware of the nature of the American social dynamic and how it monitors the ingredients of class stratification in American society.... Therefore, the functional role of the Negro intellectual demands that he cannot be absolutely separated from the black or white world. (451–52)

For both Cruse and West, the crisis or dilemma for the black intellectual is her attempt to fit comfortably and simultaneously in both worlds, neither of which embraces her. West, in particular, considers the push-pull movement of the black intellectual between two poles—the racist white society and the anti-intellectualism of the black community. At any given moment, the black intellectual might seek an uneasy refuge in either world, although cognizant of being an anomaly in both.

At the end of his essay, West states that "the predicament of the black intellectual need not be grim and dismal" (146). Even after quoting James Baldwin's representation of the black intellectual as "a kind of bastard of the West," West contends that "[t]he future of the black intellectual lies neither in a deferential disposition toward the Western power nor a nostalgic search for an African one" (146). There is, West argues, a middle ground which allows for dialogue with and within both cultures.

Neither West nor Cruse addresses the question of language, however, and it is language, the means by which we not only communicate but also make sense of the world, which will force the black intellectual to privilege one community over another. How, for example, can the black intellectual bring academic and vernacular language together so that both communities will embrace that union? Would the vernacular language defer to the more prestigious language of academia and stand out only in its exotic fanciness, like placing an African fetish statue amid some New England landscape paintings? A funny image, I grant you, but can it function as a metaphor for the kind of criticism current in black scholarship? My point is this: that even as black critics look to the vernacular culture for tropes and language to represent critical paradigms in African American literature, they represent this culture in the kind of sterile academic prose which, in my mind, strips the vernacular of its power and pleasure. The traditional image of academia is the ivory tower; I would love to refigure it into the Tower of Babel—all kinds of voices with their own inflections and cadences which we all would respect even as we struggle to learn the different languages. But the Tower of Babel represents confusion, and in academia, voices other than its own are mere babble. Thus, if "native" language provides one of the means by which an outsider can gain access to another culture, college students are denied such access because there is no place for vernacular language in the classroom. Smell the ammonia?

III. My Personal Resistance to Cultural "Funkiness" in the Pedagogical Act

In my discussion of the body as text, the African American intellectual, and academic discourse, I have focused on perceptions of "appropriateness"—external expectations of the teacher/professor and their impact on the very act of teaching itself. These expectations, however, signal the outright tyranny of certain ideological or traditional signifiers of appropriateness within the academy because they allow only a rarefied space for privileging expressions of the vernacular culture. Within this space, the vernacular receives only an appreciative nod or rather cursory gesture: it does not control or inform every aspect or activity within the classroom. But given the privacy of the classroom and the power I have to establish and maintain the focus of the course, why do I allow these signifiers of appropriate pedagogical practices and professorial attire to inform my own teaching and scholarship? If I am truly a child of the sixties who has known for a long time that the revolution will not be televised but who believes that teaching can be a revolutionary act, why continue to engage in such "unrevolutionary" behavior?

One reason is my understanding of perceptions of vernacular culture which many people, both inside and outside of the culture, retain. Often, references to African American cultural features create an occasion for laughter or ridicule. One example is the term "voodoo economics," an expression which has assumed an undisputed place in our lexical playground. It's used on programs as diverse as *MacNeil-Lehrer*, *Wall Street Week*, and *Good Morning, America* and found in newspapers from the *New York Times* to the *Milwaukee Journal*. When that expression was first used, however, I remember a Haitian scholar's horror and dismay that the word for a religion which he and many other Haitians practice would be used so profanely, casually in reference to a capitalistic economic theory. Clearly, the person who coined the term "voodoo economics" did not consider constructions such as "United Methodist economics" or "Presbyterian economics," and certainly not "Jewish economics," because such an expression would unleash the smell, the very stench, of anti-Semitism, allowing it to rise and converge with other anti-Semitic acts of violence. But voodoo—one may disrespect the religious beliefs and practices of Haitians.

Such ridicule, such disrespect, constitute acts of violence on the vernacular culture. Disinfecting dialogues will not allow such violence to occur since they do not offer space for its inclusion. So, this racial/gendered subject simply avoids the potential for violence to her history, background, and culture. She is keenly aware, however, of that potential and that it is, in many instances, simply suspended in the classroom. Once outside of that rarefied space, the violence may reveal itself in all of its craziness, all of its horror. Thus, the revolutionary inclinations of the black woman professor may become a mere gesture, as they are tempered by her desire to have some respite, albeit temporarily, from the racism which has been her unwelcome companion from the day she came to understand what a difference a color makes.

Another reason for resisting "the personal" in the classroom is an admittedly personal one. I simply enjoy the sense of exclusivity, even as this reveals my romantic desire for a mysterious, impenetrable, black essence. This desire is not as crude as the one expressed in the slogan "It's a black thang—you wouldn't understand." It is, however, an appreciation—no, a need—for (the sense of?) familiarity and intimacy which is possible among African Americans. Certainly, the features of this intimacy are learned, like the vocal expressions in call and response. With continued use, however, culturally inscribed words and gestures constitute one's personal/cultural repertoire, which facilitates spontaneous, seemingly natural, responses to cultural signs and symbols. Things not said are understood; you know what to do. This sense of intimacy is necessary bread when I feel displaced and dispossessed—the "Nobody knows the troubles I've seen" days or the "It bees that way sometime" days. It's a look exchanged between you and another black person which says, "Yeah, uh-huh." It's having the drums tell you what to do and, not bothering to contemplate the implications of such an act, you do it.

In *Loose Canons*, Henry Louis Gates states that "[a]ny human being sufficiently curious and motivated can fully possess another culture, no matter how 'alien' it may appear to be" (xv). Gates also refers to Edward Said's comments that "[i]t is the role of the academy to transform what might be conflict, or context, or assertion into reconciliation, mutuality, recognition, creative interaction" (quoted in Gates xv). Together, Gates and Said's statements point to the absurdity of my desire for an essential (not even strategic) blackness and suggest that my construction of a disinfecting dialogic in the classroom actively deters racial reconciliation and understanding. My response is that every pedagogical act is constructed not only by the professor's knowledge but also by an ideology informed by her still evolving personal history. Although her knowledge is available for display, her personal history may make her overly protective of those socially constructed cultural memories and features. And, until our fight against racism and sexism is more successful, my attempts to "keep it clean" may persist.

I would like to conclude my talk with the following example. Last semester, during our class discussion of Rita Dove's short story "The Vibraphone," which described a character with an "Afro exploding," a German exchange student asked me to define "Afro." Amid the laughter of the black students in the class, a reaction which said, "OK, Ms. Professor, let's see you do this," I remember responding something like the following:

> The appearance of the Afro, an arrangement of the hair of blacks into a style signifying African heritage, coincided with blacks' rejection of Western culture's hegemonic declarations about the nature of blackness as well as a rejection of whiteness as the standard of physical beauty. Sometimes called a "natural," the Afro involved the following: washing one's hair and leaving it in its natural state; when dry, or barely dry, using a special preparation to untangle it; and finally using a special comb, called a "pick" which, unlike a comb, more closely resembles a quadrangle and has five or so long, extended teeth. The structure of the pick allows for the simultaneous untangling and lifting of the hair in order to frame it, halo-like, around the face.

That's what she got.

What she did not get: James Brown's "I'm Black and I'm Proud"; Afro-Sheen; Angela Davis; Stokely Carmichael; H. Rap Brown; dashikis; a raised, clenched fist; "To Be Young, Gifted, and Black" (especially the Nina Simone version); Donny Hathaway's "Take It from Me, Someday We'll All Be Free"; instructions on how to—as James Brown said—"Make It Funky."

Could she have understood all that I did not give her? I don't know, since I did not give her an opportunity to do so.

Works Cited

Chow, Rey. "The Politics and Pedagogy of Asian Literature in American Universities." *d i f f e r e n c e s* 2.5 (1990): 29–51.

Cruse, Harold. *The Crisis of the Negro Intellectual.* New York: Morrow, 1967.

Dove, Rita. "The Vibraphone." *Fifth Sunday.* Charlottesville: UP of Virginia, 1985. 40–54.

Ellison, Ralph. *Invisible Man.* New York: Vintage, 1990.

Finke, Laurie. "Knowledge as Bait: Feminism, Voice, and the Pedagogical Unconscious." *College English* 55.1 (1993): 7–27.
Gates, Henry Louis, Jr. *Loose Canons: Notes on the Culture Wars*. New York: Oxford UP, 1992.
Hurston, Zora Neale. *Their Eyes Were Watching God*. New York: Harper, 1990.
Morrison, Toni. *Beloved*. New York: Knopf, 1987.
West, Cornel. "The Dilemma of the Black Intellectual." *Breaking Bread: Insurgent Black Intellectual Life*. Ed. bell hooks and Cornell West. Boston: South End, 1991. 131–46.

12 | Caliban in the Classroom

Indira Karamcheti

Now, DON'T GET me wrong: I've got nothing against Caliban—at least not more than most people. And I've got absolutely nothing against classrooms—again, not more than most people. But I'm not crazy about the combination of Caliban *and* the classroom, especially when I'm cast in the role of Caliban. I sometimes think that a lot of us academics who are blessed (or should I use the French sound-alike "blessés"?) with the "surplus visibility" (Patai A52) of race or ethnicity are cast as Calibans in the classroom, lurching between student and blackboard, our hour come round at last, rough beasts slouching (maybe even shuffling) along in the ivied Bethlehems of higher education.

We are sometimes seen, it seems to me, as traveling icons of culture, both traditional (as long as we're over there) and nontraditional (when we're right here), unbearably ancient in our folk wisdom and childlike in our infantile need for the sophistication of the West. We are flesh and blood information retrieval systems, native informants who demonstrate and act out difference, often with an imperfectly concealed political agenda. We are the local and the regional as opposed to the universality of the West, nature to its culture, instinct to its intellect, body to its brain. We are, in fact, encased in the personal and visible facts of our visible selves, walking exemplars of ethnicity and of race.

What we are not, however, is objective, impartial purveyors of truth, teachers of fact and method. We always teach, at some level, the personal but usually unspoken story of ourselves in the world. We teach with ourselves as our own most effective visual aids. The contemporary practice of choosing to insert personal, biographical details about the author into critical or theoretical articles deliberately sets out to situate and historicize authority, maybe even reveal the illusory nature of impartiality, objectivity, and authority itself. But the minority teacher does not necessarily have the choice of deliberately engaging the machinery of the personal in order to problematize authority. Authority has already been problematized by the fact of visible difference. The insistence of the personal preexists the decision to engage in the practice of self-inclusion, the politics of the personal. Indeed, the minority teacher is already known, *in personal terms*: ethnicity, race, is, among other things, an already familiar genre of personality. It is a familiar if not always understood category both of analysis and of interpretation. The more elusive issue for the minority teacher is the establishment of authority, of objectivity, of impartiality—that is, of those attributes traditionally associated with the performance of teaching. What I hope to examine in this paper is the problem of the personal as it establishes or works against authority in the classroom for the teacher marked by race or ethnicity. What is the nature of authority in this particular case? What are its sources and limits? In what ways is it dependent on the personal? Can the genre of race be used to create a more supple form of authority in the classroom, perhaps by foregrounding ignorance, active or inactive, or perhaps through the strategies of performance?

The entanglement of the personal—the facts of race and ethnicity—with the professional—a teacher's authority to speak with credibility, and thereby to educate, to lead out—came home to me when I first began teaching, as a TA, at the start of my graduate school days. I taught freshman composition in the English department at the University of California, Santa Barbara, a predominantly white, upper-middle-class campus in southern California. I realized pretty quickly that my person in the classroom was a bit of a shocker for some students. On the first day of classes, I would deliberately wait until a few minutes into the class period to allow people time to locate a new classroom in a new school, then make my entrance, walk to the table at front and center of the room, and put down my books. It was interesting to have students approach me, and, speaking very loudly and slowly, inform me that that place was meant for the teacher. Correspondingly, during the next subsequent days, a few students, not necessarily the same ones, would come up after class to remark, "You talk English so good!"

Most students were neither so officious nor so ingenuous. But events of this nature occurred sufficiently often to convince me that, one, I was probably sitting in the wrong place, and two, that it was admirable of me to speak English well, or, possibly, at all. By the time I was ready to leave UCSB, I was curious enough about this matter of race, authority, and the classroom to offer the choice of writing about prior experiences with minority teachers as one of several essay topics to one class. And I was intrigued enough by what some students wrote that I saved several of these essays. (I don't mean to imply that this material is in any way a scientific study, an objective, impartial, or even authoritative investigation. It's just personal.) These students of course saw that one of the issues hidden in the essay topic was the question of prejudice. And, of course, that they chose to write on this topic for a teacher whom they perceived as a minority person influenced what they wrote. Given this context, it's revealing to look at what incidents they chose to narrate, and the rhetorical strategies they employed in narrating them.

Almost all the essays began with the claim that the author personally had no prejudice; these students claimed to judge whether a teacher was good or not on purely "objective" grounds. One student wrote:

It was all perfectly normal. I walked into my third period class on the first day of school when I was in seventh grade, and I found, sitting behind the desk, a large black man in his mid forties. "So he's my new math teacher, eh?" I thought as I found my seat. "I wonder if he's a good teacher." It did not even occur to me that he would not be as good a teacher as a white man or woman.

The denial of racial prejudice, displaced as a reiterated belief in "objective" standards of good teaching, was sometimes accompanied by another kind of displacement: an easy identification of the "ethnic" teacher with the "foreign" teacher, who might often be a graduate student TA. Several students, after insisting on their lack of racial prejudice, thereupon proceeded to comment upon how irritating they found it when the ethnic instructor had such a strong accent that they had difficulty understanding. I don't want to take up this particular debate here, but rather point out the slippage between the references to foreign speakers of English in an essay on racial and ethnic minorities, especially following hard upon protestations of lack of prejudice against black and Hispanic teachers.

Some chose thereafter to comment about me, despite the assignment that they discuss prior minority teachers:

> My first reaction upon you walking into class was, "How can that little lady expect to teach a college course?" When you came in and gave a hearty "Hi" and began talking, my fears were dissolved.

Another student wrote about an African American woman teacher he very much disliked:

> Although my hatred was composed of various elements (injustice, rebellion, frustration, anger, etc.), Mrs. X's ethnicity definitely served to strengthen and perpetuate my abhorrence. Because her racial heritage had an ancient legacy of ethnic slurs and stereotypes, I was supplied with a plethora of powerful, seemingly empirical justifications. In effect, Mrs. X's physical and emblematic ethnicity further reinforced and rationalized my negative perception of her.

Immediately thereafter, the same student chose to describe me to me in these terms:

> My only other noncaucasian teacher is my current English teacher. My first impression upon viewing her Indian ethnicity was a mixture of surprise and skepticism. I was surprised by the novelty of an Indian woman teaching English and was simultaneously skeptical of her proficiency. Despite my initially disdainful response, I was very pleasantly surprised by her competence. Her spoken English was flawless, eloquent, clear, forceful, and concise. I perceived her manner as authoritative but not domineering, poised without arrogance, lighthearted yet not giddy, and open minded but not indecisive [a description that makes me feel like a decent, moderately priced Bordeaux]. Her literary discussions displayed an "impressive" range and depth of knowledge, commanded by a "very sharp" intellect.

The swollen ego engendered by this flattery, however, was quickly punctured by the next paragraph:

> Clearly, in this instance the professor's ethnicity affected my perceptions in a positive manner. Because of racial typecasting and her professional unique-ness [which, of course, is no longer as true now as it was in 1987], I had un-usually low expectations. Consequently, the more she established her compe-tency and her affability, my esteem increased geometrically. The ability to speak correctly and articulately or to skillfully direct a literary discussion shouldn't be foreign to any English teacher, but because of my assumption of an ethnic handicap I was overly impressed by her abilities. When she exceeded my ethnic expectations, I then perceived her qualities more favorably than I would have for a caucasian teacher.

The last of the student essays with which I'll burden you reaches some in-teresting conclusions that I've increasingly come to agree with. This student makes the point that the competence of minority teachers is directly related to the correlation between their race or ethnicity and the subject they teach: an African American woman who taught physical education ("Not only was this teacher good, but she was doing something we all knew she could do. Are black people not suppose [*sic*] to be more athletic than white?"); a "Mexican" teacher who taught Spanish III ("He, like my PE teacher was doing something that all of us, as students, knew he was capable of, teaching his language"). On the other hand, an African American man who taught biology is judged in retro-spect as not competent on the grounds of disorganization and inconsistency. At the time, however, this student writes:

> We let ourselves accept this teacher as "good" even though he really was not. This is very unusual when I think of how we reacted when we had a "not so good" white teacher. This teacher would be criticized without mercy because, in my opinion, we expected more out of him. My Biology teacher was black and because of the stereotype of black people being dumb we just accepted his faults blindly.

The excerpts from these student essays obviously prove nothing. But for me, they prove suggestive, if nothing else, in connecting the issues of race—as a category of the personal—and the taking or granting of pedagogical authority. While race or ethnicity alone may undermine classroom authority, it doesn't end here. The more complex issue is contained in the last essay from which I quoted: the matching of race with subject, the disciplining and containing of ethnicity into its proper and personal field.

Admittedly, these excerpts were drawn from essays written some years ago, and in a large, state university, where I, like all the other freshman composition instructors, was identified in the schedule of classes in advance only as "Staff," so that my appearance in the classroom affronted certain expectations. I now teach in quite a different setting, a small, liberal arts college in New England with a long history of socially progressive thought and ideals. I no longer teach freshman composition, nor do I teach pseudonymously as "Staff." Instead, I teach postcolonial literature, which I refer to in more perverse moods as PC Lit. Because my university is so small, and because my subject and I exhibit a phenomenological fit, I do not experience the same kinds of issues with authority.

That does not mean, of course, that authority has ceased to be problematic. I have increasingly come to see that my authority, and that of other teachers who work within the differences of race or ethnicity, is granted within the confines of certain more or less clearly defined boundaries. And the boundaries, though flexible, are drawn within the shadow lines of authenticity, the authentic and perceivable racial/ethnic self. "Authenticity," as the grounds for authority, creates at least two different genres of personality, two already available dramatic roles and dramatic narratives which the ethnic teacher can perform. One role is that of Caliban as a kind of native informant, lurching about the island and showing Prospero its sweet and secret places, serving to provide data with which Prospero can then rule. Caliban's claim to authority is based on natural claims—descent by blood from Sycorax. He does not have access to Prospero's source of power, his books. As a postcolonial person teaching postcolonial literature, my authority, too, is somewhat dependent upon my bloodlines, my physical and visible filiation with my subject matter. My authority is somewhat dependent on my status as native informant, providing others with data which can then be theorized, so that I serve as the metonymic figure for my entire field of study. Since that field covers 85 percent of the world's land mass this sometimes seems a largish burden. In any case, it's a representational responsibility that's difficult to fulfill. Genetic authenticity is ultimately always on a sliding scale of greater and lesser degrees of raciality: a slippery scale of more colored than thou. The hierarchies of races and ethnicities in the United States cannot support the construction of genetic authority for very long. The role of native informant is also ultimately thankless to fulfill. In my discipline, real power and authority lie, not in the role of native informant, not with Caliban, but in theory, with Prospero.

At my current university, there is another narrative which has a prepared role for the racialized body: the narrative of resistance. Resistance, as a methodology for the examination of literatures produced by "others," has the real and valuable function of focusing attention on what those others who have been disenfranchised or exploited by colonialism, institutional prejudice, and so on, have done. Placing "others" center stage has salutary political and disciplinary effects in studying literature. But the hunt for resistance on the part of the subaltern figure can and in some ways has already become a formulaic approach that provides too easy, too gratifying solutions to long-enduring social, historical, political, and economic inequities. According to the narrative, resistance is discovered in every margin and periphery: show me an other, a subaltern, a marginalized figure; I'll show you resistance. The narrative of resistance has a ready-made role for Caliban: the authentic, organic intellectual (read revolutionary) seeking to overthrow Prospero's rule, the postcolonial guerrilla fighter waging battle in the belly of the beast. The politicization of the role is clear, and brings Caliban closer, if not close enough, to the sources of power, Prospero's books.

But Caliban's resistance is no real threat. The postcolonial playing the role of the academic revolutionary is safely contained within that recognizable role of resistance: the narrative can become a simplistic "there is oppression; voilà, resistance. I'm OK; you're OK." This is to confuse the real and important—and political—work that is the proper work of academia with a misdirected call to replace it with popular, "grass roots" action. The unspoken subtext here is certainly an anti-intellectualism, more certainly a distrust of the native or subaltern intellectual, most certainly a sense that the "authentic" postcolonial is the grass-roots peasant, living oppression, not the indigenous or cosmopolite intellectual, theorizing postcoloniality.

Shakespeare's *Tempest* does not offer a figure for the hybrid postcolonial intellectual. But Aimé Césaire's *A Tempest*, his revisioning of Shakespeare's play from the viewpoint of the colonized, does. Césaire's Ariel is not Shakespeare's figure of radical difference, longing to escape the narrative. Césaire's Ariel is a mulatto, the house slave against Caliban's field slave, the native intellectual, having an identity crisis (as Césaire's Prospero derisively mocks him), deeply implicated in the very structures that enslave him, seeking to mediate and achieve synthesis between exploiter and exploited. Within the classroom, this Ariel role becomes that of the mediating figure of the indigenous elite. At its limit, Ariel's flightiness is transformed into transcontinental flight: the hybrid cosmopolite, jet-setting everywhere, at home everywhere, belonging nowhere, alighting in the classroom momentarily to magic up a literary repast, perhaps to lead the class on a whirlwind literary tour of the global, postmodern, literary bazaar.

The last of the potential roles lying in wait for the minority teacher in the classroom is, of course, Prospero himself. The minority teacher can cast himself or herself as the traditional authoritarian personality, the hard-driving, brilliant, no-nonsense professional for whom the personal has nothing to do with anything: John Houseman in racial drag. This role plays visual and epistemological games, and ultimately it, too, establishes its own authority in reference to a standard of authenticity. Denying the visual evidence of race or ethnicity, this role insists on the authenticity of guild membership—card-carrying status in the union of academic professionals, usually demonstrated, at least at the current time, by the use of complex poststructuralist concepts, language, and theory to analyze postcolonial, minority subjects. Caliban can speak with the master's voice, perhaps even be transformed into Prospero.

This cataloging of some of the various performative roles available to the minority teacher is of course both schematic and oversimplified. One major subject missing from this discussion of the genres for representation is that part of the personal which cannot be made shapely, which cannot be sanitized into safe or viable forms for pedagogical purposes. Caliban says that Prospero has taught him to speak and his profit on't is that he has learned how to curse. I'm not suggesting that minority teachers need to have their mouths washed out with soap. I am suggesting, rather, that this passage can point out to us that the position of marginality teaches its own discourse, precisely because it is not an inborn, natural category but something learned: that one is not born minor, but becomes minor, to use JanMohamed and Lloyd's phrase (9); or that one is not ethnic, but becomes ethnicized, to use Rey Chow's terms (25). Built into difference is real resistance to authority, to Prospero's voice, to offering fictions of authority. Minority discourse is characterized more by subversion, interrogation, critique than construction. We are all gadflies to some extent; the best of us are lethal gadflies. But teaching, at least traditional ideas of the role of the teacher in the literary studies classroom, insists that criticism be constructive, that analysis lead to the new, improved model. I suggest that minority discourse does not necessarily lead to the construction of a newer model, does not give something to offer up at the altars of positivistic belief. Yet this is a pressure that is exerted in the classroom by students, and certainly within the world of scholarship. The pressure to provide intellectual guides, schema, tropes for analysis that will lead to more and more accurate, subtly nuanced interpretations has already produced analytical blueprints such as blues ideology, signifyin', or the more simplistic uses of resistance.

Of course, analytical methodologies can be useful, offering us ways to think about and understand the unfamiliar. They can be constructive and generative, or, at least, give us the illusion that they are. A harder issue for me is the problem of anger, the issue of rage named in the idea of cursing. Anger, by contrast, is useless, destructive, degenerative, at least in reputation. Certainly, anger seems to me antithetical to the dialogue of teaching; yet anger is a real and present fact of the personal. And if minority teachers can be figured as Calibans, Ariels, impersonators of Prospero, at what level does anger move against Ferdinand, Miranda, the children of Prospero, and his heirs? This leads me to the last of the points I'd like to make. In fact, as should be no surprise, the personal, while it seems to be the grounds upon which the minority teacher constructs his or her myths of authority, is not the goods in which one trades. Rather, the personal remains a matter, if not for repression, then for generic shaping. One does not present the personal, one represents it. For the minority teacher especially, I think, who has historically been allowed into academia in the guise of the native informant, the use of the personal poses problems. To refuse to engage the personal, to silence it, is one way of resisting the commodification of the multicultural body, the modern-day skin trade, the postmodern trading in the flesh.

However, the personal, at least as it concerns the genres of race and ethnicity in this country, is irrepressible. It cannot be silenced; it is inevitably part of the equipment with which one teaches, willingly or not. The only ways of speaking it are through a playful, inventive, eclectic use of preexisting genres—subversion once again. If the authority derived from the grounds of authenticity is ultimately self-defeating, the performance of race, of ethnicity, can provide a more supple, a more reflexive, a more powerful because more challenging authority. But this should be a Brechtian performance, which alienates the viewer from the spectacle, discomforts rather than fulfills audience expectations. If we Calibans, knowing our hour has yet to come around, do not slouch toward Bethlehem, yet we may shuffle off to Buffalo as guerrilla theater or neo-blackface minstrel show.

Performance and guerrilla theater are strategic, and they are also at the same time, I think, symptomatic. They are strategies for seizing control of the machinery of representation but also always symptoms of powerlessness . . . as well as power. The demand on the minority teacher for the personal (a demand which often forms the grounds for pedagogical authority) appears in many places: in teaching strategy, in subject matter, certainly in the power dynamics and the erotics of the classroom. More important, it moves the marketplace into the classroom. The personal is something we narrativize and produce as part of the package we sell. The personal is part of our academic, economic product. Academia is neither Bethlehem nor Jerusalem, although it is, or can be, both. But it is useful to remind ourselves that it is also an industry.

To state that what we do in academia is part of the free-market economy is a commonplace. It is also a statement to which many of us have a great deal of resistance. We (and I'm speaking specifically here of teachers, although I think this is no less true of students) want to believe (and traditional thinking reinforces) that teaching is more than a trade of supply in accordance with demand. We would like to believe that, in fact, while we may be peddling our wares with the other moneylenders in the temple, we are nonetheless tearing down the walls of Babylon, laying the foundations of a new Jerusalem, helping a new world order be born in Bethlehem.

I am not suggesting that these are alternatives between which we need to choose—that we are necessarily either on the side of the angels or of the devils, either tradesmen or selfless priests or revolutionaries. As always, things are not so simple. Instead, what seems to me more interesting is to look at the ways in which we struggle between knowing that we are in business and our desire to be working for a cause. Our difficulty with reconciling vocation with avocation has a great deal to do with the prominent place accorded the personal today. To reduce the teaching of postcolonial literature, as well as other subjects concerning difference or "otherness," simply to a disciplinary body of knowledge which can be transmitted impersonally—to leave out the personal—is to accede to the view that this is only a business. The minority teacher transmitting that discipline personifies several things: not only the body of knowledge (pun intended) but also of political virtue. The minority teacher becomes the manifest demonstration of solidarity with the struggle. The personal becomes a way to redeem our trade.

But the personal in this case is nonetheless curiously impersonal: it is, after all, not the facts and substance of an individual teacher's life that are desired, but the generic substance of the minority self. In this sense, the ethnic teacher is involved in a kind of skin trade, but even more in an impersonation. The minority teacher performs a generic ethnicity in which the personal is simultaneously a symptom of powerlessness within academia and a strategy for gaining power (as is identity politics in general). The ethnic impersonation releases the minority teacher from trading in the individually personal, while enabling him or her to do business in academia. If the minority teacher has traditionally been allowed into the groves of academe as a native informant, on the basis of the authority of experience, then the impersonation of the personal allows him or her the experience of authority.

A version of this article also appears in *Radical Teacher*, 1993.

Works Cited

Chow, Rey. *Woman and Chinese Modernity*. Minneapolis: U of Minnesota P, 1991.
JanMohamed, Abdul, and David Lloyd, eds. Introduction. *The Nature and Context of Minority Discourse*. New York: Oxford UP, 1990. 9.
Patai, Daphne. "Surplus Visibility." *Chronicle of Higher Education* 30 Oct. 1991: A52.

13 | In-Voicing
Beyond the Voice Debate
George Otte

CERTAIN CONTROVERSIES GO right to the heart of what writing teachers do, giving us polarized answers to questions about what kind of writing we should assign and what qualities we should look for in it. Often such answers sort out into the opposing camps of personal writing vs. academic writing, but those camps are so variously defined as to blur (as well as dichotomize) our sense of what is going on. I think we can get a clearer sense by attending to conceptions of voice.

Admittedly, there are problems with definition here too. Surely not all would subscribe to the definition of voice given by a proponent of "authentic voice" like the late Donald C. Stewart, who defined "the fundamental quality of good writing" as "the presence of the individual writer, a presence made visible by what I choose to call an authentic voice" ("Cognitive" 283). Yet that sense of a speaking self, a self-characterized author, is no less there in the arguments made by those who adamantly oppose the valorization of "an authentic voice." For example, in a famous formulation, David Bartholomae says the student "must become like us.... He must become someone he is not. He must know what we know, talk like we talk" (300).

These days, champions of adapting to academic conventions are at least as likely to be found on the left as on the right: Patricia Bizzell, for instance, argues that "politically oppressed students need to master academic discourse" (193). And we have poststructuralist visions of the self-realized authorship so dear to Don Stewart. For example, resisting Bartholomae's dictum, Joy Ritchie invokes Bakhtin to describe a "dialogic" writing workshop in which the students "did not become 'someone they were not,' as Bartholomae suggests students must.... They became more themselves, the people they are continuing to become" (171).

The common thread throughout is the sense of a speaking self. What varies is how that self is defined or located: whether it is discovered or constructed, emerging or adapting, characterized primarily by its own integrity or by integration with what is around it. But again, the metaphorical polarities should not obscure commonalities. No one on either side of the argument supposes the speaking self is essentially static. Whether an authentic voice is discovered and then developed or an inchoate academic voice gradually learns the appropriate moves and modulations, there is work to be done, progress to be made. (This is important; it gives the teacher something to do.)

And this progress is made by practice in varying contexts and goals. Both conceptions of the speaking self are explicitly transactional (even dialogic). Adaptability, adjustment, acculturation—the great imperatives of the academic camp—are acknowledged by the proponents of authenticity as well: Stewart called his voice-centered textbook *The Versatile Writer*. The question is not whether there are accommodations to be made and roles to be played but what priority or effect they have with respect to the writer's identity. According to Bartholomae, "The struggle of the student is not to bring out that which is within; it is the struggle to carry out those ritualized activities that grant one entrance into a closed society" (300). Stewart, by contrast, holds that the discovery of "authentic voice" entails "a kind of revelation in which you not only begin to see yourself through the eyes of others, but also acquire a fundamental sense of individuality, which transcends the roles you play in life" (*Versatile Writer* 8). We might say that one's allegiances on this issue sort out depending on whether one is interested more in the dancer or the dance—and it's good to recall Yeats's sense of the difficulty in distinguishing them.

The analogy is also useful because dance is performance, and we can get sidetracked down epistemological dead ends. Concern for voice—academic or authentic—may have less to do with ideas about the fragmentation of identity or the social construction of self than with what sort of voice the listener wants to hear. Questions about voice ultimately boil down to the students' question: "What does the teacher want?"—but now posed by the teaching profession to itself. And the two supposedly opposed answers given may boil down to one: the teacher wants to hear something that sounds like the teacher.

That's a point (charge?) I'm going to have to develop, but first I want to say why it's worth developing. Arthur Applebee has established that far and away most of writing instruction is evaluative rather than heuristic, a matter of prescription and judgment rather than discovery and development. For the students, the object is always to meet the teacher's requirements. The teacher who advocates exploratory, student-centered, speak-for-yourself writing may simply seem to complicate the requirements, to have a more complex or submerged agenda, and to appear still more directive and intrusive a pedagogical presence than other teachers who have gone before (needing to fly in the face of so much the student must presumably unlearn). The advocate of academic discourse is hardly in a better position: invoking discipline-focused practices on light acquaintance with other disciplines, often begging the question of writing across the curriculum, speaking on behalf of an entire institution from one relatively marginalized corner of it, this teacher seems on shaky ground to be (as Sheryl Fontaine points out) the classroom's sole authority on academic discourse. In either case, the teacher is inescapably the evaluator of students' work. The inescapable question, then, is the students': What does the evaluator want?

And what is it teachers want? What, in our eyes, makes writing good? An interesting (but ultimately troubling) answer is the anthology *What Makes Writing Good* (1985), put together by William E. Coles, Jr., and James Vopat. The idea for the anthology dates back to a 1981 conference, where Coles discussed what he thought was the best student paper he had ever received. Those in attendance were asked to think about what student writing they would choose as best—and why. Ultimately, forty-eight contributors were asked to supply papers (and to provide commentaries on those papers). Though they were a varied lot—theorists, empirical researchers, linguists, popular authors, all "names" in composition representing a wide range of perspectives—the student papers they selected were emphatically not so diverse. There were no research papers, only two essays that analyzed texts, and four examples of professional writing. Of the forty-eight samples, thirty—over three-fifths—were personal-experience essays.

That fact alone is enough to raise eyebrows. What principle of selection is operating when the best scholar-teachers say that the best college writing they've seen is experiential writing? We can begin to answer the question—though not without provoking more questions—by noting that their most common criterion for defining what is best is "honesty" or "integrity" or (yes) "authenticity."

But in what does such a quality reside? That's not an easy question to answer, not least of all if we ask the "authentic voice" advocates. Dona J. Hickey opens her recent textbook *Developing a Written Voice* by saying that voice "is just plain hard to talk about. It's hard to define, it's hard to explain its features, and it's hard to find an organized way of introducing and teaching it to others. Still, we all know it when we hear it" (v). Peter Elbow describes voice as "something mysterious and hidden. There are no outward linguistic characteristics to point to in writing with a real voice. Resonance or impact on readers is all there is" (*Writing* 312). In fact, I. Hashimoto has devoted an entire article to what he calls the "anti-intellectual, evangelical appeals for 'voice' " (77), partly to explain the fuzziness of such definitions.

Lester Faigley, in analyzing the *What Makes Writing Good* anthology, homes in on the appreciations of presumed honesty; he suspects the perception of honesty is a function of "writing about potentially embarrassing and painful aspects of one's life" (121), especially since he finds contributors such as James Britton and Steve Seaton contending that a student's willingness to do so is proof of good teaching: it "betokens an unusual trust in the reader she has in mind, her teacher. Such a relationship of trust must be the outcome of successful teaching . . . over a period of time—something that must be *earned*, can't be *demanded*" (79). Faigley is not so sure, having "read narratives written for large-scale assessments that deal with intense personal events such as the experience of being raped, yet the writer had no knowledge of who would read the paper" (121).

Faigley's own explanation is that, because students and their writing are "judged by the teachers' unstated assumptions about subjectivity" (128), "[t]he student selves we encounter in *What Makes Writing Good* are predominantly selves that achieve rationality and unity by characterizing former selves as objects for analysis . . . " (129). They have learned to accept change, acknowledge contradictions (without contradicting themselves), endure but also transcend embarrassing revelations, show themselves in possession of a salutary self-consciousness. The result is not so much truth as a special sort of appearance of truth: in Faigley's words, " . . . the truths 'exposed' or 'revealed' in the essay are a series of recognitions for a college English teacher" (125). For those uneasy that an interest in personal-experience essays springs from a kind of voyeurism, Faigley raises a more damning question: Is it really, at bottom, not voyeurism but narcissism? Is it not just advocates of academic writing who say, with Bartholomae, that the student "must become like us"? Is it also the demand of those who want authenticity, honesty, uniqueness? Consider this confession from Peter Elbow:

> As I've been trying to work and rework my thoughts about voice these last four years, I have been nervous about the charge that what I am calling "real voice" is just writing that happens to tickle my feelings or unconscious concerns and has nothing to do with the words' relationship to the writer. The charge is plausible: if I experience resonance, surely it's more likely to reflect a good fit between the words and *my* self than a good fit between the words and the writer's self; after all, my self is right here, in contact with the words on the page, while the writer's self is nowhere to be found. (*Writing* 300)

Apparently, writing teachers have plenty of reason to question the authority they ask their students to acknowledge, whatever it is. The upshot of all this personal and professional soul-searching is that, regardless of whether the sort of voice advocated is supposedly acclimating itself to academia or authenticating itself, what's really sought is the master's voice. Teachers want to hear themselves.

There's an easy solution to this problem (if it's seen as a problem). If an important determinant of "voice" is (as we've always suspected) the listener, other listeners can be implicated. There's also an easy answer to the question "Who?": those other listeners immediately available are students. Collaborative learning techniques give answers to the questions "How?" and "Why?" as well, though not the sort that will please everyone. For an "authentic voice" man like Stewart, someone like Ken Bruffee, perhaps the profession's chief advocate of collaborative learning and a self-proclaimed "social constructionist[,] lives in a world in which people lose their identities in collaborative uses of language . . . " (Stewart, "Cognitive" 283).

Actually, that wasn't the case in the Bakhtin-refracted writing workshop Joy Ritchie observed, the one in which students "became more themselves, the people they are continuing to become." But there was another problem with these students writing for tough audiences of other students, one Ritchie frankly acknowledges when she says they did not emerge "from the workshop with writing that would have been entirely acceptable to many of our colleagues" (171). If they hadn't lost their identities, they hadn't necessarily gained all the requisite academic moves either.

It seems you can't please everybody—but it also seems that that's a more valuable realization than it may at first seem, one that may ultimately allow some negotiation between extremes like Bartholomae's insistence that the task of college writing "is not to bring out that which is within" and Elbow's charge that "we can't teach academic discourse because there's no such thing to teach" ("Reflections" 138). The world of writing instruction abounds in instructors who presume to say what's true for everyone. When Donald Murray says "Voice separates writing that is not read from writing that is read" (144), or *The Practical Stylist* tells the student "You should have a voice, and that voice should be unmistakably your own" (6), I hear—dare I call it a voice?—sounding more imperious (and less ironic) than Bartholomae's when he says that the student "must become like us . . . someone he is not." Whether writing teachers say one thing or the other in front of our classrooms, whom can we be said to be speaking for? A profession divided on the issue of voice—and more than a little guilt-stricken about it, regardless of the stand taken? Students whose "identities" may be convenient fictions, destabilized or constricted or determined by cultural imperatives unlike their teachers'? Colleagues in other disciplines whose discursive practices are known only a little and esteemed still less? A society (or some subset of it called the "real world") so complex one can't begin to comprehend its multitudinous stratifications and compartments?

If ventriloquism is dangerous for writing teachers, it may be just the thing for our students. The advocates of academic moves and authentic voice tend to neglect what the Summerfields stressed in *Texts and Contexts*: students are good at role playing, at in-voicing identities not their own. Typically, a student who inhabits some fictive scenario, who "pretends" to write from the position of a public figure or literary character, shows a rhetorical sophistication well beyond what might have been taught or expected. Perhaps the most famous (notorious?) example comes from Brannon and Knoblauch's "On Students' Rights to Their Own Texts": a student writing on the Lindbergh kidnapping trial adopted the approach of giving the prosecution's closing arguments. Forty teachers evaluating the piece all felt the writer "depended too much on emotions and too little on logic" to be convincing (though some allowed a certain satirical effect); actually, the student's essay was "in fact very similar" to the prosecution's summation in the trial (159–61). In this case, one student proved a shrewder judge of what a shrewd judge of a specific audience would say than a host of English teachers.

That chastening discovery poses a possibility: since advocates of both academic and authentic voice acknowledge the importance of context, perhaps the place to begin is with what thinking goes into the adoption or modulation of a voice in a particular scenario. While considering what works as a well-pitched voice in a real-life context, we might begin to discuss how much intention involves imagined reception, how much what is offered involves withholding, how much the appearance of sincerity involves choice and craft—how much the text is shaped by the context.

That student who second-guessed the prosecution's pitch seems to have underestimated the reliance on emotional appeal. Here's the student:

> Ladies and gentlemen of the jury, I whole-heartedly believe that the evidence which has been presented before you has clearly shown that the man who is on trial here today is beyond a doubt guilty of the murder of the darling little, innocent Lindbergh baby.

And here's part of the prosecution's actual summation:

> Why, men and women, if that little baby, if that little, curly-haired youngster were out in the grass in the jungle, breathing, just so long as it was breathing, any tiger, any lion, the most venomous snake would have passed that child without hurting a hair of its head.

Robert Brooke has argued that students do and should model their writing voices on those of writers they esteem, but a case could also be made that this courtroom rhetoric is the kind of voice that should be in-voiced for and by students, at least in part to allow them to consider whether they find it estimable. Again: who is speaking here, and on whose behalf—not just for whom but against whom? If this speaking self has credibility and force, in what does that reside? (Are all the images of restrained violence redirecting violence?) How do we measure the success of such rhetoric? For whom does it work?

If a student "owned" this discourse, if it seemed to come from that student's "true" self, such questions would be difficult to address. If a student didn't enact such discourse, the questions would be difficult to care about. Whatever we say about self, voice is certainly a spatchcocked affair, and writing teachers might do well to help students see as much. We might lay less stress on either "truth" and "sincerity" or "genres" and "conventions" than on choices and chances.

Norman Holland holds that, in reading, *"Interpretation is a function of identity."* Talking about student writing, we could reverse that to *"Identity is a function of interpretation."* The speaking self is less the origin of one's discourse than the representation created by it, more effect than cause. If students could be helped to read not just the voice but the in-voicing, they might make their choices, their borrowings, and their self-characterizations more carefully, more thoughtfully.

The point of in-voicing other voices is not to make for risk-free, semi-engaged games of pretend; on the contrary, it's to make apparent the risks of a practice we all constantly enact, speaking the already spoken whether by teachers or TV lawyers, evangelists or advertisements, parents or talk show celebrities. Whatever is said is not just mostly borrowed, but borrowed on interest.

Consider, for example, what happened when a would-be president made "Read my lips" an unforgettable soundbite. Invoking his predecessor's in-voicing of another Dirty Harry threat ("Make my day"), Bush crowned his bid for election with a promise made extraordinarily memorable precisely because it seemed so out of character. (He was consciously dodging the "wimp factor" at the time.) Yet, that promise broken and another election contest under way, what was memorable became haunting, doubly so as two opposition candidates delighted in reminding voters of a soundbite gone sour. This establishment in-voicing of an anti-establishment character, this use of words from a fictional figure contemptuous of words, this intentional blurring of personae and purposes and realms of discourse is rich grazing ground for discussion and analysis. But the writing teacher must come to it ready to offer more than injunctions against clichés.

Words are indeed things to conjure with. But so are the voices, the roles, the contexts associated with them. These, too, are subject to manipulation and interpretation—and in ways that are enormously consequential. Rather than advocating some take on voice, writing teachers might invite students to do self-conscious in-voicings of other voices, other roles—thus getting that all-important interpretive process out in the open.

Works Cited

Applebee, Arthur. *Contexts for Learning to Write*. Norwood, NJ: Ablex, 1984.

Baker, Sheridan, and Robert E. Yarber. *The Practical Stylist with Readings*. 6th ed. New York: Harper, 1986.

Bartholomae, David. "Writing Assignments: Where Writing Begins." *Forum: Essays on the Theory and Practice of Writing*. Ed. Patricia L. Stock. Upper Montclair, NJ: Boynton/Cook, 1983. 300–12.

Bizzell, Patricia. "College Composition: Initiation into the Academic Discourse Community." *Curriculum Inquiry* 12 (1982): 191–207.

Brannon, Lil, and C. H. Knoblauch. "On Students' Rights to Their Own Texts: A Model of Teacher Response." *College Composition and Communication* 33 (1982): 157–66.

Brooke, Robert. "Modeling a Writer's Identity: Reading and Imitation in the Writing Classroom." *College Composition and Communication* 39 (1988): 23–41.

Bruffee, Kenneth A. "Social Construction, Language, and the Authority of Knowledge." *College English* 48 (1986): 773–90.

Coles, William E., Jr., and James Vopat. *What Makes Writing Good: A Multiperspective*. Lexington, MA: Heath, 1985.

Elbow, Peter. "Reflections on Academic Discourse: How It Relates to Freshmen and Colleagues." *College English* 53 (1991): 135–55.

——. *Writing with Power: Techniques for Mastering the Writing Process*. New York: Oxford, 1981.

Faigley, Lester. *Fragments of Rationality: Postmodernity and the Subject of Composition*. Pittsburgh: U of Pittsburgh P, 1992.

Fontaine, Sheryl. "The Unfinished Story of the Interpretive Community." *Rhetoric Review* 7 (1988): 86–96.

Hashimoto, I. "Voice as Juice: Some Reservations about Evangelic Composition." *College Composition and Communication* 38 (1987): 70–80.

Hickey, Dona J. *Developing a Written Voice*. Mountain View, CA: Mayfield, 1993.

Holland, Norman. "UNITY IDENTITY TEXT SELF." *Reader-Response Criticism*. Ed. Jane Tompkins. Baltimore: Johns Hopkins UP, 1980. 118–33.

Murray, Donald. *Write to Learn*. New York: Holt, 1984.

Ritchie, Joy S. "Beginning Writers: Diverse Voices and Individual Identity." *College Composition and Communication* 40 (1989): 152–74.

Stewart, Donald C. "Cognitive Psychologists, Social Constructionists, and Three Nineteenth-Century Advocates of Authentic Voice." *Journal of Advanced Composition* 12 (1992): 279–90.

——. *The Versatile Writer*. Lexington, MA: Heath, 1986.

Summerfield, Judith, and Geoffrey Summerfield. *Texts & Contexts: A Contribution to the Theory and Practice of Teaching Composition*. New York: Random, 1986.

14 | *In Loco Parentis*
Addressing (the) Class

Susan Miller

Lᴇᴛ's ᴀssᴜᴍᴇ, but only for now, that "school" is a place where we learn to write—"we" who know about writing and difference, about the pen and the phallus, and about writing as women whose lips were sealed. Among ourselves, we have unloaded canons, dispossessed Father texts, and drastically shortened the grand récits, to place in quotation marks "literature," "science," "history," "cognition," "psychology," "culture," and most subjects we once thought as simply mastered and taught. Assuming this position, we are finally getting pedagogical, in long-imagined but almost infinitely postponed talk about teaching as personal and relational—two terms that I separate because our assumptions about having already learned about writing in school are, as I said, just for now.

We must, of course, address the postponement of this discussion. As Jane Tompkins points out in "The Pedagogy of the Distressed," we all learned early on that pedagogy is a dirty little secret, the fearsome and demeaned professional impropriety that, "exactly like sex," is "something you weren't supposed to talk about or focus on" (655). Even now, we notice that only those of us willing to deal in vernacular trades—reading and writing, stories and corrections—own up to a connection between the "personal" and "pedagogy." No astrophysicists are among us. As one of them who won a major university's distinguished teaching award said to me once, "If I became known as a teacher, my career would be over."

Assuming *that* position, it's easy enough to admit, if we consult our stomachs, that publicly linking pedagogy and the personal involves uncovering not only the "fear" that Tompkins identifies as her primary emotion as a teacher, but a particular sort of guilt, the dis-ease that most of us experience when the student/teacher subject comes up. We assume that this shame is inherited, along a story line Hegel points at us. This line moves from the Socrates of the Phaedrus (the pupil who held Lysias's scroll in the interest of learning how to write), through Rousseau's intimacies with students and those of the de Sade whose digital pedagogy as pederasty has been made to count among us, if compulsively, by Jane Gallop's description of student bodies and their extremities in *Thinking through the Body*. But, I want to argue, *our* teaching assignments are the plots of different, much shorter, still uncataloged pedagogical narratives.

Contemporary talk at this professional limit remains simultaneously resonant and blurred. The resounding "importance" of this discursive space cannot mask the fact that it contains a professionally unspeakable topic about which we may have already said too much. But its blurring disarranges even those who lately say that knowledge is writing, constructed representations with specific political agendas.

We might, consequently, begin there, where the *locus* of my title is a particular and political space. We need, that is, to understand "pedagogy" as a specific construction, assigned to those of us who teach vernacular texts, first by locating ourselves in the particular cultural formation that gave birth to our professions. It is old news by now that vernacular language studies, whose spin is not the one described in astrophysics, began in the nineteenth century as specifically *cultural* pedagogies. They were designed to colonize mass populations— American immigrants and reconstructed Southerners, East Indians and newly industrialized Britons. The people in these groups were imagined, both *as* groups and as a mass, as those for whom an only recently standardized written English and a newly designated "national" literature would replicate a failing religious means of control. As Ian Hunter, Terry Eagleton, and many other historians of the humanities explain, the study of vernacular texts was established at this political moment in England, India, and America to isolate, and to create, a new class identity, built specifically for new students in new, mass education. This class's reproduction would be assured by its receptions and renditions of itself as identified with selected secular texts. Like Eagleton in "The Subject of Literature," Hunter argues in *Culture and Government* that this new pedagogical technology has been precisely moral. It made central a curriculum that was, and is still, comprised of four pedagogical emphases: (1) information about language in rhetoric and philology, (2) a simultaneously analytical and self-"critical" sensibility, (3) an illusion of "freedom" in closely monitored self-expression, and (4) a special kind of teacher. This teacher, our forebear, is described as a friend and confidant in one 1850 document that Hunter quotes:

> It is necessary that [the teacher] place himself on such terms with his pupils as that they can, without fear, make him their confidant, unburden their minds, and tell him any little story, or mischievous occurrence. Teachers and parents, [to gain] the confidence of their children, must in fact, themselves, as it were, become children, by bending to, and occasionally engage in, their plays and amusements. Without such condescension, a perfect knowledge of real character and dispositions cannot be obtained. (Stow 156; quoted in Hunter 126)

Hunter elaborates on how modern literary education installed this strikingly familiar teacherly personae in an educational culture of "self criticism," the second element of its moral technology. The teacher of literary and literacy studies in this politically intended cultural pedagogy was not called on to reproduce traditional knowledge as a content to be mastered, but to fix a particular difference from academic *and* from home values in a newly "trained," not classically educated, "public." By this means, the school replaced the home as the primary civic unit of society. It took on monitorial duties of which it often complains, but which it nurtures in ways that replace formerly *inherited* access to moral judgments, evaluations of character, and entitlements with *acquired* status and "success." All, that is, seem endowed, or not, by mass educational institutions.

Hunter stresses the requirement that this self-critical schooling persistently places students between their informal cultural experiences and formal, institutional organizations of them as "texts." The gap between the two unsettles the student, who must oscillate between their cooperatively opposed modes. On one side, that is, this pedagogy relies on formalist categories of analysis like those that vernacular literacy lessons call "conventions," and that literary studies names as genres, structures, and intertextual influences. On another side of the student, however, is an opposing mode of interpretation—reading against immediate "experience" and "feeling" that the model teacher elicits to reveal the student subject to the institution, making it available for persuasive "correction." This production of "English" regulated a new class, requiring that pedagogy inject the institution of education *itself* into popular social registers, especially into the standardized vernacular language of a new majority who would eventually attend college.

Hunter focuses on teaching "Literature," which "is not deployed as a philological document registering the motley of cultural technologies, [but] . . . instead . . . as an ethical device inside *one* such technology: the supervisory apparatus of modern pedagogy" (258). In other words, the study of vernacular texts was constituted by three elements: a double formalist and experiential critical sensibility; selected textual objects that, as one nineteenth-century teacher said, embody our "universal ideals, our national ideals, and our race ideals"; and a particular teacher. These three components comprised what Hunter calls an "intervention in the life of the population" (263).

We might think that this analysis exaggerates the culturally required "personal" condescension and interest of a special teacher, the agent of this intervention in the "little story or mischievous occurrence," or that this mode of personal involvement was needed only in nineteenth-century Britain. But it is more chillingly emphasized in the minutes of a 1913 meeting of the American National Education Association, the organization that articulated the pedagogy by which our own public school teachers were taught. As this record puts it, "The first business of pedagogy is *pedagogy*—leading children" (*Addresses* 74). Consequently, "it is the duty of the educator to know every individual" and "to be social engineers" (76). The record states that the teacher's social duty is to educate according to each individual student's nature. Like Jane Tompkins's seemingly personal claim to teach what she calls "the ideals we may cherish" (656), these public school teachers were to turn to "end[ing] the oppression of the poor and the angering of the discontented" (77).

But these angry and discontented masses are not, as Tompkins and most of us usually suggest they are, the student's Others. They are not a vaguely defined population beyond school, a general, uneducated "society" that we create to work against. They are the students themselves. The teacher's necessary social engineering, articulated by the NEA as "The Teacher as Community Surveyor" (*Addresses* 75), is consequently described in the same regulatory taxonomy that Foucault uses to highlight practices that organize social functions once diffused throughout communities. According to these minutes, that is, the self-infantilizing teacher prescribed by Stow (above) must use personal surveillance to offer the recently distinguished *student* identity an alternative to "asylums and hospitals . . . jails and penitentiaries" (77) and, notably, the institution of prostitution. The minutes assert that "we must cut off at the sources . . . the supplies from which are recruited annually some *sixty thousand or more* prostitutes. . . . There are more such women in America than there are women . . . teachers" (77). These outlaw fates await students whose teachers do not study "their natures in childhood," by accessing their family histories, their "communities, to see where they will fit in," and "their habitats, to see whether farm or field, mine or river will receive them" (77). This American pedagogy requires a teacher to get personal about what it calls the "powers, needs and interests of the flesh-and-blood *different* boys and girls whom we know and love, for whom we labor, whom at last we are beginning to understand" (77; emphasis added). The sacrifice expected of this teacher, about whom the minutes also get personal, additionally threatens the teacher's life, but in a particularly impersonal way that is implicated in other apparatuses of the State. The minutes note that "actual statistics show that the mortality among composition teachers is in many instances actually greater than at the bloody field of Gettysburg" (94).

This intended military comparison reminds us again that the personal in this cultural pedagogy is meant to be socially regulatory. For all its seemingly traditional formation in "leading out" the individual "nature"—the teaching stressed in systematic pedagogies from Plato and Comedius through Rousseau and Hegel—this modern version of a "personal" must be understood differently. These monitoring interventions consciously manage a student body whose "nature" and attractions are, at the least, different. In his speech at the same meeting on "The High School and Democracy," Thomas Jesse Jones from the National Bureau of Education suggests that a teacher's academic knowledge may itself give way to the difference in the student's material and class-coded situation. Jones pictures a teacher of Latin throwing over her expertise to give her pupil Mary lessons of a more "useful" sort:

> If Miss Smith wishes really to help direct the great wave of democracy, she must follow Mary to her mother's home and see the mother battling bravely

> to feed, clothe, and educate her family of five children and father and mother on ten or fifteen dollars a week. She must learn what is Mary's attitude toward her hard-working father and mother. She must ascertain Mary's pleasures and evening companions. She must study the relation of housing and food to the death of Mary's baby brother. She must determine in her own mind and, if possible, help Mary to determine what useful sphere in life Mary is going to fill. These various excursions into Mary's life will probably lead Miss Smith to the study of her community. . . . Finally at the end of the school year when her mind is full of this living information, Miss Smith will decide to teach Latin in such a living style that it can no longer be called a dead language, or she will throw Latin overboard and teach another subject which Mary needs more in her daily contact with a mother who slaves all day, with children who need to be fed and clothed and washed. . . . (98)

We notice that Mary's body is not half so much fun to examine as the bodies of Phaedrus, of de Sade's homo- and heterophilic students, or of Rousseau's Emile. But, I need to insist, Mary's is the body we have been assigned to anatomize, the "subject" named as both the nineteenth-century medical term for "cadaver" and the current term for "identity." The person with whom we get personal has been culturally hailed to a lower status than its teachers. This subject is an object—of pedagogical surveillance undertaken as a mode of conversation, "involvement," and condescension. Most important, this body is collective, a "populace," not the characterized and named students in the pedagogical narratives whose genre still writes our blurred accounts.

So we examine this student body, and our relation to it, in a discourse we find uncongenial. Especially as university professors whose discourse encourages us to imagine ourselves as participants in national, if no longer universal, communities of ideas that are outside a pedagogical moment, we prefer to stay within the Hegelian story about teaching that creates us, and students, as "personally" involved. We, like Tompkins, are willing to imagine ourselves as fearful, failing to perform as our mythologized Fathers, our mentors, expected us to in *their* class. And we are willing to acknowledge that we want to talk about pedagogy and the personal as sites of a guilt that we often turn into compulsive talk, to voice-over unacknowledged erotic desires for students we can never fully master, dominate, or love enough because they will, we know, outlive and rewrite us. We can identify with unfulfilled but confessed and personal teacher's guilt, a repressed lust to reproduce sameness by breeding more people like us, more citizens of an intellectual identity politics that once placed schools and universities precisely *in the place of parents*, with all the physical intimacy enabled by the phrase. Nonetheless, we can have only little to do with those elitist pedagogues, the always vaguely unhappy lovers and martyrs to children for whom they could never do enough. We would rather represent ourselves as those unhappy lover/martyrs than as we are, those whose ethical frustration has been translated into typed regulations against fraternizing with the Other. But the students we now describe, and the ways in which we get personal with them, do take another shape. Our desire to rewrite Socrates and de Sade hides the base of another employment.

It seems doubly unfair to point out how even such painful, psychologized admissions have their own historically planted roots, to suggest that individual stories about "the personal" must, like heartfelt renditions of pedagogy, be told in quotation marks. But these confessions are neither individual nor even personal. They are constructed sites for modern texts that neither we nor students author. I am obviously suggesting that this personal, like the pedagogical I have already located in an openly stated historical agenda for cultural regulation, is a particular and specific fiction. In this myth, "personal" accounts of teaching do not primarily describe actions we have already taken. These narratives work instead as agents. They motivate culturally cooperative subjectivities for both teachers and students. They establish characters whose supposedly "natural" desires toward each other, both generative and perverse, will maintain the once Great Narrative about teaching that is now artificial.

The "loco" of *in loco parentis* is not still the *place* of parents, but now a subtextual craziness. It is the inevitable result of applying a situationally inapplicable family romance to explain intimacy between managers of the vernacular and a linguistically managed class. So the parental text we *will* admit to perverting is not the text we are in. But analyses of the "personal" still take authority from it, creating a dissonance that is a specific and modern source of guilt about pedagogy, our knowledge that we have "children" who will never inherit.

We are of course more familiar with ways in which we try to hide this possibility from ourselves in talk about personal relations to students and personal teaching histories than we are with ways to uncover its implications. For instance, reports of literary "response" and ethnographic observations in educational and composition studies often focus on "personal" cases drawn from the reading and writing processes of individual students. Like New Historicism, such research finds authority in anecdotes. There is, for example, a particular subgenre of argument in composition studies, "the University of Pittsburgh article," which regularly proceeds as a masterful reading of one student text. This reading offers a template not only for "student thought" but for engaging in a psychologized and conscious self-criticism that is globally attributed to all teachers, not to the confessing reader alone. In this and similar research, first, the originary parental model of personal interactions with students is displaced onto an authorizing method—the "case study" or "ethnographic observation"—and then it is re-personalized, apparently because the nature of its supposed "data" demands this mode of interpretation.[1] Individual students and individual teachers may, in these accounts, be imaginatively returned to the scene of our original sins—the gardens, cozy "school rooms," and other closeted spaces in which Socrates, de Sade, Rousseau, or Catharine Beecher stood in for home truths about desire. And readers are thereby reassured that their students are "people like us," younger and more ignorant, but not inaccessible or un-available to join, enter, and penetrate our discursive homes.

This published way to hide the confusion caused by ignoring the manage-rial functions of our "personal" interactions also appears in this research mode's probable source text, the talk in hallways and offices that privately re-hearses a traditional family romance. To reread Jane Tompkins, it is not entirely true that pedagogy has always been a dirty little secret, the unspeakable. We do a great deal of compulsive talk about teaching, or more precisely about students, in which we admire their body parts, named openly among my colleagues as "head," "heart," and, depending on their sex, "legs" and "buns." To name a "good head" is taken to express our perspicacity about intelligence; to certify "great buns" is taken as a statement of precisely liberatory pedagogy. But here it is the new *teacher's* empowerment in a professional underlife that fits Hunter's description of literary culture's "illusion of 'freedom' in closely monitored self-expression." Most frequently, this talk in offices and hallways cements bonds between colleagues; it rarely expresses a relationship to or desire for a particular student. Especially when it more complexly addresses the performance of a stu-dent on a paper or examination, it reassures us that we have evaluated accu-rately. This seemingly personal talk tells us that our monitoring gaze has seen the same causes and results that our partners in modern pedagogy have seen. We tell and ask about the "personal" in teaching to affirm that we are being "objective," to calibrate and recalibrate the vision we have been assigned.

It is usually at about this point that analyses like these are accused of inef-fectual postmodern tendencies and dismissed because they cannot honor the human agencies necessary to produce political change. But these analyses, like others that insist that we apply what we have learned in new schools about "writing" to those schools themselves, lead instead to political changes we probably don't want to make in mass education or in its construction of a keen and functional "personal." They require us to acknowledge that the particular modern cultural pedagogy that interpellates our teaching and disorganizes old narratives disallows our wanting to belong to the class we address, and prevents us, in both conceptual and material ways, from entering it. So an obvious, more relevant encounter with my argument might emphasize that the professional-ized textual establishment to which we belong is what Nancy Armstrong has called a "purveyor of a specialized form of [vernacular] literacy" (25). Institu-tions of mass education maintain tensions with an ancient, homoerotic, "per-sonal" relationship to students, but they do so to, as she says, "invariably per-petuate the hegemony" (25) of dyadic formations that must already divorce pedagogy and the personal from politics. The separation and identification of "teacher" and "student," like minutely described interactions between them, sustain images of a depoliticized interiority that we identify as our "normal," or "basic," lives. These oppositional human constructions allow us to focus on discussing the "personal" while we avoid its cultural placement in the same quotation marks we have placed around other forms of knowledge. We cannot explain agency to students in ways that empower their political difference from us so long as we misrecognize them, and ourselves, as innocently implicated in what are actually artful interactions.

The alternative to such misrecognition, of course, is to reimagine ourselves as the managers of the vernacular, at all its levels, that we are assigned to be, and to reveal and explain this assignment to students. This move need not be as tedious and embedded in male-coded, anti-familial Marxism as may first appear. If we take a more discursive view of the personal, we might openly distinguish it from its different, not opposite, term—the relational. "Relational" and social configurations name the important difference between the real situation and desires of students who are a "class" production, and idealized "people like us," whom we still, in now falsely "personal" frustrations, imagine them to be. A relational perspective allows us to forego the fearsome identity of an imagined individual's pedagogue, the personal that necessarily effaces the class we teach *as* a class. This view instead puts into play the social situation of mass education that is now repressed into a simple dyad between a student and a teacher, wrongly emphasizing singular and in fact *im*personal (because different from this social situation) relationships with a Socrates, a de Sade, or a Tompkins.

The fear that this retained individual "teacher's" stance addresses is an old one—that the brothers will bond, rise up, and kill and eat the Father, no matter if he is also a Mother. But this fear is also a contemporary public alarm—that becoming aware of the politics of the canon, the power of the Father texts, and the tedium of the great narratives will encourage the masses brought together in public institutions like this one to overturn the correct and carefully selected vernacular structures that contain them. We consent to both versions of this fear by many of our re-formations of pedagogy and the personal—by actively discussing how to relinquish classroom oppression, share authority, and value multiple "voices" and liberal pluralistic interpretations. Like the monitorial Lancaster System instituted for much the same purposes in the nineteenth century, current reemergences of equalizing teaching techniques diffuse the very awareness of "writing" we have so politically pursued. Such equalizations reinstate unproblematized portrayals of "student" and "teacher" as merely "taking" roles they might easily, "individually," forego. With the blessing of the institutions they preserve, discussions of such techniques reinstate guilt. And their practice prevents the distinct, and to us inaccessible, student body from recognizing itself as different from the pedagogical moral technology that was designed to contain it.

Where we stand, consequently, is at the beginning of a discussion of pedagogy and the personal that needs framing in a new discourse. The conditions that produce learning have been socialized to bring "everyone" into educational institutions, but relations within those institutions are not yet socialized or recognized in ways that replace our desire for the security of a regime of truth—thus our compulsion to talk about students. The textual unconscious of our "personal" narratives about teaching re-establishes authority for the monitorial functions of mass education while suppressing the socialization within institutions that is their logical but unintended outcome. Similarly, the mentoring relationships we so insistently but ambivalently portray offer a space where we can continue to imagine privatized relationships in decidedly public spaces. Finally, new pedagogical and scholarly discussions of student and discursive "communities" reinstate identity politics, covering over the actually fragmented, associational, and urban situation of knowledge making in their returns of repressed desires for unified, exclusionary groups.

It may seem that I have rejected all that is empowering for both students and teachers in long-awaited discussions like this book—all hope of renovating institutions we already agree to dismantle. But there is, I think, an alternative both to misrecognizing ourselves as pedagogues and to misrecognizing our students as the meritocratically motivated, Jeffersonian elite whom we believe our teachers taught. We have in fact many examples that students are not collectively silenced, and that we need to question our "seriously academic" and "moral" reasons to reject the authority of their differences from us. Consequently, to get personal in a post-Hegelian and post-Oedipal context about an alternative pedagogy and its politics, I want to end with another sort of narrative. Its unconscious limits on what we can say about pedagogy and the personal are more elastic than those that create the so-called empowering mode of individualistic teaching, which has done less than Ross Perot has to change the participatory curve of the now "educated" masses. It is a perhaps trivial, but telling, exemplary interaction, outside our expectations of either pedagogy or its personal accounts. It took place not in a private space inhabited by me and a student, but where our self-misrecognizing, "loco" portrayals of the personal are rarely set, a classroom. In conservative Mormon Utah where I teach cultural studies, our last class meeting of the fall featured a usually indirect but for this occasion "serious" female student asking if I preferred large or small blue books for writing exams. Before I could answer, the ex-Marine now security police male student next to her announced, "You know that size doesn't make any difference—only what she said, 'the point.' " And another woman's voice called out, "You wish! That's what they always want to think. You wish it were true, but it's not." I looked curiously around the room, wondering how the returned missionary who uses Althusser and Mouffe to explain the collective identity of the Mormon community was taking this in. But I did finally answer—"I hesitate to share this now, but I prefer large ones."

There is, of course, a pedagogy here, a subtextual way of teaching that assumes that the students in a class do embody a class, a collective whose interests are not always mine, especially in this last evaluative pedagogical moment. There is an institutional imperative—an exam, a prescription for its writing, and a certain amount of responding anxiety, expressed as the first student's question. But there is also, undeniably, a visibly different text of the "personal," written by the students as interactions with each other in which they overcome anxiety by making a dirty joke, without regard for my comfort. That I was (precisely) their straight man, not their "teacher," is abundantly clear, as is their difference from me and from the institution's interests at this moment. We were, then, "relational," not "personal" with each other in this public space. My privatized interests, like their "individuality," were suspended, finally turned to laughter at a personal matter I am reluctant to share.

Note

1. I would like to make it clear that I am not discussing every publication that examines student texts, but those that take a student's writing to be an emblem of a general, scientistically verified inference.

Works Cited

Addresses of the Fifty-First Annual Meeting Held at Salt Lake City, Utah, July 5–11, 1913. Proc. of the American National Education Association. Ann Arbor: Association Secretary's Office, 1913.

Armstrong, Nancy. *Desire and Domestic Fiction: A Political History of the Novel.* New York: Oxford UP, 1987.

Eagleton, Terry. "The Subject of Literature." *Cultural Critique* 2 (1985–86): 95–106.

Gallop, Jane. *Thinking through the Body.* New York: Columbia UP, 1988.

Hunter, Ian. *Culture and Government: The Emergence of Literary Education.* London: Macmillan, 1988.

Tompkins, Jane. "The Pedagogy of the Distressed." *College English* 52 (1990): 653–60.

Contributors

Chris Amirault, a doctoral candidate in the Modern Studies concentration in the Department of English and Comparative Literature at the the University of Wisconsin-Milwaukee, is researching the history and culture of the patient in the modern era. He is the author of a recent essay in *Discourse*.

David Crane is a doctoral candidate in the Modern Studies concentration in the Department of English and Comparative Literature at the University of Wisconsin-Milwaukee. He teaches courses in film and media studies and has been co-president of the UWM graduate assistant labor union.

Arthur W. Frank is Professor of Sociology at the University of Calgary. He is the author of *At the Will of the Body: Reflections on Illness* and editor of the "Case Stories" series for the journal *Second Opinion*. His essays have appeared in such journals as *Sociological Quarterly, Theory and Psychology,* and *Literature and Medicine*.

Jane Gallop, Distinguished Professor of English and Comparative Literature at the University of Wisconsin-Milwaukee, is the author of *The Daughter's Seduction, Reading Lacan, Thinking through the Body,* and *Around 1981: Academic Feminist Literary Theory*.

Madeleine R. Grumet is Dean and Professor in the School of Education at Brooklyn College-CUNY. She is the author of *Bitter Milk: Women and Teaching* and essays in such journals as *Cambridge Journal of Education, Journal of Curriculum Theorizing,* and *Phenomenology and Pedagogy*.

Gregory Jay, Professor of English and Comparative English at University of Wisconsin-Milwaukee, is the author of *America the Scrivener: Deconstruction and the Subject of Literary History* and the editor of *Modern American Critics: 1920–1955* and *Modern American Critics since 1955*. His essays have appeared in *Boundary 2, Cultural Critique, Diacritics,* and *College English*. He is cofounder of Teachers for a Democratic Society.

Cheryl Johnson is Assistant Professor of English at Miami University in Ohio. Her work has appeared in *Feminist Collections, The Cream City Review, College English,* and *Discourse.* She is completing a book about the relationship between language and ideology in black women's fiction.

Lynne Joyrich is Assistant Professor of English and Comparative Literature at the University of Wisconsin-Milwaukee. Her book *Re-Viewing Reception: Television, Gender, and American Culture* is forthcoming from Indiana University Press. Her essays have appeared in such journals as *d i f f e r e n c e s, Discourse,* and *Camera Obscura,* and in anthologies on television and mass culture.

Indira Karamcheti is Assistant Professor of English at Wesleyan University. She is working on a book, entitled *Postcolonial Theory,* about the development of post-colonial studies as a subdiscipline in academia.

Joseph Litvak is Associate Professor of English at Bowdoin College. He is the author of *Caught in the Act: Theatricality in the Nineteenth-Century English Novel* and essays appearing in such journals as *Texas Studies in Literature and Language, English Literary History,* and *PMLA.* His work-in-progress is entitled *Class Acts: The Politics of Sophistication from Austin to Proust.*

Susan Miller is Professor of English and member of the faculty of the University Writing Program at the University of Utah. She is the author of *Rescuing the Subject: A Critical Introduction to Rhetoric and the Writer; Written Worlds: Reading and Writing Cultures;* and *Textual Carnivals: The Politics of Composition.*

George Otte, Associate Professor of English and Director of the Writing Program at Baruch College-CUNY, is coauthor of *Casts of Thought: Writing in and against Tradition* and *Writers' Roles.* His articles have appeared in the *Journal of Advanced Composition* and the *Journal of Basic Writing,* among others. He is completing a book entitled *The Issue of Error.*

Naomi Scheman is Professor of Philosophy and Women's Studies at the University of Minnesota and the author of *Engenderings: Constructions of Knowledge, Authority, and Privilege.* Her essays have appeared in *Critical Inquiry* and in *(En)Gendering Knowledge: Feminists in Academe* and *A Mind of One's Own: Feminist Essays on Reason and Objectivity.*

Roger I. Simon teaches at the Ontario Institute for Studies in Education, University of Toronto. He has written extensively in the area of critical pedagogy and cultural studies and is author of *Teaching against the Grain: Texts for a Pedagogy of Possibility.* Simon's current work concerns the ways commemoration constructs relationships between history and collective memory.

Index

Kaplan, E. Ann, 60–61*nn*5,9
Karamcheti, Indira, 6–7, 8–9, 18*n*7
Keyssar, Helene, xiv, 81–88, 88*n*13
Kierkegaard, Søren, 33
Kimball, Roger, 108, 115
Knoblauch, C. H., 151–52
Kristeva, Julia: and mimesis, 39, 44; and the gaze, 44; and pedagogy, 99

Lacan, Jacques, 44, 90
Lack, 28–35 *passim*
Larson, Sue, 107
The lecture, 28–35; and supplement, 29; and transference, 31–32
Lesbianism. *See* Queer/Lesbian/Gay
Lévi-Strauss, Claude, 60*n*4
Levinas, Emmanuel, 92, 103–104*nn*3,15
Lewis, Magda, 104*n*11
Litvak, Joseph, xii, 9–12, 14
Lloyd, David, 144

Masculinist culture, 19–21
Master's voice, 150
Mayne, Judith, 61*n*15
McCarthy, Cameron: and multicultural models, 118; and essentialism, 119; and curriculum, 125
McDaniel, Judith, 81, 84, 85
Melancholia, 19–26
Mellencamp, Patricia, 58
Meyer, Richard, 27*n*2
Miller, Susan, xiv, 2, 13–14, 16, 17*n*1, 82–88
Modleski, Tania, 60–61*n*9
Mohanty, S. P., 90
Morgan, Robert, 103
Morley, David, 60*nn*6,7
Morris, Meaghan, 61*n*12
Morrison, Toni, 129
Morton, Donald, 126
Mothersill, Mary, 107
Multiculturalism, 117–27, 129–36, 138–46
Mulvey, Laura, 60–61*nn*6,9
Murray, Donald, 151

Newton, Ester, 18*n*8
Nurturance, 64–77, 79–88

Oliver, Kelly, 45
Olney, James, 38
Otte, George, 4, 6–7, 17, 18*n*6

Pagano, Jo Anne, 75–77
Passeron, Jean-Claude: reproduction and teaching, 14–16, 18*n*4, 70–72; model students and teachers, 74, 76

Patai, Daphne, 138
Peers, 96, 107, 155–64
Performative: brownnosing, ix–xiv, 3; and teaching, 3–4; during delivery of papers, 13; and Judith Butler, 16, 103–104*nn*5,6; and de Man, 19–20; and homophobia, 19–21; costume, 36–44; and *The Prime of Miss Jean Brodie*, 46–60; and gender dynamics, 79–88; "teaching as a Jew," 91–94, 102–103; and essentialist teaching, 129–36; and voice, 147–53
Petro, Patrice, 61*n*15
Pierce, Bonny, 103
Pinar, Bill, 38
Piontek, Thomas, 60
Pitt, Alice, 103
Ponet, James, 103*n*3
Portuges, Catherine, 18*n*3; teaching and institutional authority, 67–68; students and teachers, 73–74. *See also* Culley, Margo; Keyssar, Helene
Postcoloniality: and alterity, 90–94; and classroom, 138–46
The Prime of Miss Jean Brodie, 46–60
Prospero: and impersonation, 7; and power, 138–46
Purpel, David, 103

Queer/Lesbian/Gay, xii, 9–12, 19–26, 103*n*1, 106–15

Race: and essentialism and authority, 117–27, 129–36; in classroom, 138–46
Radicalism, 106–115
Reagon, Bernice, 104*n*14
Reproduction: and impersonation, ix–xiv, 1–5; in *The Prime of Miss Jean Brodie*, 46–60; and "good teacher," 64–77; and doctoral study, 94–100; and cooptation, 106–15; and voice, 147–53; and cultural discipline, 155–64
Resistance, 142–43
Rich, Adrienne, 81
Ritchie, Joy: and dialogic writing, 147, 148; and voice, 151
Rosenberg, Sharon, 103
Rousseau, Jean-Jacques, 4, 18*n*3, 155–60 *passim*
Rubin, Gayle, 60*n*4

Sade, Marquis de, 155–63 *passim*
Said, Edward, 136
Sartre, Jean-Paul, 38
Scheman, Naomi, 3–4, 9–11, 17*n*2
Schenke, Arleen, 103